3.

SATHER CLASSICAL LECTURES

Volume Twenty-eight

REPRESENTATIVE
GOVERNMENT
in Greek and Roman History

REPRESENTATIVE
GOVERNMENT
IN GREEK AND
ROMAN HISTORY

J. A. O. LARSEN

UNIVERSITY OF CALIFORNIA PRESS
BERKELEY AND LOS ANGELES   1955

University of California Press

Berkeley and Los Angeles, California

Cambridge University Press

London, England

Copyright, 1955, by

The Regents of the University of California

Library of Congress Catalogue Card No. 55-6998

Printed in the United States of America

By the University of California Printing Department

PREFACE

In these eight lectures an attempt has been made to trace the relationship of some of the chief Greek and Roman political institutions to representative government and to determine the extent to which this form of government actually was used. The lectures are printed approximately in the the form in which they were delivered, except for the addition of certain details, particularly in chapters i and ii.

The book is a summary of the results of research extending over a period of more than thirty years. A part of the subject, in fact, was discussed in my doctoral dissertation. In spite of the length of time devoted to it, the study is, in a sense, incomplete. My preliminary investigations have covered neither the *koina* of Asia Minor nor the western provincial assemblies as thoroughly as the leagues and federal states of Greece proper. The work in the one area largely centers around Lycia; in the other, on Gaul. Nevertheless, I hope that no material which would alter the general picture to any extent has been omitted.

I owe thanks to innumerable scholars of the past and present. To my old teachers of ancient history, the late E. M. Walker of Queen's College, Oxford, and the late W. S. Ferguson of Harvard; to many colleagues with whom I have discussed problems, especially the late R. J. Bonner of Chicago, B. L. Ullman, now of the University of North Carolina, and Gertrude Smith of Chicago; to colleagues in other universities who have exchanged views and reprints with me, especially M. Cary of the University of London and André Aymard of the Sorbonne; to Sterling Dow of Harvard and H. J. Carroll, Jr., of Pomona College for advance information concerning their study of representation in the Athenian *boule;* to numerous libraries and librarians; to the Social Science Research Council for a grant-in-aid which enabled me in 1930 to devote six months of uninterrupted study to my chosen subject; to the Uni-

versity of California for inviting me to deliver the Sather Lectures
of the year 1953–54 and thereby helping me to punctuate these
studies with a semicolon if not a period; to my colleagues at the
University of California, who, during the stay of Mrs. Larsen and
myself in Berkeley, have extended every possible aid and courtesy;
and finally to Mr. Harold A. Small, Professor W. H. Alexander,
and the staff in general of the University of California Press for
help in the preparation of the manuscript for printing.

J.A.O.L.

Berkeley, California, June, 1954

CONTENTS

I
The Problem

REPRESENTATIVE government, for the purposes of the present study, can be defined simply as government in which the ultimate decisions on important questions are made by representatives acting for their constituents and having authority to make such decisions according to their own best judgment. To illustrate, when it is stated in a document that certain representatives cannot be held to account by their constituents—or, as the Greeks put it, are not subject to *euthyne*—for decisions made in the assembly,[1] this means that they are true representatives and not messengers merely recording the will of their constituents. Where such a body has the final decision on fundamental questions of legislation and foreign affairs, representative government exists. It is not necessary to enter into the various debates about how representation should be arranged and what elements in the state should be represented. Both a government based on representation by trade unions and professional groups, and one based on representation by geographic districts, are representative governments. Nor does it make any difference whether the state in question has universal suffrage within the citizen body or suffrage limited in some way by property qualifications, sex, or the like. Both an oligarchy and a democracy can possess representative government. In ancient times, of course, the most liberal suffrage was the universal manhood suffrage of the democracies. Now it would be natural to expect that democracies, with their larger body of voters, would develop representative government more readily than oligarchies. Actually just the opposite seems to have been the case. Greek democracy maintained as one of its most fundamental doctrines the belief in the collective judgment of the masses as superior to the judgment of experts and, therefore, for long was loath to surrender any important decision to representatives. Oligarchy, with its sus-

[1] For notes see pages 191 ff., below.

picion of the masses, was more ready to delegate decisions of this kind to representatives.

The antithesis of representative government is direct government. This is something the modern state at times tries to secure through the use of initiative and referendum. The Greek and Roman city-state, on the contrary, secured direct government by the use of primary assemblies in which all adult, active, male citizens had a right to take part.[2] All students of Greek history are aware of the importance of the Athenian primary assembly, the *ekklesia,* but it may be well to recall some of the decisions made by this body. It was the *ekklesia* which decided in 431 that the Athenians should abandon the countryside and withdraw within the walls; the *ekklesia* which in 427 condemned the Mytilenaeans to death and next day reversed the decision; the *ekklesia* which voted assessments of tribute on the Athenian subjects including the assessment of 425/4 with its huge increase in tribute; the *ekklesia* which in 416 voted the expedition to Sicily and late in 414 voted not to recall the expedition but to send reinforcements; the *ekklesia* which—this time subject to some manipulation—passed the bills that made possible the establishment of oligarchy in 411. It would be easy to cite many other examples of important decisions made by the Athenian assembly; but only one more will be given, in order to emphasize the point that the assembly could also act as a law court. It was the assembly which in 406 condemned to death the victorious generals after the battle of Arginusae. On that occasion, dominated by a mob spirit, it even disregarded constitutional safeguards intended to prevent and correct overhasty or irregular action. Farther, direct government can hardly go.

Actually, the rule that all adult male citizens could take part in the meetings of the assembly, at least in states as large as Athens, was honored more in theory than in practice. Only in very small communities would it be possible for the majority of the adult males to turn up for frequent meetings. Not only was the disinclination to waste time on tiresome details of government as great among the Greeks as with us, but attendance at meetings demanded a sacrifice which many could not afford to make. Thus in Attica many farmers lived a day's journey or more away from Athens. Consequently the decisions of the assembly were made not by a majority of the voters, but by a majority of that relatively small percentage which happened to attend.³ The fact that a quorum of 6,000 obviously was regarded as high suggests that the normal attendance was considerably less. Naturally the element which attended was the one which could do so with least effort. Hence, by the simple act of fixing the place for the meetings, it was possible to give the advantage to one element in the state or another. In Athens the meetings were normally held within the city and so favored the townsmen over the farmers, and it was undoubtedly the former who in 431 carried the decree to abandon the countryside.⁴ On the other hand, the assembly at Colonus in 411—which prepared the way for oligarchy—undoubtedly was convoked outside the city walls at a time when the enemy was abroad, in order to discourage the attendance of the unarmed democratic lower classes who lived within the city.

In spite of the limitations resulting from the circumstance that only a small percentage of the qualified voters normally attended the meetings, the primary assembly was the fundamental institution of the Greek democratic city-state; and one gains the impression that in the many moderate oligarchies the primary assembly was equally fundamental. The chief difference between an oligarchy and a democracy was that in an oligarchy the right to vote and to hold office was limited by a property qualification or in some other way. Thus in the Boeotian cities in the period preceding the King's Peace of 386 there was a property qualification for active citizenship. The voters were divided into four *boulai* or councils, each of which functioned in turn while the other three combined to serve as the assembly to which the proposals of the council were submitted. In Cyrene similarly, in the government which existed in the last part of the fourth century, the "Ten Thousand" functioned as a primary assembly.⁵ Likewise in Athens, when property qualifications for active citizenship were introduced in 322 and again in 317, the *ekklesia* undoubtedly continued to function as a primary assembly open to all active citizens.

If we glance for a moment at Rome, the same prominence of the primary assembly is to be noted. There is, however, one marked difference between the way the Roman and the Athenian assemblies functioned. At Athens the vote was counted by heads, and a majority of the voters present decided the issue. Thus democracy was possible under the Athenian system. In Rome, on the other hand, democracy had much less chance because the votes were always taken by voting units and this made it possible to favor certain elements in the population. Thus the propertied classes were favored in the *comitia centuriata.*⁶ Other factors which tended to prevent the development of democracy in Rome need not detain us. It is enough to note that the Romans, too, clung to their primary assemblies even at a time when the potential voters were numbered in the hundreds of thousands and even millions.⁷

The importance of the primary assembly in ancient times has so impressed scholars that it has been difficult for them to believe that representative government could actually have been tried by the Greeks and Romans. Two points, however, should be noted at the outset. In the first place, even the fully developed Greek democracy contained so much representative machinery that little more than a shift in the emphasis on the various organs of government was needed to transform it into a representative government. In the second place, the fully developed democracy and the theory of democracy on which it was based came relatively late—not before the fifth century B.C.—and did not long remain unchallenged. Thus there was an opportunity for the development of representative government both before the democratic theory and system had evolved and again after democracy had lost its popularity. In neither case would it have left much of a mark on theory. If it existed before the development of democratic theory, it antedated any important formal Greek political theory; if it developed later, it was overshadowed and colored by earlier theories. As a matter of fact, the later development of representation came in federal states, while political theory, even in Roman times, concentrated on the city-state. The ancient cities, both while independent and later as municipalities of the Roman Empire, seem to have retained their primary assemblies, in fact or in fiction, to a very late date. Consequently there was little opportunity for any theory of federal representative government, and what little there was tended to assimilate the federal state to the city-state. This should be easy to understand when it is remembered that the very word "cosmopolitan" involves a comparison of the world to a city-state, and that Rome continued to be regarded as a city-state even when she was considered the mistress of the world.

The two points mentioned above, the representative elements in the government of a city-state and the late development of democracy, will have to be discussed briefly. To begin with, the representative machinery within the city-state, the organ of government which obviously calls for most consideration, is the *boule* or council which prepared the business for the assembly and supervised innumerable details of government.[8] It is widely recognized that the *boule* of Athens was so composed as to constitute a cross section of the citizen body and to give all sections of Attica representation approximately in proportion to their citizen population. Possibly, later investigations may show that scholars in their first enthusiasm have sometimes exaggerated the exactness of the proportion, but the general conclusion will continue to stand.[9] The subject is so important for the present investigation that it is necessary at least to be aware of the nature of the evidence. All generalizations so far have been based on only a small part of the evidence soon to be made available. In 1927 I made a survey of the material then on hand, in a study which remains unpublished.[10] Even that material is too much to be presented here. Since then the evidence of a mass of additional inscriptions has been added through the excavations in the Athenian Agora or civic center.[11] Many of these have been published, but some still remain to be deciphered and made available. Of all this only a sample can be given. Justice cannot be done to the whole subject except by a separate study of considerable size. Such a work is now being prepared by Professors H. J. Carroll, Jr., of Pomona College and Sterling Dow of Harvard.

During the fifth century the Athenian council or *boule* consisted of five hundred members chosen by lot, fifty from each of the ten

tribes, to serve for one year. The ten tribes mentioned were artificial
subdivisions of the citizen body as reorganized by Cleisthenes in
508 B.C. They have been called tribes because "tribe" is the standard
translation of the Greek name *phyle,* and because they maintained
the fiction of kinship in the worship by each of a hero or mythical
ancestor. The tribes obviously were intended to be approximately
equal in population, but naturally could not be and were not
exactly equal. The tribal contingents in the council took turns, in
an order determined each year by lot, to serve as the *prytaneis,* a
presiding committee both of the council and, whenever the assembly met, of the latter body also. The collective name for the
committee and for the period for which it served is *prytany.*[12] In
the Hellenistic Age the number of tribes was increased and varied
somewhat from time to time. Since the tribal contingents continued to contain fifty members each, this in turn caused changes
not only in the number of tribal contingents and prytanies, but
also in the total membership of the council. This, however, does
not affect the general picture except so far as the creation of new
tribes offered an opportunity to readjust representation. Thus the
first step in securing representation in the council approximately
in proportion to population was taken when each tribe was given
fifty members; but for Athens, and probably for many other cities,
this is only the beginning of the story. The Athenian tribes contained varying numbers of local subdivisions called demes. The
composition of many tribal contingents has become known
through inscriptions listing members by their demes. When these
inscriptions began to be published, it was possible for the French
scholar, Hauvette-Besnault, to reach the conclusion as early as 1881
that the repeated representation of the same deme by the same or
approximately the same number of representatives could not be
due to chance.[13] This conclusion was definitely proved correct when
the *editio princeps* of Aristotle's *Constitution of the Athenians* was
published in January, 1891, and was found to state that in his day
the members of the *boule* were still chosen by demes. Formerly
other magistrates elected by lot had been so chosen, but on account
of the prevalence of bribery the selection of most of them had been

transferred to the tribe as a whole.[14] Once it was established that the members of the council actually were chosen by demes, which meant that a certain number of seats was assigned to a deme in advance, many interesting conclusions could be drawn. It was obvious that the representation was based on population, and even if the adjustment of representation to population was not perfect, it was possible to use information concerning it as a guide to the relative size of the citizen body of the various demes. To use an illustration, even without the direct statement of Thucydides (2.19.2), the fact that Acharnae had twenty-two representatives would almost allow the conclusion that Acharnae was the largest Attic deme.[15] Hence it is no accident that most of the evidence on the representation of demes available in 1933 is tabulated in Professor Gomme's study of the population of Athens.

As an illustration of the mass of evidence available, three inscriptions showing the representation of the tribe Aigeis in the fourth century may be cited. There is, in the first place, a complete list available for 341/0 b.c.[16] With this can be compared incomplete lists for about 350 and for 335/4 b.c.[17] The complete list, that for 341/0, shows twenty demes, with the number of representatives varying from one to six. The preserved part of the list for about 350 gives us the representation of twelve demes. For one deme it has one less (Kydantidai, 1 for 2) and for two demes each one more (Bateis 2 for 1, Phegaieis 4 for 3) than the later list. Otherwise the two lists agree, which means that they agree 9 out of 12 times.[18] From the figures given it is easy to deduce that if the earlier list were preserved in its entirety there would be a discrepancy for at least one other deme. Obviously, for every representative added to one deme, one must be withdrawn from another deme, and vice versa. The list for 335/4 gives the numbers for seven demes only, and for all seven it is in agreement with the list for 341/0, the list which chronologically is the middle one of the three. This in itself is significant though not so very startling, but, more important, the seven include two in which there were differences between the two earlier lists. Thus the picture is: several differences between the first and second lists, complete agreement between the second and third. To be sure, if the third list had been preserved in its entirety the agreement might not have been so perfect. Nevertheless, it now looks as if there had been a readjustment of representation between 350 and 341. Of course, it is impossible to tell from this one example whether there had been a general readjustment or whether it was confined to the one tribe. It would be possible that tribal officials made readjustments within single tribes, so that evidence drawn from one tribe would prove nothing either about a general readjustment or about readjustments in other tribes.

This one example will have to suffice. It may be said that lists from other tribes, also, show slight variations in the representation of demes. Carroll and Dow report that in the period from 408/7, the year of the earliest prytany list preserved, to about 224/3 B.C., the evidence suggests that there were no general reallocations except such as were occasioned by the creation of new tribes. At other times, divergences of one, such as in the example we glanced at, are common, but larger divergences are extremely rare. In fact, Carroll and Dow are inclined to believe that the quotas laid down by Cleisthenes were retained unchanged through this entire period except for alterations made when new tribes were created. As for the other divergences, they suggest that when demes—especially very small ones—could not themselves supply their entire quota, these made arrangements with other demes. This, rather than readjustments made by tribal officials, is probably the best explanation of the divergences observed. In any case, the evidence shows that the system of quotas was largely or totally abandoned about 200 B.C. The retention of the system as long as this is important, for it shows that at least Athens retained a system of representation in proportion to population for the *boule* throughout the period in which the institutions of the city-state may have served as models for the governments of federal states. Probably even before 200 B.C. new federal governments would look for models to other federal states rather than to cities. By drawing on other information concerning population, Carroll and Dow will also be able to throw some light on the question of how close a correspondence there was between the numbers of representatives assigned to the various

units and their actual population. Here it must be noted that the
question is not whether Athens did or did not employ a system of
representation in proportion to population in the *boule,* but rather
how accurate and successful the system was. This is a question
which can be asked appropriately about most modern representative systems.

For the date of the introduction of the system there is no direct
evidence, but it is natural to connect it with the formation of the ten
tribes and the council of five hundred by Cleisthenes. For the use
of the lot in selecting members, we have contemporary evidence
which shows that it must have been adopted by Athens before
453/2 B.C., the year in which Athens imposed the same system on
Erythrae.[19] The evidence bearing directly upon the proportionate
representation of the demes is somewhat later. Aristotle's *Constitution of the Athenians* was written late in the fourth century. Moreover, though there are many fourth-century inscriptions, only one
is available from the fifth century, namely, a partial prytany list
from 408/7 (*IG* I², 398). This may be due in part to the accident of
preservation; almost certainly it means that the practice of in-
scribing prytany lists on stone was relatively late. This is not the
only Athenian institution for which there is little epigraphical evidence for the fifth century, and thus the absence of evidence is not
too significant. Hence, until negative evidence turns up—and I do
not think it will—it is natural to believe that the system goes back
to Cleisthenes.

Representation of demes in proportion to population meant virtually the representation of most elements of the citizen body in
proportion to their numbers. This was a natural result of the fact
that the members of one deme consisted largely of farmers; of
another, of handicraftsmen and workers, and so on. To be sure,
it is probable that country demes sometimes were represented by
members living in the city. Membership was hereditary and members who moved from the country to the city and their descendants
retained membership in the deme of their ancestors. Aristotle (e.g.,
Politics 1318b11), it may be noted, speaks of the tendency of
farmers to stay away from assemblies. Any maladjustment of repre-

sentation resulting from this practice cannot have been great. More serious, if correct, is the claim that there was a tendency to exclude the very lowest classes and to have membership largely monopolized by men of property.

Members of the *boule* had to be thirty years or more of age and could serve only twice in a lifetime.[20] The only source for the latter detail is Aristotle's (*Const. Aths.* 62.3) description of the government of Athens as it was in his own time. He does not tell when the rule originated and, naturally, he does not tell how long it remained in force. He does, however, give the rule as an exception to the general prohibition against holding any particular magistracy more than once in a lifetime. This implies that the permission was granted because otherwise it would be difficult or impossible always to secure enough members.[21] A glance at what little is known about the population of Athens shows that this must have been the case in the fourth though hardly in most of the fifth century.[22] The total citizen population in 480 b.c. has been estimated tentatively at 140,000. According to modern census statistics the number of males reaching the age of thirty in a year would be about 900 to 1,100. By 431 the numbers have risen to 172,000 and 1,100 to 1,340. Thereafter there was a decline, and for 400 the numbers are as low as 90,000 and 560 to 680 respectively. Later there was some increase in population, but it apparently never got back to the level of the most prosperous part of the fifth century.

These statistics naturally cannot claim complete accuracy, but they are the best that are available. They suggest that through much of the fifth century it cannot have been too difficult to supply even 500 new councilors a year, but that with the decline of population it must have become difficult if not impossible to do so. Even if there were more than 500 men reaching the proper age every year, there would always be some who were disqualified and some who avoided having their names submitted as candidates. Moreover, of those otherwise qualified, not a few must have been required for the many other magistracies of the state. This may well have caused the adoption of the rule that former members should be permitted to be reëlected once and serve twice in a lifetime. With this rule in force—whether it was a new rule or not—there once more was an adequate supply of candidates. This is suggested by the apparent rarity of records of men who had served twice, and seems proved by the practice of selecting alternates to be available if a regular member should die or be rejected at the scrutiny of new members. It appears that these were selected by the demes at the time of the sortition of their members.[23] The alternates need not complicate our reckoning to any extent, for obviously those alternates who did not become members were not disqualified from standing as candidates at later elections. They need to be considered only so far as their mere existence shows that the sortition of the members did not exhaust the list of candidates. To be sure, there were demes which occasionally did not furnish all their regular members and thus must have failed also to select alternates. Some examples of this, however, does not prove that there was a general shortage of candidates. The situation may rather have been due to maladjustment caused by shifts in the population. This may have produced a situation in which some demes had an abundance of candidates while others suffered from a shortage. In such cases, as already suggested, arrangements may have been made with other demes. In spite of some cases of this kind, it is still possible to argue, as has been done for the fourth century on the basis of a study of inscriptions and careers, that the poorer members of the community did not normally serve on the council.[24] The evidence is difficult to interpret, and all will not agree, but there seems some reason to believe that a disproportionally large number of men of property served in the council. This would be in accordance with the constant efforts in the century to keep the government in the hands of the "better" people. Yet the numbers of those available for service was not such that the tendency can have been excessively great. The conclusion is that, in spite of some maladjustment of representation due to shifts in population, some abstention on the part of farmers, and possibly some overrepresentation of men of property, all classes and elements of the population were represented in the council pretty much in proportion to their strength.

The system of a council subdivided into prytanies and similar

subdivisions and, as a result also, the proportionate representation
of the various parts of the citizen body in the council, seem to have
been very common in Greek cities.[25] Two examples for which we
have unusually early evidence will be considered briefly. Chios is
shown by an archaic inscription to have had a popular *boule* with
fifty members chosen from each tribe.[26] For Erythrae, an inscription has already been cited which shows that in 453/2 the city was
given a *boule* of 120 members. If another difficult and rather
neglected inscription really belongs to the same period, it can be
added that the *boule* was subdivided into prytanies, though not
necessarily ten as at Athens.[27] In fact, it is likely that Erythrae had
three tribes and, as a result, three prytanies a year with forty members in each.[28] Since this arrangement is found early in the fifth
century and again in the third century, it is likely that it antedated
the Athenian intervention and was retained unchanged for centuries. The likelihood that the intervention was preceded by a
period of rule by tyrants supported by Persia (*ATL* III, 254-255)
does not supply any argument to the contrary. The tyrants certainly
would not alter the preëxisting tribal system and may even have
retained the magistrates. If not, the general plan of the older system
was restored after the overthrow of the tyrants. Hence the Athenian
decree of 453/2 regulated the manner in which the *bouleutai* were
to be chosen, but retained unchanged a system of the subdivision of
the year into three prytanies of four months each and the use of a
multiple of three in determining the size of the *boule* as well as of
other boards of magistrates. If proof is needed that the *prytaneis*
for any single prytany were the members of one tribe and not a
group chosen from all three tribes, it is found in the fact that they
numbered forty and that forty is not a multiple of three. Wherever
it came from, the system of three tribes cannot be due to Athenian
influence. Hence the examples of Erythrae and Chios—the popular
boule of which may well be earlier than Solon—indicate a development in Ionia independent of that in Attica.

The example of Erythrae also suggests that the Athenian system
was not unique in actually utilizing in the *boule* a large percentage
of those eligible to serve. The proviso in the decree of 453/2 to the

effect that no one could serve in the *boule* more than once within a period of four years must mean that there would not be enough eligible candidates if service was limited to once in a lifetime or, as in Athens, twice in a lifetime. That such regulations as those in the Erythrae decree were intended to provide for the service of most of those who were qualified is suggested by the regulation for the *boule* of Cyrene from the last quarter of the fourth century B.C. providing that membership was to be limited to men over fifty, but that if not enough of this age were available, the deficiency should be made up from those over forty (*SEG* IX, 1. 16–19). At Erythrae, since election was by lot, it must have been anticipated that there normally would be some choice. Even so, it is likely that most of those who were eligible actually served at some time and that those men over thirty who took an active interest in politics served in the *boule* say every fifth or sixth year. In some moderate oligarchies, such as the cities of Boeotia at the time of the Peloponnesian War, all active citizens were divided into four groups which took turns in functioning as a *boule*.[29] Similarly, in the constitution "for the future," drawn up in 411 and connected with the government of the Five Thousand at Athens, the active citizens—those above thirty with the necessary property qualification—were divided into four divisions each of which was to serve as the *boule* a year at a time (Arist. *Const. Aths.* 30). Since the *boule* in this case was authorized to make definitive decisions itself, the government described would amount to a mild experimentation with representative government. The interesting and vexed question whether the constitution described by Aristotle was the one actually adopted cannot be discussed here.[30]

This feature, the participation of all or most of the active citizens in the actual work of the government, however, is not as important for the present investigation as the existence of a representative council. With such a council functioning, it is clear that all that was needed to create a representative government was to give the council final authority on major issues. This naturally brings up the question why, when they had such admirable representative machinery, the cities clung so tenaciously to direct government.

The answer is not merely that many Greek states were so small that it was possible for all the citizens to gather in a single meeting. Direct government through primary assemblies actually was used by states with areas so large that the distances made it impossible for many of the citizens to attend meetings regularly and with populations so great that, if all had turned up, the assembly would have been hopelessly unwieldy. This is true not only of federal states but also of many city-states and most obviously so of Athens. Therefore, there must have been some plausible reason for retaining the supremacy of the primary assembly, and this must have been more than mere belief in the ability of the ordinary citizen to administer the government or in his right to take part in its work. If that was all, the purpose could be accomplished by election to office by lot, so that all had an equal chance to be elected, and rotation in office, so that all were given their turn to serve. There must have been some more specific reason for retaining the primary assembly.

This specific reason is to be found in the belief that the collective judgment of the masses was superior to that of experts, a theory that was enunciated not only for politics but for music and poetry as well. This is a doctrine which by implication can be traced back as far as to Aeschylus' *Suppliants* and which was retained even by Isocrates while he attacked other features of extreme democracy.[31] Thus, after the restoration in 403, when democracy ostensibly was accepted by all except a negligible number of extreme oligarchs, it must have been this aspect of it which first and foremost was emphasized and retained. Moreover, this ostensible acceptance of democracy seems to have been widespread and was not confined to Athens. The effect of this in delaying the final adoption of representative government in federal states will have to be considered later.

Notice, however, that the development of this democratic theory was relatively late and can hardly be traced back farther than to the period of the Persian War or, at the very earliest, to Cleisthenes.[32] Some of the elements of the theory of popular government certainly go back to the days of Cleisthenes, but the prevailing theory of the time seems to have placed emphasis on the republican magistrates as responsible to the people and as held to account by it in contrast to the irresponsible tyrant who regarded himself as accountable to no one. In fact, the supremacy of the assembly does not seem to have been included in the original reforms of Cleisthenes, but to have been introduced a few years later. Before this, the council of five hundred must have been very nearly supreme in the state except so far as it shared leadership with the older council, the Areopagus.

This means that not only democratic theory but democratic government was relatively late to develop.[33] The chief evidence is to be found in an inscription which contains fragments of a decree or law limiting the power of the *boule*.[34] Included in this is also the oath taken by members of that body. From references in the oath to putting questions to vote in the *boule* and *ekklesia* it has rightly been concluded that this must be the bouleutic oath. Hence it is natural to believe that when the bill states that the *boule* cannot act on certain questions without consulting the "entire *demos*," this means that the right to take final action on these questions formerly belonged to the *boule* and is now being taken away from it. Thus the inscription throws light on the relative powers of the council and assembly both before and after the bill was passed. For this reason it is possibly the single most important inscription in existence for the study of the history of the Athenian constitution; but, probably because it is so extremely fragmentary, it has not received the attention it deserves and has not been included in shorter selections of inscriptions or in source books. It has been studied mostly in connection with the right to inflict the death penalty.[35] This is well and good as far as it goes, but it has tended to obscure the further implications of the document. The acts which cannot be performed without the participation of the "entire *demos*" include, besides the infliction of the death penalty and the imposition of high fines, also the making of war and, undoubtedly, the concluding of peace. References to the five hundred, the *boule,* the *prytaneis,* and the *ekklesia*[36] make it likely that the document dealt in considerable detail with the relative powers of the *boule* and the *ekklesia*. The number of acts listed as not to be performed without consulting the "entire *demos*" must have been considerable.

The phrase here translated "entire *demos*," that is, all the voting members of the citizen body, is known only from this inscription and hence is difficult to interpret. It has been translated by others "full assembly" and has been taken to refer to the requirement of a quorum of 6,000, the number required for ostracism and certain other acts.[37] This is a plausible interpretation in itself, but it does not fit the contents of the document, which does not distinguish between different kinds of meetings of the *ekklesia* but rather between the *boule* and the *ekklesia*. Hence, it is likely that the phrase δῆμος πληθύων refers rather to the entire people or body of voters in opposition to the small part of it present in the *boule*. It may be objected that *demos* alone, without the modifier, would be enough to indicate this, but it would not be unnatural in an act which practically transferred the supreme power from the council to the assembly to use some modifier to emphasize that questions were hereafter to be submitted to the *entire* people. This emphasis, in turn, may well be due to the new doctrine of the superiority of the collective judgment of the masses. The phrase, of course, tells nothing about how well attended meetings actually were.

The language of the inscription gives one additional bit of information about procedure. It seems to have provided that the *boule*, for instance, could not declare war "without [consulting] the entire people." This implies both that earlier the council could declare war without consulting the people and that after the new requirement the *boule* still remained the agency which declared war; and so too with other acts listed in the document. This must mean that the *boule* could consider any number of things, and only when it wished to take positive action on a subject on which the people had the final say was it necessary to bring a bill before the people. Negative action, on the other hand, must often have been taken by the *boule* without ever informing the people that a subject had been taken up. To use one illustration, foreign ambassadors may have submitted to the *boule* many proposals which never were brought before the assembly.[38] Thus, even when the *boule* officially possessed only the right to consider in advance the questions to be acted upon by the *ekklesia,* it may have made many important negative decisions by the simple expedient of deciding not to submit a question to the people.

But what is the date of the bill transferring the decisions on many important questions from the council to the assembly? It is usually believed that our inscription is connected with the restoration of democracy after an oligarchic interlude, and so it has been dated about 410 B.C., but it is recognized that the contents must in part or even in their entirety be older. It is hardly necessary to point to the archaic character of the language. It is enough to notice that the assembly long before 410 possessed many of the powers mentioned. On the other hand, the decree cannot belong to the original reforms of Cleisthenes, for the implied period in which the council possessed final authority in vital matters must be placed after his reforms for the simple reason that also at that time it had five hundred members. Thus the date of the reform must be later than 508 B.C. This once established, it is gratifying to find that the conclusion is in agreement with the tradition of the Greeks themselves. In the days of Aristotle it was believed that the oath still sworn by the members of the *boule* originated in the archonship of Hermokreon, which seems best placed in 501/0 B.C.[39] No matter how little faith one may have in the accuracy of the evidence for this period of Greek history, it must be admitted that this makes sense. It separates the act both from the reforms of Cleisthenes and from the reforms which followed soon after Marathon[40] and associates it with another measure strengthening the power of the assembly, namely, its election of the ten generals. Hence the date should be accepted with that slight mental reservation which one must always make when one has the evidence of only a single source. When once it is established that the measure came a few years after the reforms of Cleisthenes, it is a matter of little importance to determine to what extent our document is a transcription of the original bill and to what extent it includes subsequent modifications and additions.

A somewhat startling by-product of this demonstration of the late origin of democratic theory and democracy, and of the early prominence of the *boule,* is the conclusion that the *boule* was so powerful that it can almost be said that Athens for a few years possessed a representative government. Can this possibly be correct? So far as the meager evidence available allows us to determine, it is correct. Moreover, if we get away from the point of view that Greeks must always have insisted on direct government, this is exactly what we should expect in the course of devolution from monarchy to democracy. It is generally recognized that in Greek states monarchy was followed by aristocracy and oligarchy, and that the power of such governments was largely concentrated in a council of nobles or rich men. What more natural than that in the course of development of popular government an effort should be made both to render this council less exclusive and to set up a more popular council as a rival? The transformation of the old council of nobles into a council consisting of former magistrates, as in the Areopagus at Athens, did little for the lower classes as long as the council conducted the elections and thus was self-perpetuating.[41] Hence the organization of a popular council alongside the Areopagus. This meant the partial substitution in the government of one council for another; but what a difference there was between the councils! The oldest form of the earlier council had meant rule by the nobles; the council which consisted of former magistrates and which itself elected the magistrates meant rule by a closed self-perpetuating oligarchy. If such a council can be called representative at all, it represented only a small part of the people. Of course, it largely acted for and represented the state, but this does not constitute representative government of the kind under consideration in the present study. On the other hand, the popular council, at least as transformed by Cleisthenes,[42] represented the entire citizen body.

The experience of Athens was hardly unique, though direct evidence from other cities is rare. Aristotle, however, recognized representative government in a city-state as one form of oligarchy, and noted also the tendency to make the *boule* the chief organ of

government in democratic states which lacked pay for offi
for participation in meetings.[43] This last observation may b
in part on the experience of Athens and suggests that an in
with a powerful popular *boule* was a common stage in the d
ment from aristocracy to democracy. Actually an inscriptiu.. ου..-
taining fragments of an enactment supplies evidence of this for
one other state, namely Chios, where at an early date (cf. n. 26)
there was created a popular *boule* which stood alongside of a more
aristocratic or conservative one, much as at Athens the council of
four and later of five hundred stood alongside the Areopagus. The
adjective "popular" applied to it apparently was used to distinguish
it from another council, so that the existence of the aristocratic
council already mentioned can be taken for granted. This *boule*
seems to have been so powerful that the government of Chios at
the time was practically a representative government. It was made
up of fifty representatives from each tribe, but since we do not
know how many tribes there were we do not know its size. Appeals
could be made to it from the decisions of magistrates, and there was
one regular meeting each month to handle other business of the
people and to attend to the cases which had been appealed during
the past month. The council, apparently, was competent to handle
all business on behalf of the people,[44] though the law is most specific
about its judicial competence. If we could be sure, as some scholars
have maintained,[45] that the members were elected by vote and not
chosen by lot, we should be able to classify it as closer to a modern
representative assembly than anything else we know in early
Greece. However, though it is perfectly possible that the members
were elected in this manner, it is not safe to draw this conclusion
from a single expression the exact connotation of which we do not
know. It may mean no more than that the members were taken
fifty from each tribe. It matters little. The important point is that
a smaller body was authorized to act on behalf of the citizen body
and thus to represent it.

The name applied to this council both in the Chian and the early
Attic inscription is *boule,* and this continued to be, even down to
Roman times, the most common Greek word for the council of

the city-state. This name makes it possible to reconstruct tentatively the evolution of the institution. Our two inscriptions emphasize the judicial activity of the council; but that cannot have been the activity which seemed most important when the name was adopted. The word means also "council" or "plan," but the related verb *boulesthai* means "to will" or "wish," and *boule* too must originally have meant a wish or desire, or an act or expression of will or wish, and then, later, the council which expressed its will.⁴⁶ The verb *bouleuein*, "to deliberate," is almost certainly a later derivative. When *boule* was adopted as the name for the aristocratic council, it must have been because the council was asked by the king to express its wish or will on matters laid before it. This use of the name goes back as far as the Homeric poems. Particularly interesting is *Odyssey* 3.127–128, where the word is used in two successive lines, once about the council and once about the thought or plan of individuals. At first the judicial activities of the council must have been few, partly because there was no appeal from the verdict of the king or magistrate, but probably rather because those who were wronged relied more on self-help than on courts and litigation. The judicial activities of the council too can be traced back as far as Homer and probably developed as a check on the arbitrary power of the king and magistrates. Naturally, where a more popular council was organized in opposition to a more aristocratic one, it would endeavor to acquire both judicial and deliberative authority. On the deliberative side, the early Athenian *boule* once could deliberate and make a decision without referring the question to the assembly; later, on all important questions, it could only deliberate in advance on measures to be submitted to the assembly and draw up the bills to be presented to it. In technical language, the *boule* thereafter became a probouleutic council.

The early history of the federal state seems to show the same development. First there was a *boule* with final authority, but later its power was limited and final authority was vested in a primary assembly. This development will have to be discussed in the next chapter, but, even without the evidence from the federal state, the development of the city-state is enough to indicate that the Greeks at a relatively early stage, before 500 B.C., were adopting the natural expedient of permitting smaller councils to act on behalf of the citizen body and thus had begun to evolve representative government. The process was checked before a theory of representative government had been developed and has left practically no mark on literature. Instead, the theory of democracy and of the superiority of the judgment of the masses over that of the experts not only caused the city-state to adopt direct government with a primary assembly, but also saddled the federal state with this form of government so unwieldy and impractical for it.

Our problem will thus be to study the return of representative government, and this will involve primarily the federal state. First, however, it will be necessary to sketch the early development of the federal state and the use of representation in the semifederal alliances or leagues such as the Peloponnesian and Delian leagues and their successors. After that will come the federal states proper and, as a sequel or continuation, the federal confederacies and assemblies of the Roman Empire. The latter are important for perspective. Though they had little political power, it is clear that they did constitute the machinery of representative government. Thus the question of the return or adoption of representative government in the federal state becomes primarily a question of date. On the date in turn will depend the answer to the question whether the representative machinery had much to govern or whether it was in large part only a potential representative government. The date for the adoption or readoption of representative government which will be defended in this study will be a little before 200 B.C. This is the date of its adoption by the Achaean Confederacy, and there the adoption came so early that the government was still a real government.

II
Early Tribal and Federal States

ANCIENT GREEK governments and political institutions always displayed considerable variety. This may be even more true of the period from the seventh to the fifth centuries than of later periods. Some of the forms of government will have to be noticed. Special interest attaches to the Boeotian Confederacy of the period 447–386 B.C. with its representative government. Not too many have recognized the character of this government and even fewer have proceeded to draw the obvious conclusion that representative government was well known in Greece as early as the days of Pericles. In fact, this form of government, rather than some other of which no description is available, is probably to be regarded as normal at the time for federal states. A glance at other states, though not too conclusive, confirms rather than refutes this theory.

The tribal state is the most backward and the federal state the most advanced type of state known from ancient Greece. The tribal or ethnic state or society is commonly regarded as the forerunner of the city-state. The tribes usually occupied what for Greece were fairly large districts, lived in open villages rather than in cities, had no recorded law, relied on kinsmen and self-help for defense against crime and enemies, and possessed little government except leadership in war. Characteristic of such society was the practice of bearing arms while going about one's normal business. Thucydides (1.5.3–6.2) mentions the survival of this practice in parts of Greece in his own time (*ca.* 460–400). The reason for linking the ethnic state and the federal state is that federal states normally were the result of development within ethnic states. If several cities grew up within the territory of a tribe and did not become completely independent city-states but retained some tie with each other, the natural result was a federal state. This is probably best illustrated by Boeotia. The line is not always easy to draw.

22

Thus it was possible for a group of subtribes, though not urbanized, to have sufficiently strong central and local governments to constitute a federal state. The continuity of development from tribal state to federal state is shown by the use of the Greek word *ethnos*, "nation, people," about both types. The word suggests a tribal or national state, but it was also one of the more common names applied to federal states. Hence *poleis* and *ethne* could be used to cover all normal Greek states, *ethne* including federal as well as ethnic states.[1] It should be borne in mind that ethnic states remained in existence to a late date. It is true, however, that the districts in which they survived and which were slow to develop cities had small part in Greek artistic and literary activities.

The federal state hardly demands definition. It is a state in which citizens are under the jurisdiction of both a federal government and the government of a member state. In Greek federal states the member states normally were city-states. This may suggest to some that the term "federal state" is a misnomer and that it is a question of the central government and mere municipal governments, but such a conclusion would be a mistake. The city-state, small as it often was, differed completely from the modern city. The latter, after all, is a mere city, while the city-state included territory outside of the city proper and no doubt frequently included more farmers in the citizen body than members of all other professions combined. It is also a question of attitude. To a Greek, his city-state was his country, and it was a great concession to allow it to become subordinated to any authority. That is one reason why so many of the efforts to unite Greek cities took the form of permanent alliances of free states.

A Greek descriptive name—in a slightly anglicized form—for a federal state is *sympolity*. The first element in this compound noun indicates that it refers to the sharing of something or participation in something. It is hardly necessary to know Greek in order to see that what is shared is citizenship. Similarly, since an alliance involves participation and coöperation in fighting, *symmachy* is used as a name for the alliances mentioned above.[2] Sympolity is applied also to other mergings and sharings of citizenship—for instance,

when two cities are combined into one,—but in employing it as a
technical term for a Greek federal state we are following late
Greek usage. Nor are the other meanings of the word likely to
cause confusion. What does cause trouble at times is that *sympoliteia* as a name for a federal state seems to have come into use
only at a relatively late date. It does not seem to be attested in literature before Polybius,[3] but was hardly new at the time and
appears to have been used earlier in documents.[4] The use of *sympoliteia* for a federal state was probably not adopted before the
Greeks had become fairly well acquainted with the institution.
This means that there was a transitional period in which federal
institutions existed but without an adequate vocabulary to describe
them. For the earliest organizations, we do not find clear descriptions in the sources, but must determine whether they were symmachies, sympolities, or more primitive tribal states by the institutions described. The ancient description may even be misleading.
Consequently, the classification of organizations is not always easy,
and this difficulty is particularly aggravating when it comes to
naming them. When our sources speak of action by "the Lacedaemonians and their allies" or by "the Achaeans," we almost have to
adopt some sort of name for the organizations involved if we are
to discuss their institutions.

The names used will be most helpful if they suggest the nature
or classification of the organizations; but that, as I have already
indicated, involves difficulties. Hence there is a temptation to avoid
the issue. There is a Greek word, *koinon,* which can be applied to
almost anything individuals and states have in common or in
which individuals and states are combined, from the smallest club
to the United Nations. It is a temptation to choose an English word
which can have almost as many meanings and to call all organizations in which states are combined "leagues," whether they are
symmachies, sympolities, tribal states, or religious associations, as
the Boeotian League, the Peloponnesian League, and the Amphictionic League. This is precisely what has been the normal usage,
including that of the recent *Oxford Classical Dictionary,* and it
agrees with the common usage of other countries.[5] A number of

scholars have tried to avoid this,[6] and it is advisable to do so. In earlier articles I have taken the line of least resistance and followed the common usage, and there actually is something to be said for not trying to be more precise than the Greeks themselves. However, in a work in which several types of organizations are considered and in which federal states are particularly important, it seems advisable to adopt a term which at least will set off the federal state from the rest. For this purpose I have chosen "confederacy." Any choice has to be arbitrary. Probably "commonwealth" would be the best translation for *koinon* as applied to a state, but "confederacy" has in its favor that it has been used by others and is related to *confédération,* which has been used by a number of French scholars. Hence I shall use "confederacy" for federal states, for instance, the Achaean Confederacy, and retain "league" for symmachies and other combinations of states and tribes. It may be impossible always to be completely accurate, and thus an organization which approaches close to a federal state may at times be called a league.

Descriptions of all Greek federal states cannot be included in the present work. For those who wish to survey this entire field there are fairly adequate handbooks available, though even the best at times omit material desirable for an understanding of the institutions considered.[7] All that it will be possible to do is to mention some of the best-known states and trace the development of their institutions with special reference to representation. Ethnic states will not be considered separately, but only as an initial stage in the development of federal states.

The federal state, however, if we regard it as springing from the ethnic state, has very old roots. The tribal groups of Greece, out of which the federal states grew, seem to go back to the period immediately after the Doric migration. Judging by survivals and Homeric institutions, we can take for granted at the outset government by kings, councils of nobles, and popular assemblies. The last-named, in the period immediately after the migration and in some places much later, must have been assemblies of men under arms. The primary assembly of the Aetolians retained this characteristic to the time of the Roman conquest. There were, of course, local differences, perhaps depending upon the extent to which a district was or was not affected by the Doric invasion. For Aetolia we have from as late as 426 B.C. a description of a typical tribal system with three tribes and subtribes (Thuc. 3.94.4–5), although, as we shall see later, the Aetolians may already have been on the way to develop a federal state with an efficient central government. On the other hand, Attica with her boasted autochthony may have had a certain amount of government from urban centers—Athens herself, Eleusis, and others—continuously from Mycenaean times and may not have passed through a period as a tribal state. It is difficult to know whether the same may have been true of other parts of Greece. One possibility is Achaea. The people there in a sense formed an ethnic group, but the tradition of Achaea as a unity goes back as far as Herodotus, and by him it was already described as consisting of parts. Was there a string of settlements or palaces along the north shore of the Peloponnesus that survived from Mycenaean times? And was there a king who was supreme over all or most of these and held them together till kingship was replaced by a republican form of government?[8] Indications point to a relatively strong Achaea in the period of colonization and during the conflicts for control of the Gulf of Corinth in the fifth century. The early Achaean Confederacy may thus have been one of the very oldest Greek federal states, though our information is scant and unsatisfactory. Yet the ethnic or national composition of the people is of the greatest interest. Linguistically the Achaeans are classed as Northwest Greeks.[9] This means that at the time of the Doric migration the country was overrun by the invaders in sufficient quantity to color the language, but the name of the people, Achaean, is a name which more and more is becoming recognized as a name for a pre-Doric Greek people. Does this mean that the Achaeans consciously clung to the tradition of descent from the greatest Greek people of pre-Doric times? If so, the two elements of the population must have intermarried and blended more quickly than in other parts of the Peloponnesus. At least, we have no reports of conflict between them such as we have for neighboring Sicyon (Herod. 5.67–68). Is this successful blending of the two stocks the reason why the Achaeans early were willing to make citizens of non-Achaeans and to annex their communities as integral parts of the Achaean state?

For evidence of what a federal state may have been at this early date it is necessary to turn to the Ionian League, an organization which at first glance seems almost more shadowy than the early Achaean Confederacy.[10] It is a little difficult to know how to classify this organization. Its Ionic patriotism suggests an ethnic state, but it actually was a league of cities. Its sanctuary, the Panionion, where festivals were held (Herod. 1.148), has made some think of an amphictiony, but a federal sanctuary with festivals and meetings held in connection with them is possible even in a highly developed federal state. Its preoccupation with wars may suggest a symmachy, but governments of federal states were also concerned largely with foreign affairs. It probably can best be classified as a very loosely organized federal state. This conclusion is based on the most plausible theory of the development of the League, namely, that it originated as a monarchy and developed into a league of cities. When it is remembered that there was a king of the *koinon* of the Ionians at a later time, the theory becomes almost a certainty. This king, like the king archon of Athens, must have been a survival from the old order and a real kingship.[11] Moreover, his retention by title, no matter how tenuous his power, shows that the old government was never completely overthrown, but that it was transformed by devolution like the governments of so many Greek states, notably Athens, where the process was completed, and Sparta, where the process was arrested and the kings retained. Thus the powers that were taken away from the king must have been assumed by other officials. Hence some sort of central administration or authority must have existed, and it must have been this which summoned the extraordinary meetings at times of emergency. Of the exact nature of this machinery we know nothing. The Ionians regarded themselves as a people, but as far back as we have any knowledge cities existed among them, and thus the subdivisions or members were not tribes, but cities. Hence it seems best to describe the League as a loose or incipient federal state, though there is no specific evidence for a federal citizenship. On the other hand, there is no doubt about the citizenship of the cities, which tended at times to ignore the central government and to go their own way.

Undoubtedly it was this tendency of the cities to independence that was the cause of the proposal attributed by Herodotus (1.170) to Thales that the Ionians should have a single *bouleuterion* or place for deliberation, that this should be at Teos, since it was centrally situated, and that the other cities should continue to be inhabited as before but should be regarded as demes. This proposal is probably to be dated fairly early in the sixth century. The language of Herodotus should not mislead us into thinking that Thales' proposal envisaged a state something like Athens after the synoecism. Teos was a relatively small city and would have been completely overshadowed by Chios, Samos, and Miletus.[12] Such cities could never have stood in the same relation to Teos as the demes of Attica did to Athens. The reference to demes, though it suggests subordination, also suggests a certain amount of local government for the component parts. This is so obvious, even for Attica, that an important study of the government of the demes there is entitled *La Vie municipale en Attique*.[13] From this point of view even Attica had some semblance of a federal state. In Ionia, where the "demes" composing the larger state would themselves have been cities with the citizen bodies subdivided into tribes and these undoubtedly into other subdivisions corresponding to the Attic demes, the federal element would be much stronger.

It is impossible to make even a plausible guess about the precise nature of the executive of Thales' federalized Ionia, but something more can be said about the deliberative authority. It is natural to believe that the meetings at the Panionion were at first meetings of a primary assembly in the sense that all citizens of the twelve Ionian cities who were present had a right to take part. In practice it no doubt came nearer, but only slightly nearer, to conforming to this name than the assembly of the Amphictionic League. A real primary assembly, even moderately well attended, would be impossible for an organization including several large cities with two of the largest, Chios and Samos, situated on islands. Hence the natural way out would be to establish representative government, and this would come all the more naturally if Chios, and possibly also other of the cities, already had experimented with it. What little evidence we have points in this direction. The proposal to establish a single *bouleuterion* suggests that a *boule* or council was to be the chief deliberative body of the League. Moreover, it is known that shortly before the battle of Lade in 494 B.C., the Ionians sent *probouloi* or representatives to a meeting at the Panionion.[14] Thus even without the reforms proposed by Thales the League possessed a representative assembly. Finally, let it be said that in all likelihood the proposal of Thales is historical; if not, it is almost equally important that Herodotus should have considered it historical. It was not impossible for Greeks of the fifth century to envisage a federal state with a strong central government.

What has been said about the proposal of Thales makes it unnecessary to say much more about the Ionian League as it actually existed. All the chief actions of the League reported concern foreign policy. After the capture of Sardis by Cyrus in 546, the Ionians and Aeolians sent envoys to Cyrus requesting from him the same terms as they had received from Croesus. Cyrus repulsed the overtures and made a treaty on the terms suggested only with Miletus. The rest of the Ionians gathered at the Panionion and decided to send a joint embassy to Sparta. The language used by Herodotus (1.141) suggests that separate instead of joint action would have been possible. The Aeolians, again with some cities abstaining, decided to coöperate in sending the embassy (Herod. 1.151). It is unnecessary to follow this farther, but it may be noted that the Aeolians must have had an organization somewhat like that of the Ionians. Another meeting is reported to have been held at the Panionion after the conquest (Herod. 1.170). During the Ionian Revolt the *koinon* of the Ionians once sent a fleet to Cyprus, and it is reported that this fleet was bound—so those who served in it declared—by instructions received before sailing (Herod. 5.108–109). These instructions must have been given as the result of a decision taken at a meeting. Finally, there was the meeting of *probouloi* which preceded the battle of Lade and which took charge of the plans for the campaign (Herod. 6.7). Several of these meetings obviously were extraordinary meetings called to deal with an emergency. Hence, if we believe that regular meetings were held annually in connection with the festival of the Panionia, it is clear that there also existed some authority which could call additional meetings. If the suggestion made above, namely, that the devolution from kingship produced some other kind of federal executive, is accepted, the explanation is simple. It was this executive which called the meetings. The deliberative assembly, like the one about which we have information, was in all probability a council or assembly of delegates. It is possible that a primary assembly survived, though, as we have noted, it cannot have been well attended. On the other hand, since the theory of democracy had hardly yet begun to emphasize the role of the primary assembly, it is possible that it had been allowed to lapse. The business transacted, such as the negotiations with Cyrus, suggests that the League was able to deliberate and make permanent plans for the future of the entire group of cities. On the other hand, the history of the period shows the cities, except for occasional coöperation, going their own way. Had it not been for this tendency, the Ionian Confederacy—as it then would have to be called—might well have become our earliest fully developed Greek federal state, and its government, in all likelihood, would have been a representative government.

To summarize, if this reconstruction is correct, the Ionian League illustrates both the possibility of passing directly from kingship to federalism and likewise the difficulty of maintaining a federal state when the constituent cities grew too large and too independent in their outlook. Another possible example of development from monarchy to federalism is to be found in Asia Minor in the Lycian Confederacy, but there the initial stages were hardly Greek and the development into a republican federal state came later.[15] There is the additional difference that wars against local dynasts and pirates seem to have forced the Lycians to coöperate down to the time of the suppression of piracy by the Romans and thus to develop an organization with considerable cohesion and unity. In such a case a sympolity was, fully as much as a symmachy, a result of the need of coöperation in foreign affairs.

The earliest federal state for the constitution of which we have a fairly adequate description in a literary source is the Boeotian Confederacy of the period 447–386 B.C. It is also the clearest example we have for early Greece of representative government in a federal state. The description is contained in a fragment of a Greek history on a papyrus first published in 1908 and named from the place where it was discovered, the *Hellenica Oxyrhynchia,* or "Greek History from Oxyrhynchus," a village in the Fayum in Egypt.[16] The work has been recognized as a first-class piece of history writing, but though a huge literature has been published on the subject, the authorship has not yet been determined,[17] nor can it be discussed here. It seems safe to say, however, that the detailed account of the first part of the fourth century was written not too long after the events narrated and that its origin can be placed in the fourth century. The description of the Boeotian constitution is given in connection with events of 395 B.C., but it is clear that the constitution described is essentially that which was adopted when Boeotia recovered its independence in 447 and which was retained down to the King's Peace of 386 B.C. A few references in Thucydides allow us to see both that this constitution was in force during the Peloponnesian War and that it underwent some minor changes at the time.[18]

The description of the constitution is found in the eleventh chapter of the *Hellenica Oxyrhynchia.* It gives first a brief statement about the governments of the cities within the Confederacy. In each city there were four *boulai* or councils, containing not all citizens but all those who were qualified by the possession of a certain amount of property. Each of the four took its turn in acting as a presiding and probouleutic body and in preparing the business to be put before the other three, and what was then adopted by all was final. In other words, one of the four did approximately the work of the *boule* of Athens, while the other three served as the *ekklesia* or primary assembly of all active citizens, though the language implies that each *boule* voted separately and that a negative vote of one of the four would prevent the adoption of a measure.[19] The length of the term of service of a *boule* is not known for certain, but the example of the federal *boule* suggests a term of one-fourth of a year. The federal council also was divided into four parts, and in view of the Greek tendency to elect officials for a year's time it is a plausible guess that councilors were elected for a year and that each of the four divisions took turns to serve as the council—or one might almost say the prytany—for one-fourth of the year. The obvious parallelism of federal and local institutions suggests the same term for the local councils.[20] In any case, governments of the cities were based on a principle of direct government fully as much as that of Athens. It is likely that each *boule* contained, as it were, a cross section of the body of active citizens, and that the functioning *boule,* for practical purposes, made all decisions, with the result that approval by the other three was purely formal. But such practical surrender of the decision to a smaller body does not mean the abandonment of direct government.

The government of these cities in which the right to vote and hold office depended on a property qualification was oligarchic or, more specifically, timocratic. Thucydides indicates that it was so regarded by contemporaries when he reports a plot in 424 to substitute for it democracy (4.76.2), and in another passage specifically refers to the Boeotians as oligarchic (5.31.6). We are not told what the property qualification was, but, considering the prominence of the Boeotian infantry, it was almost certainly the hoplite census.[21] This means that those who served in the cavalry and heavy infantry were included. It is possible that a law reported by Aristotle (*Pol.* 1278a25) excluding from office those who had engaged in trade within the preceding ten years belongs to this period, and that only landowners were admitted to active citizenship. Whether, as in some oligarchies, there was also a high age qualification for active citizenship, is not known. In any case, the Boeotian cities supply one of the best illustrations we have of Greek moderate oligarchy. Since the Confederacy was composed of these cities, it was just as oligarchic as the cities.

The number of cities in the Confederacy governed in the manner described was ten. On the other hand, there were eleven of what might be called representational districts or units. The explanation is that a city might include one or more such units or might form only a fraction of a unit. Each of these districts supplied to the federal army approximately 1,000 hoplites and 100 cavalry; and to the federal government, one Boeotarch and 60 *bouleutai* or councilors. They also sent judges to the federal courts and contributions to the federal treasury in the same proportion. In short, all participation in federal affairs was regulated in the same manner. Obviously we have here a system of representation in proportion to population. It may seem strange that even contributions to the federal treasury were determined in this manner. However, the system of payments to federal treasuries in proportion to representation in the federal council seems to have been used extensively. It was still in use in the Aetolian Confederacy in the last part of the third century B.C.[22] This system, whether that was the purpose or not, must have served to discourage any effort on the part of a city to secure more than its due representation, since each additional representative would mean a corresponding financial burden. Hence, it is likely that the representation in proportion to population in federal states was approximately correct. In Boeotia it does not seem that Thebes, the largest city, had an excessive number of representatives. As to the figures given, the numbers of councilors are, of course, accurate, but hardly so the numbers of soldiers. Our source itself designates these as only approximate. Undoubtedly all men of military age and the required property qualification who were physically fit were liable to service no matter what their actual number. It is possible that the totals, 11,000 hoplites and 1,100 horse, are approximately the numbers on the military lists but that these were never attained in any particular mobilization; yet it is more likely that the actual numbers on the lists were somewhat smaller. The numbers at Delium in 424 are given by Thucydides (4.93.3) as 1,000 cavalry, 7,000 hoplites, and 500 peltasts[23]—not to mention more than 10,000 light-armed troops. The reference to these last suggests that the unenfranchised Boeotians outnumbered the active citizens, and

their use in the army suggests that the day might come when they
would prove a danger to the oligarchic form of government.

The eleven units of representation were set up as follows: Thebes
controlled four units, two on her own behalf and two on behalf of
Plataea and a number of other small towns near the border of
Attica which had once been grouped together; Orchomenus with
Hysiae—or probably rather Hyettus—controlled two; Thespiae
with Eutresis and Thisbe, two; and Tanagra, one. Thus four cities,
Thebes, Orchomenus, Thespiae, and Tanagra, together with the
smaller towns combined with them, accounted for nine of the
units. Each of the other two units was made up of three towns
which took turns in supplying a Boeotarch and which probably
each sent twenty councilors to the federal *boule*. One group consisted of Haliartus, Lebadea, and Coronea; the other, of Acraeph-
nium, Copae, and Chaeronea.[24] The statement concerning these six
indicates so clearly that they were separate towns within the League
that there is no disagreement about their status. On the other
hand, there has been a tendency to look upon the smaller towns
grouped together with the larger cities as constituting separate
cities.[25] The language of our sources, however, shows that these
towns were merged in or combined with the larger cities.[26] In all
likelihood their status was not one of subjection,[27] but rather one
of sympolity or union with the larger city—sympolity in this sense
being used to indicate a union or merging of two or more cities
into one state. Thus, to use an illustration, Eutresis and Thisbe
undoubtedly continued to exist as towns, but their citizens were
citizens of Thespiae just as the citizens of the towns and villages
scattered throughout Attica were citizens of Athens. Such absorption into a larger community may at times have been due to compulsion and may then have resulted in dissatisfaction.

Thus the ten cities of the Confederacy were the four large cities
mentioned above and the six small cities which together formed
two of the eleven representational units of the League. There
probably were some changes from time to time, particularly after
the destruction of Plataea in 427. In all likelihood it was at this date
that Thebes absorbed the cities which formerly had been grouped

around Plataea and thus doubled her representation. Then, in connection with events of 424 B.c., Thucydides (4.76.3) speaks of Chaeronea as belonging with Orchomenus, while in the *Hellenica
Oxyrhynchia* she appears as one of the small independent towns,
and so it would seem that she was detached and set up as a separate
city some time after this date. A map showing the approximate
boundaries of the territories of the ten cities is given by Eduard
Meyer.[28] A glance at this will suggest that Thebes did not have too
large a representation in proportion to her territory. Even so, her
representation was large enough to give her a preponderating influence—an influence which undoubtedly was increased by pressure on smaller members. Thus Thucydides (4.133.1) reports for
423 B.c. that the Thebans accused the Thespians of pro-Athenian
sympathies and dismantled the city wall. Such an action must have
been due to some ruling of the federal authorities, but the impetus
came from Thebes. In fact, does not the accusation of "Atticism"
suggest a charge brought by the Thebans before a federal court or
the federal *boule?* When a few years later the *demos* of Thespiae—
undoubtedly the disfranchised lower classes—rose against their
magistrates, Thucydides (6.95.2) again reports that the Thebans
came to the aid of the authorities, and that some of the revolution-
aries were arrested while others fled to Athens. In this affair, it is
clear that the oligarchs of Thebes came to the aid of the oligarchs
of Thespiae, and probably no ruling by the federal authorities was
needed. Such incidents show that one bond which held the League
together was the class interest of the oligarchs, and that the democratic party at times had to be held down by force of arms and
intimidation.

If we now turn to the federal government proper, its most remarkable feature is that it was an out-and-out representative government. The *Hellenica Oxyrhynchia* states that each of the eleven
units of the League contributed sixty councilors, and that the meetings were held in the Cadmea, the acropolis of Thebes, but it has
nothing to say about a larger assembly.[29] Moreover, a chance reference by Thucydides indicates both that the federal council had the
final decision and that, like the local councils, it was subdivided

into four sections. In fact Thucydides (5.38.2) speaks of them as the "four *boulai* of the Boeotians, which have complete final authority."[30] The remark comes in the account of the complicated diplomacy of the year 420 B.C. (Thuc. 5.36–38). Two Spartan ephors concocted the plan of reaching an understanding with Argos, the old enemy of Sparta, through the help of the Boeotians and the Corinthians. The Boeotians were themselves first to make a treaty of alliance with the Argives and then help to bring about an understanding between the latter and the Spartans. The ephors laid the matter before Boeotian and Corinthian ambassadors, who happened to be in Sparta. On their way home these, in turn, reached an understanding with certain Argive magistrates. All this the Boeotian ambassadors reported to the Boeotarchs, who were ready to go ahead with the plans immediately. Soon also Argive ambassadors arrived and complete agreement was reached. The agreement, however, was obviously restricted to a few officials who were playing the game of secret diplomacy. The first step was to negotiate a treaty between the Boeotians, on the one hand, and the Corinthians and some of their associates, on the other. This treaty was submitted by the Boeotarchs, who obviously expected a routine confirmation, to the four *boulai* without any information about the understanding with the Spartan ephors. They thought that, even so, the *boule* would follow their advice. Here the shift to the singular shows that Thucydides really had in mind the federal council which was divided into four sections. The members, however, could see nothing in it except a proposal for a treaty with the Corinthians, who then were at outs with Sparta, and so rejected the proposed treaty for fear of antagonizing the Spartans. Therewith the whole matter was dropped.

This story caused trouble when the *Hellenica Oxyrhynchia* was first published, for the account in this work spoke only of four councils in each of the Boeotian cities and had nothing to say about four councils in connection with the federal government. Hence a view which actually was maintained was that Thucydides meant, or should have meant, the four councils in each of the cities within the League. This would mean that such questions as treaties would have to be submitted to the separate councils in every city. This interpretation has by now been so generally abandoned that it hardly needs to be refuted in detail. It may suffice to say that submission to all separate city councils could have worked only if the Confederacy had been free from local antagonisms. In Boeotia, where measures favored by one city would have been opposed by other cities, it could never have worked.[31]

The hesitation to accept a federal council of 660 members divided into four sections seems to have been due to a failure to look at the question from the ancient Greek point of view instead of the modern. A council of 660 members seems an absurdly large representative body for a state as small as Boeotia; the Greeks, however, appear to have hesitated to delegate final authority to a small body. Even their probouleutic councils, which did not have final authority, tended to be large. Hence they had to be subdivided, and if the federal council was to be subdivided, what more natural than that it should be subdivided on lines similar to those of the councils of the cities?

A result of the hesitation to entrust authority to small councils was that the large councils in their turn left most of their work to smaller groups. In the Boeotian federal council a division of 165 members undoubtedly served as a probouleutic body for the others and did most of the work. But even a body of 165 men is too large to serve successfully as a committee. Hence, as the story told by Thucydides implies, most of the important and confidential work was left to the Boeotarchs, while the council did little but give formal approval to their work. It looks as if the government of the Boeotian Confederacy was in theory a government by a representative assembly of 660 members but in practice a government by a representative committee of 11 members.

The Boeotian Confederacy is shown to have been a true federal state by the strength of the central government and by the definite demarcation between the spheres of the federal and local governments. This has been questioned, but wrongly so.[32] The Confederacy definitely possessed the government of a state with a board of executive magistrates, a large representative council, a treasury and income, and a federal court or courts. This is enough to indicate that for all intents and purposes there existed a federal citizenship. The strength of the federal government is indicated also by the fact that it imposed uniform local governments upon the member cities. The existence of a federal treasury is significant, but less so, for even an alliance, such as the Delian League, could possess a treasury. Moreover, it seems that the central authorities did not themselves collect taxes, but, as we have already noted, that quotas were contributed by the cities in proportion to their representation in the federal government, that the local authorities themselves supplied pay or expense money to their councilors,[33] and that the latter were paid only when on duty. The members were sent by the various sections. Hence it is clear that they were elected locally. Probably the most plausible conjecture is that in every city one-fourth of its representatives were chosen by vote by each of the four local councils.

In the federal government the chief executive officials were the Boeotarchs and the chief deliberative body was the *boule* or four *boulai*. War, the army, diplomacy, and treaties belonged to the sphere of the federal authorities. The incident of the proposed treaty with Corinth which was rejected by the councils indicates that the Boeotarchs were in charge of diplomatic negotiations and often did not even inform the councils about what was going on. It also suggests that the Boeotarchs were in the habit of submitting motions to the councils and having them accepted. Thus the actual probouleutic power belonged more to them than to the group of 165 councilors who probably possessed it officially. In the army it is clear from Thucydides' account of the battle of Delium (4.91–93) that the Boeotarchs were in command and that on any specific occasion one was in supreme command. At Delium it was Pagondas, a Theban, but it is not known how the commander was selected or for how long any one Boeotarch held the supreme command. The marshaling of the army by units suggests that the various contingents of hoplites were commanded by their own Boeotarchs.[34] Apparently the authority of the commander-in-chief did not include the right to decide how all troops should be drawn up.

At Delium the Thebans were drawn up twenty-five deep, the others as chance would have it. This, while it suggests that the Thebans had already begun the advances in military technique for which the period of Epaminondas is generally given the whole credit, also indicates a surprising amount of local autonomy in military affairs. The various divisions sent their contingents and occupied the positions assigned to them in the line of battle but drew up their men as each contingent saw fit.[35] Probably the actual decision was made by the Boeotarch in charge. If so, not all the other Boeotarchs adopted the Theban plan.

From the Boeotian Confederacy we learn, first and foremost, that the earliest Greek federal state of which we have anything like an adequate description possessed a representative government. What are we to conclude? It seems natural to conclude that the same is probably true of some of the less well-known early federal states. In the second place, a consideration of the Boeotian institutions and a comparison with other information shows that the constitution must have been a conscious creation and a product of oligarchic theory. The whole elaborate arrangement of city and federal government smacks of theory and artificial construction. Moreover, there is a kinship, though it cannot be traced here in detail, between the Boeotian constitution and the oligarchic movement in Athens which forged the constitution of Draco, produced the attack on democracy by the "Old Oligarch," and found expression in opposition to the democratic movement and particularly in the oligarchic revolt of 411 B.C. The chief difference is that while the Athenian oligarchs could do no better than construct a government which lasted a few months, the Boeotian oligarchs produced one which lasted about sixty years. If the oligarchy was the creation of theory, so must the representative government have been. But this, be it noted, was accepted only for the federal government. For the local governments, the principle was rather that of rotation in office—that is, in the four councils—of all sound men of property.

These points have not entered sufficiently into our thinking about Greek history and political institutions. Even the simple fact that the Boeotians possessed representative government has been noted only by very few,[36] while several of those who have described the institutions adequately enough have failed to take the last step and draw this conclusion. Even more rare has been the realization of the significance of the conscious adoption of representative government in a state adjoining Attica precisely in the Periclean Age when democratic theory and enthusiasm was at its height at Athens. This must mean that, at least in oligarchies, representative government was the accepted form of government for federal states. This does not mean that all federal states had adopted it, for some may well have preserved and developed the old primary assemblies. On the other hand, it is wrong to treat the one clear piece of evidence we possess as a description of something exceptional which was completely unnoticed by other Greeks. To do so is to carry over a point of view developed before this evidence was discovered. Moreover, since Athens once actually imitated features of the Boeotian city governments, it is inconceivable that the representative character of the federal government should go entirely unnoticed. The reason we have so little information about representative government in other Greek federal states of this period may well be the check to the development of federalism caused by the dissolution of federal states as a result of the King's Peace of 386.[37]

Suggestions of the existence of representative government in other early Greek states have been made at times, but the evidence is not always convincing. Thus, to take one example, Thessaly early acts as a unit and in such a way as to exhibit some of the characteristics of a federal state. As late as the fourth century the head appears to have been an official called *tagos,* elected—when he was elected, for the Thessalians sometimes had no *tagos*—for life. To outsiders such a monarchial head naturally appeared to be a king, and he is sometimes so called in our sources.[38] But the *tagos* was not an absolute monarch, and the Thessalians possessed also some sort of deliberative body. To go back no earlier than to 510 B.C., the Thessalians in that year, by a decision of this body, sent their "king" and a thousand horse to Athens to aid Hippias against the

Spartans (Herod. 5.63.3). The alliance or friendly understanding, which was not new at the time, was interrupted by later events, and Athens entered into a new alliance with Thessaly in 462 (Thuc. 1.102.4). Early in the Peloponnesian War the Thessalians, in virtue of their old alliance—undoubtedly that of 462,—sent a division of cavalry to aid the Athenians (Thuc. 2.22.3). There is a reference to commanders of the contingents of the cities; some are mentioned by name, and, it is stated that from Larissa there were two, one from each faction. This must refer to the oligarchic faction and the more popular, not to say democratic, pro-Athenian faction. At the time the latter faction must have had the upper hand, for we can hardly believe that Thessalian nobles favored sending help to Athens merely on account of their obligations under a treaty. A few years later, in 424, when the Spartan Brasidas crossed Thessaly, the majority was still friendly to Athens, and Brasidas was met with the objection that he was committing an injustice in crossing Thessaly without the common approval of all.[39] Nevertheless the pro-Spartan group was able to get him across Thessaly unmolested. According to Thucydides, this was because an arbitrary oligarchy (*dynasteia*) counted for more than responsible or constitutional government. This probably means that the powerful nobles were able to act without submitting the question to the assembly or council which should have decided. What was the nature of this body? A. H. J. Greenidge argued that it must have been a council composed of delegates and called it "the earliest instance of political representation on a large scale in Greece."[40] This statement was written before the discovery of the *Hellenica Oxyrhynchia* had revealed the Boeotian constitution. With our present knowledge, representative government in Thessaly in the fifth century would seem even more natural than it did when Greenidge wrote. Unfortunately, the language of Thucydides seems to imply an assembly to which all Thessalian citizens were admitted. In Thessaly, a land of serfs, this at most would mean all the free men of the country; but even so, an assembly would be very unwieldy, and consequently it may have been relatively easy for the nobles to usurp the real leadership.

The case for representative government is somewhat stronger for the Chalcidic Confederacy, a younger contemporary of the Boeotian.[41] The federal state of the Chalcidians was organized probably about 432 in connection with the revolt of Potidaea and what has been taken as the synoecism of a number of near-by towns with Olynthus. It is true that the usual interpretation of the account of Thucydides (1.58) suggests the creation of a unitary state consisting of one city and its territory, in the manner of Athens and Attica, and there have been scholars who have maintained that this was all that there was. Thucydides, however, commonly speaks of the people as Chalcidians, thus indicating that the state was regarded as the commonwealth of the Chalcidians rather than as the city of the Olynthians. It is true also, as Professor D. M. Robinson has remarked in connection with the publication of an inscription referring to the *polis* of the Olynthians, that "the official name of the state was 'the Chalcidians.' "[42] It should be reasonably clear that the *koinon* which is mentioned in a treaty of the Chalcidians with Amyntas of Macedonia[43] refers to the federal state or government in opposition to the *polis* of the Olynthians. Thus in the few inscriptions we possess we have references both to the federal government and to one of the cities within the Confederacy. Another inscription preserving fragments of a treaty between the Chalcidians and Philip II of Macedon contains a reference to the federal magistrates.[44] Almost equally conclusive is the speech attributed by Xenophon (*Hell.* 5.2.12–19) to Cleigenes of Acanthus, an envoy who came to Sparta in 382 B.C. to request intervention against Olynthus. Whether the words are those of Cleigenes or of Xenophon matters little; in either case we have the evidence of a contemporary. He speaks of cities being forced into a sympolity with Olynthus and being compelled to use the same laws. This suggests a federal state, but is not fully conclusive, for sympolity could be used about absorption into a unitary state. More conclusive is reference to the right of intermarriage (*epigamia*) and the right to acquire real estate (*enktesis*) in each other's communities. Such a statement has no meaning unless the cities continue to have a corporate existence within the Confederation.[45] Finally, it may be mentioned that there is in Polybius (9.28.2) a reference to the Confederacy as a federal state in which Olynthus was the leading city.

The evidence cited disposes of the theory of a unitary state. It is easy to understand Professor Robinson's enthusiasm[46] at finding at last a document referring to the city of Olynthus. Naturally the document confirms the existence of the city as a corporate unit, and, since it refers to the sale of a house which had once been the property of the city, it shows that Olynthus, like other Greek cities, could and did own real estate; but it does not supply a shadow of an argument for the conclusion that the city of the Olynthians is the same as the commonwealth of the Chalcidians. The evidence at the same time tends to invalidate the theory that a unitary state was created in 432 and that a confederacy was formed later by the addition of other cities. The addition of cities to a unitary state does not create a federal state, but only a larger unitary state. The substitution of a federal state for something else, whether a unitary state or a looser tribal state, must be due to a conscious creation of a new constitution. Such an act can be placed most convincingly in 432, a time at which a major change is known to have been introduced. This seems reflected in the language of Thucydides. He is much more inclined to speak of the Chalcidians, while Xenophon often speaks of the Olynthians, thus mentioning the capital instead of the Confederacy. The usage of Thucydides suggests that the later state of the Chalcidians, in other words the Chalcidian Confederacy, was in existence at the time of the events he describes, and that must mean that it goes back at least to 432. It is possible but very unlikely that the closely organized federal state goes back still farther. As for the usage of Xenophon, it may not be out of place to recall our own tendency to speak of London and Paris when we mean Great Britain and France. It may be more to the point to recall that the seat of the federal government was Olynthus and that the capital probably was so large as to dominate the Confederacy, as Thebes did the Boeotian Confederacy of the fourth century B.C. and Demetrias the Magnesian of the second.

For the form of the government there is no direct evidence. It has been concluded on the basis of a reference to talk about the Thracian gold mines in the *demos* of the Olynthians that the government was democratic[47] and that the chief organ of government therefore was a primary assembly. This may have been the form of government, but it should not be necessary to point out that the evidence cited hardly proves the conclusion drawn. *Demos* need not refer either to a primary assembly or to a democracy, but simply to the people of Olynthus. Probably the best argument for a democracy is that a primary assembly meeting in the capital can be a perfect instrument for the domination of a federal state by that capital, for the simple reason that it is much easier for people living near than for people at a distance to attend meetings. But would democracy be a form of government acceptable to the enemies of Athens? Hence it is not surprising that it has been argued that the government was aristocratic or oligarchic and imitated the form of government of the Boeotian Confederacy.[48] This is very likely, but it cannot be definitely proved. The prominence of the Chalcidic cavalry would suggest, if anything, a narrower oligarchy than that of Boeotia.[49] Even so, it is possible that the Chalcidic Confederacy merely had a high property qualification for active citizenship and employed a primary assembly. On the other hand, the example of Boeotia makes it natural to believe that the constitution makers of the time, when they drew up a constitution for an oligarchic federal state, would give it a representative government, and so it is likely that this was the form of government of the Chalcidic Confederacy.

One final point about this confederacy. It is clear that for a federal state it was strongly unified both politically and economically. We have already noticed a reference to a uniformity of laws. This may suggest primarily uniform local governments in the cities, as in the Boeotian Confederacy, but Aristotle (*Pol.* 1274b23) refers to a lawmaker who drew up laws for the Chalcidians of Thrace concerning homicide and inheritance, and so it is possible that the uniformity of law went farther than mere constitutional matters. On the economic side, the possession by citizens of *enktesis,* the right to acquire landed property in the other cities of the Confederacy, is important as evidence of the manner in which already at this early date the creation of federal states was beginning to break down the economic barriers between cities. Yet, as far as the development of federal government is concerned, the reference to the collection of the customs for the federal government in the seaports and other ports of entry (Xen. *Hell.* 5.2.16) is even more important. The actual collection undoubtedly was conducted by tax farmers. Also a treaty of the Confederacy with Amyntas of Macedon (Tod, 111) shows that the customs duties were under the control of the federal government. In thus allowing the federal government a direct source of income the Chalcidians seem to have been in advance of the Boeotians. The same is true also of two other states on the northern frontier of Greece. A chance remark in one of the speeches of Demosthenes (1.22) suggests that by his day the federal government of Thessaly had taken over the customs. The same is suggested for Epirus for about 300 B.C. by a grant of exemption from the payment of duties made by the central government to an Atintanian.[50] This clearly was the simplest way to give the central government a regular and direct source of income, and it is rather surprising that we do not have more evidence of its use for that purpose. In fact, it rather seems to have fallen into disuse. So far as we can judge by the evidence now available, the lead in exploiting this source of income for the federal government rather than the local governments was taken by the Chalcidian Confederacy.

To conclude, the examples of the Boeotian and Chalcidian confederacies indicate a strong movement toward federalism in the fifth century. They also indicate that the federal governments of the time went far in creating uniform institutions in the cities within the confederacies. On the side of economic centralization and the breaking down of barriers between cities the best evidence comes from the Chalcidic Confederacy. For representative government the best evidence comes from Boeotia; but there is also the strong likelihood that the Chalcidic Confederacy and possibly other contemporary states had adopted the same form of government, and the near certainty that even earlier the Ionian League was on the way to develop into a federal state with representative government. Nevertheless, later in the fourth century, it will be seen that federal states regularly adopt governments with primary assemblies. Something has happened to check the natural development toward representative government. This seems in part to have been the wide adoption of the theory of democratic government with its glorification of primary assemblies and of the collective judgment of the masses. In the second place, it seems to have been discovered by statesmen who wished virtually to subject the rest of the confederacy to the capital that a primary assembly meeting in the capital was an excellent instrument for that purpose. The development may also have been influenced by the fact that some of the new organizations were created in opposition to Sparta, the traditional champion of oligarchy, and so naturally adopted a democratic organization, and, by that time, a democratic organization meant a primary assembly. This development will be taken up later, but first it will be well to glance at the tendencies toward the development of representative government in what started out as alliances concerned exclusively with foreign affairs.

III
Representation in Greek Permanent Alliances

THE CHIEF permanent alliances or symmachies to be considered are the Peloponnesian League, the Delian League, the Second Athenian League, and the Hellenic League of Philip II of Macedonia and his successors.[1] Of these, the first served as the instrument for Spartan leadership in Greece; the second and the third, as instruments for Athenian leadership; the last, as an instrument for leadership and attempted unification of Greece by Macedonian kings. Hence their history is a large part of the political history of Greece from the sixth century before Christ to the Roman conquest. Naturally it will be possible to deal only briefly with their institutions, and with their history scarcely at all except in relation to the progressive development of these institutions. An attempt will be made to show that these leagues, while theoretically alliances of completely autonomous states, tended to develop more and more of a machinery of government and to establish control over the members. Great advances were made in the Second Athenian League, but the highest development was reached when the Hellenic League of Philip and Alexander guaranteed to protect the members against revolution at home. When that was done, the organization had advanced far along the road toward federalism and, given time and opportunity, might well have reached the goal.

The history of the movement begins with the Peloponnesian League. In the sixth century before Christ, Sparta gathered to her side a considerable number of allies in the Peloponnesus. At first these merely had separate treaties with Sparta, but before the end of the century the group was transformed into the Peloponnesian League.[2] Thereafter, when Sparta proposed a war of the League, she could call a meeting of the assembly, and if a majority voted for war, the members were obliged to take part and obey her orders.

Next, before the formation of the Delian League, comes the Hellenic League organized in 481 for the prosecution of war against Persia, and the Hellenic League as reorganized at Plataea in 479. The first was a symmachy organized for a limited objective, which seemed to have been attained with the victory at Plataea. At that point, when the Persian War proper was considered completed,[3] an effort was made to transform it into a permanent Hellenic League.[4] As such it did not function successfully for any length of time. As a result, little is known about the details of its organization. It may be enough to note that it was not considered defunct when the active conduct of the naval war was taken over by the Delian League. The latter was organized late in 478 and placed under the leadership of Athens. Its main purpose was to continue the naval war against Persia. Thus, ostensibly at least, it was not founded to be an instrument for augmenting the power of Athens, but the fact that it was transformed into an Athenian empire is only too well known. Naturally, what will concern us in the present study is chiefly the institutions of the League before this transformation. The Athenian empire, in turn, went under in the Peloponnesian War, which Sparta fought for the freedom of Greece and won with Persian gold only to show herself a more arbitrary oppressor than her opponent had been. This gave Athens a chance to organize a new league, the Second Athenian League, in 378 B.C., to uphold the freedom of the Greeks against Sparta.[5] This League seems to have been founded on a wave of enthusiasm, with Athens promising to abstain from all the abuses of which she had been guilty in the days of the Delian League. So far as institutions are concerned, the Second Athenian League marks an advance. It was also successful at first in winning the supremacy of the sea for Athens and her allies, but how short-lived this success was is indicated by the fact that a few years later Athens joined Sparta in a fight against the rising power of Thebes, one of the earliest members of the League. This is symbolic of the confusion and rivalry of a period which teemed with peace congresses, plans for coalition, and even talk of Panhellenic peace and unity, though unity in the form of union against the barbarians. This culminated in the Hellenic League, frequently known as the Corinthian League, organized by Philip II of Macedonia, continued by his son, and revived by later kings. It was the most advanced and statesmanlike of all the symmachies, but the hegemony—that is, the leadership—was held not by a Greek city but by a Macedonian king, and there was the rub. Probably even more disastrous in the long run was the absorption of the kings in larger problems. The leadership of Greece was still coveted, but it was rather for the sake of prestige and as a source of soldiers to keep conquered barbarians in order than for its own sake. This League will hereafter be referred to simply as "the Hellenic League." Other versions or attempts at organizing Hellenic Leagues, such as those of 481 and 479 and the one founded by the Macedonian king Antigonus Doson in 224/3 B.C., will be more fully identified.

These leagues were permanent alliances of free states under the hegemony of a state or later of a king. The hegemony meant the executive power and primarily the right to command the armed forces of the league. The permanent tenure of the hegemony by one specific power meant that the leagues, while they did have assemblies to determine their policies, did not have elected executives. This is one of the most marked differences between a symmachy and a federal state; the latter always has a central government of a sort. The freedom of the members of the symmachies was so emphasized by the ancients that it need not be demonstrated. The term, of course, might be deceptive and the theoretically free states might actually be under the control of the power holding the hegemony. That these leagues were permanent alliances, in the sense that they were made for an indefinite period or for all time, may not be quite so clear. For the Peloponnesian League the evidence is indirect, though pretty convincing.[6] Actually the Peloponnesian League was the most enduring of its kind. Meanwhile we hear only of threats of secession, when members claim that their rights are being violated, and of the counterclaim that secession is a violation of the oaths of the members, in other words, contrary to the fundamental law or constitution of the League. For the Delian League we have direct evidence. When it was formed,

members sank red-hot iron into the sea as a symbol of its perpetuity.[7] Such a pledge may seem strange in connection with the
formation of a league organized with a specific objective, the free-
ing of the Greeks from Persia. When a league was made permanent
under these circumstances, it must have been because by that time
it was taken for granted that symmachies of the kind should be
permanent. If so, the tradition must have been established by the
example of the Peloponnesian League. Thus also the case for the
latter league is strengthened. For the Second Athenian League
the best evidence for permanency is the treaty between Athens and
Corcyra by which the latter was admitted into the League (*SIG*[3],
151; Tod, 127). This is definitely marked as a treaty for all time.
It is not unlikely that the decree by which the Athenians early in
377 issued an invitation to join the newly formed League also
contained a reference to its permanency. A few lines of the document were chiseled out in antiquity. They have been restored by
Silvio Accame in such a way as to indicate that one purpose of the
League was to make peace, or the general peace (*koine eirene*),
endure forever.[8] Such a clause must mean that the League itself
was to endure forever. Finally, the Hellenic League of Philip II
expressed the idea of permanence through an oath of allegiance to
himself and his descendants.[9] Probably the Greeks had a tendency
to consider their obligations extinguished with the death of the
king to whom they had taken their oath, but Alexander the Great
surely made it clear that this was not his interpretation. It could
also be objected that in Macedonia the succession was not certain.
Even so, there can be little doubt that the oath was meant to be a
pledge of loyalty to Philip and his successors and that Philip intended the League to be permanent. Undoubtedly, the later and
looser Hellenic League of Antigonus Doson founded in 224/3 B.C.
similarly was meant to be permanent. Thus, from the sixth century
B.C. to the Roman intervention in Greece, permanent alliances
under the hegemony of a city-state or a king were a constant and
prominent factor in Greek interstate relations.

Naturally, permanent symmachies were not the only interstate
organizations in ancient Greece, nor were those few that have been

mentioned the only ones of their kind. Alliances could be organized also with a limited objective and for a short time. Such an organization was that of the Greeks organized in 481 for the conduct of the war against Persia, which has already been mentioned, and such probably was also the organization of the opponents of Sparta in the Corinthian War early in the fourth century.[10] Since the *synedrion* took charge of propaganda, shaped policies, and received subsidies from Persia, it was more than a mere council of war; and since it was organized in 395 and was still available at the time of the visit of Pharnabazus and Conon in 393, it is clear that it was not a mere convention meeting for a few days. Yet, since there is no indication that it was intended to be permanent, it is best regarded as a temporary symmachy. It is also interesting as a symmachy which did not entrust the hegemony to a single power. This suggests that there may have been considerable variety in Greek interstate relations. A further demonstration can be found in the many conventions of the century called to deal with the questions of peace and Greek interstate relations with the objective of establishing a *koine eirene,* a general or common peace, in Greece. Interesting as these conventions are, they cannot be discussed here except to note that arrangements for a general peace mean little unless there are sanctions for enforcing the peace. If those who sign the peace guarantee to coöperate in enforcing it, they become allies, and we have a symmachy. To what extent the conventions drawing up the peace treaties also organized symmachies is a complicated question and need concern us only for its bearing on the Hellenic League of Philip II. It is clear that the latter League, both during his lifetime and that of Alexander, placed a great emphasis on the *koine eirene* and that the members of the League could be referred to as "those who share in the common peace." As a result, it has at times been maintained that the League organized by Philip was not a symmachy but a league for peace. Since it was pretty clear that, when war was voted against Persia and when Alexander later had allied contingents serving on his expedition, an alliance existed, another version was that the league for peace was organized first and was followed later by a symmachy.

The simplest reply would be that the exact nature of the League
does not matter from the point of view of the present study. A
league of states with a hegemon and an assembly would in any case
be in the same line of development as a symmachy and would be
equally useful for a study of the development of institutions. Yet,
that I may not appear to avoid an issue, let it be said that what
Philip II organized seems to have been a symmachy from the
outset. It is so referred to in a second-century arbitration in which
earlier settlements are mentioned.[11] In the document the organization connected with the arbitration was a symmachy. This, in turn,
also demolishes the theory of a league of peace followed by a
separate symmachy, for had there been two such organizations the
work of arbitration obviously would have belonged to the league
of peace. However, if this argument is not convincing, let us take a
look at the oath of allegiance sworn by the members of Philip's
original league, the oath which, it has been alleged, contains no
references to a symmachy.[12] Unfortunately our copy of the oath is
very much mutilated and even in the part preserved we have less
than half of each line. This is a situation which lends itself admirably to endless disputes about the correct restoration. I shall try to
avoid citing any doubtful interpretations and shall even readily
admit that a plausible restoration of the preserved lines can be made
without inserting the word *symmachia,* and that since the word
has not been preserved we cannot be sure that it was used. But
even the absence of the word from the original document, if that
could be proved, would not settle the issue. The substance of the
document is more important. The oath clearly contained a pledge
not to overthrow the kingship of Philip, not to violate the treaty
or fundamental law of the League and, as far as was possible, to
prevent others from doing so. It even contained a promise to go to
war under certain conditions, and in that connection there is a
reference to the *synedrion* and the hegemon. If a league with obligations which may involve its members in war, with a hegemon
or commander-in-chief of its armed forces, and with an assembly
to determine its policies is not a symmachy, then what is?

Reference has already been made to advances and developments

in the institutions connected with the symmachies. These developments concern the assembly, approaches toward the formation of
a federal executive, and growth of a body of law which to some
extent involved even civil law.

To begin with the assemblies, the assembly of the Peloponnesian
League was subject to the call of Sparta and met only when summoned by her. If a member of the League desired a meeting, it was
necessary first to induce Sparta to call a meeting, and the Spartans
were likely, before doing so, to vote on the issue at stake themselves,
as they did in 432, when Corinth wished action taken against
Athens. In this way Sparta was able to prevent any proposal dis-
tasteful to herself from being brought before the assembly. Probably most students of the question believe that Athens held a
similar position in the Delian League.[13] This, however, is carrying
over a procedure which is known from the Peloponnesian League
but is contrary to what little evidence we have for the Delian
League, and the scholars who do so seem hardly to be aware that
they are generalizing about the procedure in symmachies from
one example, the earliest and least developed one in the entire
group. In the Delian League it is likely that at the beginning
regular meetings were held every year on the island of Delos. Meetings at the beginning of the campaigning season would be natural
in a league organized to conduct a war, and Thucydides (1.97.1)
does inform us that at first the allies discussed the policies of the
League in the meetings of the assembly. Moreover, he represents the
revolting Mytilenaeans as saying that the allies had been unable to
unite to oppose the Athenians successfully because they were outvoted (3.10.5). The implication is that they were free to bring up
what they wished in the assembly but that it was useless to do so
because they were outvoted by the many states which followed the
leadership of Athens. Most conclusive, however, is the statement
in the same speech that the Mytilenaeans had equality of vote with
the Athenians, thus indicating that the Athenians, instead of being
in a position to decide in advance whether questions were to be
submitted or not, merely had a single vote in the assembly like the
most insignificant member. Nor is it necessary to presuppose a

privileged position for Athens in order to explain her rapid usurpation of power. The usurpation can be explained easily enough by the tendency of the smaller states to vote with Athens because of her prestige and especially because Athenians commanded the fleet and Athenians administered the treasury of the League. In the Second Athenian League, a century later, the situation was different. The members of the assembly of the allies seem to have established themselves at Athens and to have been on hand permanently. Under the circumstances, they must have been available for meetings on short notice even if there were no regular meetings at fixed intervals. Since the assembly—as we shall soon see—had a presiding officer or, more likely, committee of its own, the summons pretty certainly was issued by this committee, but we can be sure that it never refused to call a meeting if the Athenian authorities desired one. The Hellenic League of 337 b.c. and later, on the other hand, held its regular meetings at the Panhellenic Games and, in addition, made provision for the calling of extraordinary meetings. In this connection, may I say once and for all that the continuity between the Hellenic League of Philip II and Alexander the Great and the League as renewed by Demetrius Poliorcetes in 302 b.c. is now so well established that I regard it as sound to use information from both periods for drawing a composite picture of the League's institutions. The information about the time and place for the meetings comes from the long inscription from Epidaurus connected with the renewal (*IG* IV², 1, 68).

Greater changes and progress are to be found in the system of representation in the assemblies. In the Peloponnesian, Delian, and Second Athenian leagues each state had one vote. This does not necessarily mean that each state had only a single representative present, but that each member state voted as a state and had a single vote. This is pictured most clearly for the meeting of the Peloponnesian League in 432 at which the Spartans called in turn on each *polis,* large or small, for its vote (Thuc. 1.125.1). The one league for which we have evidence of variation in the size of the delegations is the Second Athenian League. According to the account by Diodorus (15.28.4) of the founding of the League, it was agreed that each city, large or small, was to control one vote. Here it may be well to note that the name used for the assembly is *synedrion* and, for the members, *synedros* or, in the plural, which is the form used most frequently, *synedroi*. Diodorus is a late historian who commands little respect in his own name but who often draws on excellent sources—here, in all likelihood, the contemporary historian, Ephorus. At any rate, for interstate organizations and conventions of this period the account of Diodorus is the best we have and, as a whole, is better than that of the other contemporary, Xenophon. The latter, with his aggravating habit of completely ignoring some of the more important events of his time, has nothing to report about the founding of the Second Athenian League. However, when we turn from the statement of Diodorus that each city had one vote, to the inscriptions, we find that there are a number of references to delegates of particular states. Thus we hear of a single delegate from Carystus (*SIG*³, 190; Tod, 153), probably also a single delegate from Tenedos,[14] but another document refers to the *synedroi* of the Mytilenaeans and the *synedroi* of four other cities of Lesbos (*SIG*³, 164; Tod, 131), thus indicating that Mytilene, at least, had several delegates. The most usual interpretation is that each city had one vote but that it sent as many delegates to Athens as it wished. Another is offered by Accame, who holds that since each city had one vote, each also had one *synedros*. He has argued, consequently, that in the last inscription cited the stonecutter made an error in copying the document. Accame, therefore, has amended it in such a way as to remove the reference to the several delegates of Mytilene.[15] The amendment, from our point of view, improves the language of the document, but such emendations are dangerous and here it is unnecessary. Another departure from the normal interpretation is the conclusion that Diodorus is wrong and that the member communities were represented in proportion to their size or population.[16] This is possible, for the Second Athenian League marked a decided advance on earlier symmachies in other respects, and why not in this? The system of representation in proportion to size or to military strength is definitely attested for the Hellenic League of 337 (*SIG*³,

260; Tod, 177), but why need it be new at the latter date and not a part of the great creative work of those who organized the Second Athenian League forty-odd years earlier? Viewed thus broadly, the question becomes merely one of the date of adoption of this particular form of representation in symmachies. In spite of the attraction of the earlier date, it seems best to vote with the majority in favor of the later date and to conclude that Diodorus is right and that the members of the Second Athenian League each had one vote. The main evidence, aside from what has been cited, is an Athenian decree dealing with the admission of Corcyra, Acarnania, and Cephallenia into the League. In connection with their representation in the assembly, the decree merely states that all the cities are to send representatives.[17] Again the inscription is somewhat fragmentary, but enough has been preserved to make it reasonably certain that it contained no statement concerning the size of the delegations. Such looseness of statement would be almost unthinkable if the number of votes assigned to the states varied, particularly since those mentioned in the present document were large and on the system of proportional representation would have had several representatives each. One of them, namely Acarnania, seems to have been an entire federal state. Thus it is most likely that representation in proportion to size was first adopted in symmachies in connection with the organization of the Hellenic League by Philip II in 337 B.C. Nor must the extent of the change be underestimated. It was more than a mechanical reform. It must have tended to produce the impression that the assembly was no longer an assembly of representatives of separate states, but an assembly of the Hellenes in which each section of Hellas was represented in proportion to its importance. The league was still regarded as a league of independent states, but in the method of representation it was subtly tending to foster national consciousness and to create a national federal state.

Is there a name for the assembly of a symmachy corresponding to the term *boule* for the council and *ekklesia* for the assembly of a city-state? The name which was used in the Second Athenian League and the Hellenic League is *synedrion*.[18] It may be recalled that the name seems to have been used also for the assembly of the temporary symmachy of the Corinthian War (Diod. 14.82.2 and 84.5). For the earlier leagues it is possible that no formal name had been adopted for the assembly. That of the Delian League has often been called *synodos* on the basis of the usage of Thucydides, but when the latter speaks of the Delian League (1.96.2 and 97.1)—as well as in the one passage in which he uses the word for a meeting of the assembly of the Peloponnesian League (1.119)—the word clearly means "meeting" rather than "assembly."[19] The expression "the *synodoi* [meetings] of the *synedrion* [assembly]" used in connection with the Hellenic League (*IG* IV,[2] 1, 68. 70) will suggest that the name of the body attending the meetings was the *synedrion,* but this evidence is from 302 B.C. What evidence we have for the earlier period points in another direction. Herodotus (6.7; 7.172) uses *probouloi* for the delegates to the assemblies of the Ionian League and of the Hellenic League of 481. *Probouloi* occurs also in the decree which according to Plutarch (*Arist.* 21.1) was proposed by Aristeides at the Congress of Plataea in 479. There it is used about the members to be sent to the future meetings of the Hellenic League. This is a word which clearly suggests that the delegates were to act as councilors and were to do so on behalf of others, but it does not suggest any convenient name for the council or assembly, unless it should be *boule,* but that does not seem to have been used for the assembly of symmachies. Thucydides, in the one passage in which he applies *synodos* to a meeting of the assembly of the Peloponnesian League, refers to the members as ambassadors (*presbeis*), a word which indirectly indicates that they acted on behalf of separate states. Probably in the early symmachies, at a time when, in all likelihood, delegates were chosen separately for each meeting, people merely spoke of meetings of delegates and ambassadors. Later, when the assembly was looked upon more as a standing institution, it was natural to adopt some specific name for it. As far as the etymology and meaning are concerned, *synodos* would have done as well as *synedrion,* but the latter was the word which came into general use, as is attested by both literary and documentary sources. It probably was already in use for the council of the Amphictionic League. *Synedrion,* though used also as equivalent to *boule,* was common as a name for councils of symmachies and the like and for other interstate conventions.

Before leaving the assemblies, it may be well to note that the assemblies of the Peloponnesian, Delian, and Second Athenian leagues did not function in quite the same way even though in all three the members seem to have possessed equality of vote. In the Peloponnesian League, Sparta did not vote in the assembly, but brought questions before the allies and asked for the vote of the allies. In the Delian League, the fact that the Athenians themselves had an equal vote with the other members indicates that originally they were not supposed to have any privileged position in determining the policies of the League. This, to be sure, did not prevent them from transforming the League into the Athenian empire. In the Second Athenian League, Athens was not represented in the assembly, and the assembly did not have an Athenian as chairman. The theory seems to have been that the policy of Athens and her allies was determined by the Athenians and the allies acting in agreement with each other. The problem of the extent to which the Athenians were limited in their own freedom of action by the obligations to their allies is too complicated to be discussed here. Whatever the theory was, in the long run Athens became the predominant partner. In the Hellenic League, as is attested by the long inscription dealing with the renewal of the League in 302, the decision of the assembly was final (*IG* IV², 1, 68. 73). This naturally did not prevent the king who held the hegemony from influencing and probably at times even dictating the measures adopted.

Now a word about the members of the assembly. It will be remembered that the two names applied to the members of the earliest assemblies were *presbeis,* or ambassadors, and *probouloi,* or councilors deliberating on the behalf of others. Of these two names the latter seems, on the whole, the more appropriate one. It is both possible and probable that the members often voted in accordance with what they knew was the public opinion of their communities. At times when the issue to be considered was known in advance, they may even have received instructions before they left home.

Nevertheless, the impression gained from the reports of meetings and actions of assemblies is that there were real debates at the meetings and that the members were called upon to use their judgment. The occasions for genuine decisions at the meetings must have become progressively more numerous. In the Second Athenian League it must often have been impossible to get instructions from home. For that reason the states which could afford it may well have found it desirable to have more than a single representative on hand. This may indirectly have made it possible to send *synedroi* along on embassies and other executive missions without interfering with the efficiency of the *synedrion*. Yet members must at times have felt themselves under constraint, and some may even have been punished at home for their votes in the assembly. That may well be the reason for the rule adopted in the Hellenic League in 302, if not before, that members were not to be held to account at home for their action in the *synedrion* (*IG* IV², 1, 68. 75 f.). It is hardly necessary to say that this has been interpreted as a measure enabling the king to make the members subservient to himself, but so far as institutions are concerned it is this independence from the home authorities and this theoretical right to rely upon their own judgment which mark the *synedroi* as true representatives rather than ambassadors.

Except for the participation of *synedroi* of the Second Athenian League in executive work already referred to, the chief development of executive machinery came in connection with the chairmanship of the assemblies. Earlier, most of the executive work fell to the power holding the hegemony. To it belonged primarily, as the word itself indicates, the command of the armed forces of the League, but also much else, and at the outset specifically the right to call and preside over the meetings of the assembly. The substitution of an independent chairmanship can be traced with confidence as far back as to the Second Athenian League. Some proviso for a presiding officer or committee independent of the hegemony must have been included in the constitution or fundamental law adopted when the League was organized in 378 B.C. Otherwise it looks as if the increase of the business to be transacted by a league tended to increase the burden imposed upon the power holding the hegemony and consequently also the influence possessed by this power. Thus, the regular contributions or tributes levied in the Delian League were administered by a committee of ten Helleno-tamiae, or treasurers of the Hellenes, who were Athenian citizens and elected in Athens. The arrangement apparently was made merely because there was no federal executive machinery, and the easiest and, at the time, the most natural way to take care of the task was to hand it over to the power holding the hegemony. Naturally, in time, when the treasury was moved from Delos to Athens, and Athens assumed control of the assessment as well as the administration of the tribute, this placed a great and oppressive power in her hands. It was hardly so at the outset. As has been pointed out by the authors of *The Athenian Tribute Lists* (III, 230 f.), though the League was intended to be permanent, it was not the intention that the tribute should be permanent. In fact, the periodic revision of the assessments indicates this; the tribute was to correspond with the needs and conditions of the time, and it must at first have been assessed subject to the approval of the assembly. Yet, even so, the entrusting of the financial administra-tion to the city holding the hegemony was a dangerous measure. The same danger was involved in similar arrangements set up in the Second Athenian League a century later, only there the situa-tion was even more acute because the shortage of funds developed more quickly. In this respect, in spite of all Athenian promises of good behavior, the Second Athenian League marks no progress.

The most significant advance actually made by the Second Athenian League was the acquisition by the *synedrion* of the right to have its own presiding officers. The publication some thirty years ago of a long document connected with the revival of the Hellenic League in 302 (*IG* IV², 1, 68) revealed that in that organization five *proëdroi* were chosen by lot from among the members of the *synedrion* to preside over and control its meetings. Hardly anyone would hesitate to admit that this means that the institution goes back as far as 337 B.C. There were some who also noticed that the *proëdroi* suggested the influence of Athens, where *proëdroi* were adopted for the assembly about 378 B.C.,[20] at a time when Athens not only founded the Second Athenian League but also adopted a number of domestic reforms. Since the *synedrion* was present in Athens continuously, was subject to call when needed, and was the recipient of communications and complaints, it seemed hardly too bold to conclude that it was the Second Athenian League which first adopted *proëdroi* for the *synedrion* of a symmachy. At any rate, in 1927 I ventured the conjecture that the League must have had a presiding committee similar to that of the Hellenic League, and that its members probably were called *proëdroi.*[21] Since then this conjecture has been proved correct in the main, though we do not know the size or name of the committee. In fact, as far as the evidence now available is concerned, there might have been a single chairman instead of a committee, but from what we know of Greek institutions as a whole this is very unlikely. The fact that only a single individual is mentioned in the document does not prove that a committee did not exist. The evidence consists of an inscription first published in 1936 in which is preserved part of a decree of the *synedrion* passed in 373/2 B.C.[22] The chairman, whose name is lost, was a Theban. The important point is that he was not an Athenian. In all likelihood he was one of a committee, and, as already suggested, the members probably were called *proëdroi.*[23]

The administration of justice was very likely the field which afforded the greatest opportunity for the symmachies to increase the power of the central authorities in such a way as to approach a federal state in practice if not in theory. An impediment to this development was lack of the necessary machinery. The symmachies had no separate courts or judges, and consequently the assembly had to serve both as a deliberative body and as the judiciary. In making this statement I am contradicting the conclusions reached by some of the ablest scholars who have examined the Second Athenian League and have claimed a separate judiciary for it. On this point, however, it would seem that the use of the much-debated and rather dangerous comparative method is warranted. The Hellenic League did not have a separate judiciary, and in other respects it seems to mark an advance over the Second

Athenian League. It would be most strange if the latter should possess a separate judiciary while the Hellenic League had none. Hence we should not accept the notion of a separate judiciary for the Second Athenian League if any other reasonable explanation of the evidence is possible. Another explanation is not only reasonable, but is also actually more in accord with the evidence.

It was natural that symmachies should be founded without any special judiciary. It was their duty to act and not to judge; yet it was inevitable that from time to time intervention against a delinquent member should be discussed, and the assembly must then have conducted some sort of trial to determine the guilt or innocence of the accused state. There must have been some activity of this kind even in the Peloponnesian League. In the Delian League it actually helped Athens to impose her control upon the allies through the judgment of the assembly in cases of revolt or secession. In the Second Athenian League there was an opportunity for action not only against offending states but also against individuals, and since the *synedrion* was permanently present in Athens and possessed its own chairman or chairmen, it was better able to take care of such additional activity. The need for greater activity was largely due to the surrender by the city of Athens of jurisdiction over her own citizens to the assembly of the allies. This was done through the decree of 377 B.C. inviting states to join the League and indicating the favorable terms upon which they were able to do so (*SIG*³, 147; Tod, 123). As for the promises of good behavior in the future, provision was also made for action against Athenian citizens who violated these promises.

In the document just mentioned there are two important passages dealing with the judiciary activities of the *synedrion*. In the first (lines 41–46) it is provided that if an Athenian has acquired property illegally in one of the states belonging to the League, any one of the allies who wishes may report the offense to the *synedroi* of the allies. The *synedroi* are to [confiscate and] sell the property. Half the money realized is to be paid to the informer and the rest is to go into the treasury of the allies. Here the *synedrion* is authorized to pass judgment on the offending Athenian, but apparently the only penalty is to be the loss of the illegally acquired property. Probably even more startling than the jurisdiction over Athenian citizens is the implied jurisdiction of the *synedrion* within the various states belonging to the League and the assigning of the money realized not to local treasuries but to the treasury of the League.

Another passage (lines 51–63) is more troublesome. It provides that any Athenian who makes a motion in violation of the decree is to lose his citizenship, his property is to be confiscated, and a tenth of it is to go to Athene; he is to be liable to trial before the Athenians and the allies on the grounds that he is overthrowing the symmachy; he is to be punished by death or banishment from Athenian and allied territory, and if he is condemned to death he may be buried neither in Attica nor in allied territory. This is the passage on the basis of which it has been argued that there must have existed a joint court of Athenians and allies.[24] An analysis of the situation and of the normal procedure of the League should lead to another conclusion. The procedure for determining the policies of the League was based on the assumption of agreement between the *synedrion* of the allies and the assembly of the Athenians. Why not, then, take the view that the legal procedure was based on the assumption of agreement between the Athenian court and the court of the allies, that is, the *synedrion?* The offender under this procedure was an Athenian and the offense was committed at Athens. Thus the offender would not normally be accessible to the allies at all. It is unthinkable that the Athenians in such cases should expose their own citizens to a mixed tribunal. The illegal acquiring of property abroad by Athenians is quite another matter. It is a far cry from renouncing extraterritoriality to inviting foreigners to come in and sit in judgment on your own citizens. What, then, can the reference to trial before the allies mean? If it is remembered that the condemned man, dead or alive, so to speak, was to be banished from the territory of all allied states, the explanation is simple. It must be that after the Athenians had condemned their citizen, the allies were asked to confirm the judgment.[25] It is also possible that when the Athenians were slow to act, the *synedrion* could take the initiative and conduct, as it were, a preliminary trial and then request the Athenian authorities to take action against the offenders.

In the Hellenic League, as in the Second Athenian League, the judicial activity fell to the *synedrion*. Thus we hear that during their term of office the five *proëdroi* had full charge of the meetings and could discipline offenders, but when their term was over they could themselves be brought to trial before the *synedrion;* the Athenian orator Aeschines (3.161) complained that the Athenians had not surrendered Demosthenes nor allowed him to be brought to trial before the *synedrion* of the Hellenes; Alexander the Great in his letter to the Chians (*SIG*³, 283; Tod, 192) stated that traitors were to be liable to trial in the *synedrion* of the Hellenes. But this is not the place to collect all the evidence or to discuss the subject at any length. The examples given are enough to indicate that in the Hellenic League also there was a tendency to acquire jurisdiction over individual offenders. Jurisdiction against offending members can almost be taken for granted. One example will be cited as an illustration of how the *synedrion* could take care of an increased burden of work. We have record of an act of arbitration between the two little islands of Melos and Kimolos performed by the people of Argos in virtue of authority delegated to them by a decree of the *synedrion* of the Hellenes (*SIG*³, 261; Tod, 179). This promising development was, of course, soon cut short.

Causes for action by the league authorities were, no doubt, at first chiefly the delinquencies of states belonging to the leagues. With the Second Athenian League there was a marked increase in actions against individual offenders, or at least in rules permitting such action. The reason for this development, however, lay not so much in the original constitution of the League as in concessions later made by Athens to her allies. In the Hellenic League there seems to have been an increase in the number of occasions for intervention by the League authorities. These guaranteed to defend the members not only against attacks of outsiders but also against revolutionary movements within the states. This, of course, also meant that the *synedrion* would have to decide when measures being undertaken or proposed involved such threats. Whether such a law was a reactionary measure tending to check progress need not concern us here. What concerns us more is that an interstate organization which has acquired over its members as extensive rights as this is well on its way to becoming a federal state. Had the development been completed, the form of government would have been a federal constitutional monarchy. The question now has only an academic interest, but the development traced has a bearing on our investigations, and this is particularly true of the adoption in the Hellenic League of representation in proportion to population. With this system taken over from the city-state and the early federal state into a symmachy, it is almost unthinkable that thereafter a federal state should organize its representative council or assembly on any other principle.

IV
The Adoption of Direct
Government in Federal States

REPRESENTATIVE government, after its promising start in early Greece, received a setback in the fourth and third centuries. Instead, direct government with primary assemblies was adopted also in federal states. Yet the advances which had been made were not all lost. The councils continued to be organized on the principle of representation in proportion to population. This was the practice in city-states; it was employed in the early Boeotian Confederacy and probably in other early federal states; and it was taken over into a symmachy in the Hellenic League. Here it may be well to mention that the use of *boule* as the name for the council of a federal state suggests the modeling of federal governments upon those of the city-state. In the federal states so far considered, direct evidence for a *boule* has been found only for the Boeotian Confederacy, but it is likely that it existed in the fifth century also in the confederacy of the Bottiaeans, a neighbor and contemporary of the Chalcidic Confederacy. The evidence, unfortunately, is an imperfectly preserved copy of a treaty between Athens and the Bottiaeans (*SIG*³, 89; Tod, 68), and the crucial word has been in part restored. For the later period there is evidence for a *boule* in each of three of the confederacies to be considered, the Aetolian,[1] Arcadian, and Achaean, but, in contrast to the early Boeotian Confederacy, all three reserved the most important decisions to a primary assembly. In the Achaean Confederacy, as will be argued in the next chapter, this was true only down to 217 B.C. or thereabouts. Of the three, we actually have evidence for representation in the council in proportion to population for two, Aetolia and Arcadia. For a later period we have evidence also for Thessaly and Lycia.

The early development of federalism was largely checked by the King's Peace of 386, which stipulated that the cities of Greece were to be free. Nor were they, so to speak, left free to determine whether they wished to be free or not. Sparta was the arbiter and enforced the dissolution of federal states on the ground that cities in federal states were not free. Of major states, first to fall was the Boeotian Confederacy. There, undoubtedly, some of the cities welcomed the dissolution. It was different with the Chalcidic Confederacy. It is true that Sparta intervened at the request of a city which did not wish to be forced into the Confederacy, but it is also clear that the members were opposed to dissolution. Sparta, however, did not dissolve all federal states. The early Achaean Confederacy was her own useful ally and was allowed to continue. The best evidence for the early Achaean Confederacy as a sympolity is found in connection with events of 389 B.C. This was before the King's Peace, but it is clear that the Confederacy continued in existence after the peace. There are some indications that the Aetolian and Acarnanian confederacies also may have been in existence at the time.[2] If so, they too escaped interference from Sparta in their domestic affairs. Thus federal states could continue in existence after the King's Peace if, like the Achaeans, they were allies of Sparta, or if, like the Aetolians and Acarnanians, they were, from the Spartan point of view, remote and therefore unimportant. The case of Boeotia was quite different. She was too near and too powerful to escape attention.

The Peloponnesian and Second Athenian leagues, it may be noted in passing, could continue to exist under the King's Peace for the reason that they were symmachies which recognized the freedom of the members. To be sure, here too it made some difference who was at the head of an organization. For some time Sparta had adopted, whenever it was possible, the policy of having her allies make treaties by which the latter promised to have the same friends and enemies as the Lacedaemonians and to follow their leadership. The earliest such treaty known was that with Athens of 404 B.C. (Xen. *Hell.* 2.2.20), but there is reason to believe that Sparta had adopted the policy exemplified by it as early as 418 B.C.[3] From our point of view such treaties meant that Sparta's allies were subject allies and were deprived of any voice in their foreign policies. Had

Athens been called upon to judge, Sparta undoubtedly would have been found guilty of depriving her allies of their freedom. The Second Athenian League, it will be remembered, was founded in order to maintain the freedom of the Greeks against Sparta. The Peloponnesian League undoubtedly still claimed to be a league of free states, and since Sparta was the judge it was easy for her to acquit herself on the charge of oppressing her allies. Meanwhile Athens, too, had been acquiring allies who were virtual subject allies, but she found it necessary to abandon such treaties after the King's Peace and to start over again with treaties which recognized the freedom of both parties. These allies served as the nucleus for the formation in 378 of the Second Athenian League with its decided emphasis on freedom.

The setback given federalism by the King's Peace was only temporary and did not affect all federal states. The setback given representative government was greater and more lasting in its results. This was not because the terms of the treaty took any cognizance of representative government. It was rather because the dissolution of a federal state made it possible, as in the case of Boeotia, to make a new start and to organize the state on other lines. That the new pattern involved the use of primary assemblies was due to a number of causes, which were hardly always the same. One cause must have been the wide acceptance of the theory of democracy with its emphasis on the primary assembly and the collective judgment of the masses. In Athens, after the overthrow of the Thirty Tyrants in 403, democracy apparently was outwardly almost universally accepted, though some of those who talked democracy were not democrats, but oligarchs boring from within and trying to transform the government on oligarchic lines.[4] Undoubtedly, also, in federal states there were politicians who were anxious to manipulate democratic institutions for particular interests. Thus in a federal state with a single city considerably larger than the rest—as, for example, Thebes in Boeotia—a primary assembly could be used for giving the capital virtual control of the entire state. On the other hand, in a federal state with no large cities a primary assembly may at times have been well adapted to local conditions. This may have been true for the Aetolian Confederacy.

The history of the Aetolians is one which has had to be remade in recent years.[5] The description given by Thucydides in connection with events of 426 used to be taken as that of a typical ethnic state, while the Aetolian Confederacy as a federal state was thought to be of Hellenistic origin. This interpretation had to be changed when an inscription first published in 1939 (Tod, 137) showed that the Confederacy must have been in existence as early as 367 B.C. and that it may have been older. Under the circumstances it may be well to reëxamine the account of Thucydides. When this is done, the pattern of the ethnic state remains, but there are signs that a responsible central government already was developing.

Thucydides (3.94.4–5) lists three tribes and says that they lived in unfortified villages widely scattered. Later he mentions two subtribes of one of the three (3.96.3), which seems to imply that the other two also were composed of subtribes. When the Aetolians sent an embassy to Corinth and Sparta, there were three ambassadors, one from each of the large tribes (3.100.1). This arrangement, with settlement in unfortified villages and division into tribes and subtribes, is definitely the pattern of an ethnic state. On the other hand, the conduct of affairs by the Aetolians suggests anything but a loose and unorganized, not to say nonexistent, state. The Aetolians did not conduct their campaign in the way the Athenians would have liked, but that was because they knew too much.

The Athenian general Demosthenes had been persuaded by the Messenians of Naupactus, neighbors and enemies of the Aetolians, that conquest would be easy. When his advance is followed (Thuc. 3.96–98), it is seen that at first he had no difficulty. The Aetolians withdrew before him and allowed him to occupy place after place; but they were aware of his coming, had mobilized troops even from distant parts of the country which were not directly affected by the invasion, and fell back and fought a battle in a place of their own choosing. It looks as if they had as good an intelligence department and as efficient military organization and strategy as any Greek state. After the battle the Athenians were granted a truce to pick up their dead; that is, the Aetolians understood and observed the normal Greek practices and international law with regard to conduct after a victory. Moreover, they were not satisfied with merely repelling the invaders. They sent an embassy to Sparta and asked for help and they coöperated in the subsequent attack on Naupactus (Thuc. 3.100–102). Obviously, the Aetolians had a central government or leadership capable of pursuing a conscious and consistent foreign policy. Yet the Messenians of Naupactus, who were as well qualified as any to know the facts, had insisted that the conquest of Aetolia would be rapid and easy. It looks as if the efficiency of the Aetolians was new and a surprise even to the people of Naupactus. Apparently, the Aetolians, under the pressure of being drawn into Greek politics, had created an efficient central government. We should probably be justified in calling it a federal government, but the organization was on ethnic lines.

Later the component parts of the Aetolian Confederacy were cities. Some of these were perfectly normal cities; a glance at the rugged inland sections of Aetolia will suggest that some of the units may actually have been "country districts grouped round some village or hill fort,"[6] but this did not affect the general pattern. Since the cities had representation in the council of the Confederacy in proportion to population,[7] it is clear that the transformation must have been due not only to a gradual change in living conditions in the country, but also to some definite act of legislation or reorganization, which could be dated if we had the evidence. Probably the best we can do at present is to try to fix a *terminus ante quem*. As a *terminus post quem* we already have 426 B.C. Efforts to date the emergence of the federal state have usually centered round the occurrence of the word *koinon,* but this word can be used with so many meanings that it is impossible to use it to prove that the Aetolian state at any particular time was organized by cities rather than by tribes. Thus the inscription of 367 B.C. already mentioned shows that the transformation had taken place, not because it refers to the *koinon* of the Aetolians, but because it shows us Aetolia in possession of a central government which could make agreements on behalf of the entire state, which could be approached at any time by embassies, and which is considered capable of dealing with members guilty of violation of an agreement, and because—and here is the crucial point—the offending members were the people of an Aetolian city. By this time Aetolia must have been a sympolity of cities. For 335, more than thirty years later, Arrian (*Anabasis* 1.10.2) reports an embassy sent by the Aetolians by tribes. There is not necessarily any contradiction between this and the evidence for organization by cities, for even after the adoption of the latter system there may at times have been some consideration given to the old tribes.

The government of the Aetolian Confederacy as late as the second century before Christ included a representative *boule* or *synedrion* and a primary assembly with two regular meetings a year and extraordinary meetings called when needed. This primary assembly continued extremely active. It is hardly necessary to present proof that the primary assembly existed in the early days of the Confederacy. For the council there is the record of the honors bestowed at Athens upon an Aetolian *boularch,* or one of the presiding officers of the *boule,* in 333/2 B.C.,[8] and it is pretty sure that the council goes back at least as far as the organization by cities. Changes there may have been. Certainly the absorption of new members into the Confederacy led to the enlargement of the council. Otherwise the general pattern of the Aetolian government seems to have been the same from late in the fifth or early in the fourth century to the second century. The primary assembly may well have been a continuation and development of a primitive institution and may hardly have needed any democratic theory to bolster it up. Moreover, in a state involved in a long series of wars an assembly made up essentially of the soldiers of the state must have served its requirements well, particularly since the regular meetings were held in the spring and autumn before and after the campaigning season. Finally, when the Confederacy expanded, a primary assembly with votes taken by heads admirably served the purpose of keeping the control in the hands of the Aetolians proper and their immediate neighbors.

For the Boeotian Confederacy as reorganized after the liberation of Thebes in 379 and the Arcadian Confederacy organized in 370, it is natural to believe that the theory of democracy was drawn upon. This may well have been particularly necessary in Boeotia, where an oligarchic representative government had existed down to the dissolution of the old Confederacy in 386. One may suspect, however, that Epaminondas and others actually favored a primary assembly, because as long as its meetings were held in Thebes the Confederacy was under the control of that city. For this reason our sources have a tendency to speak about action by the Thebans in such a way that the reader is not aware of a Boeotian Confederacy, but there are other statements which imply a Boeotian organization, and there are a few inscriptions recording documents. Most important are two decrees of about 364 B.C. in each of which a foreigner is made *proxenos* of the Boeotians (*IG* VII, 2407 and 2408). Of these one is a Carthaginian and one a Byzantine. The decrees were voted by the *damos,* which must be the primary assembly; they are dated by the *archon,* obviously the highest titular magistrate of the Confederacy; and they have at the end a list of Boeotarchs, seven in number. It looks as if the representative council of the earlier Confederacy had been replaced by a primary assembly and as if the probouleutic power had been taken over by the Boeotarchs. Since no *boule* is mentioned in these inscriptions, it is possible that none existed.° This may seem surprising, but it will be remembered that in the earlier Confederacy the Boeotarchs apparently to all intents and purposes exercised the probouleutic power, and so, when the Confederacy was given a primary assembly, a separate *boule* may have seemed unnecessary. Nothing more is known about the *archon.* If, as there is reason to believe, the Thebans elected four of the seven Boeotarchs, it is easy to see that, since the deliberative power was exercised by a primary assembly meeting at Thebes, they must have had complete control of the Confederacy. In the absence of any evidence to the contrary for this period, it can be taken for granted that the vote was taken by heads or, probably more literally, by hands, so that a majority of those present decided the issue—and at the normal meetings those present were mostly Thebans.

The Arcadian Confederacy, founded in 370, is one of the most famous of all Greek federal states since its foundation was one of the more important steps in the anti-Spartan movement of the period. We have relatively adequate information about its institutions. Even so, we do not know too much, but the pattern of a democratic state with a *boule* and a primary assembly emerges clearly. The primary assembly, the Ten Thousand, is mentioned in the literary sources, while in a decree to be dated in the period 369–367 B.C.[10] we find the expression: "It was voted by the *boule* of the Arcadians and the Ten Thousand." At the end comes a list of fifty *damiorgoi*. The word, of course, means someone who works for the people, and is used as a name both for handicraftsmen and for magistrates. Here, naturally, it means magistrates or officials of some kind. The body of fifty *damiorgoi* has variously been taken to be the *boule,* or a committee of the *boule* roughly corresponding to the prytany of the *boule* of a city-state. The latter view is more likely to be correct. Fifty is too large a number for a small executive board such as the eleven, and later seven, Boeotarchs. On the other hand, fifty is too small for a democratic *boule,* and the Arcadian setup in general, including the formula indicating that a decree was voted, recalls a democratic city-state. There is, however, one difference appropriate to a federal state. The *damiorgoi* were not the delegates of a single city or part of Arcadia, but were chosen from various cities roughly in proportion to their size. Most of the cities had five each, but the new capital, Megalopolis, had ten; one city, three; and one, two. Obviously the scheme was based on five as the normal delegation of a city, with ten for an extra-large city, and a group of five divided between two smaller ones. Whether this was the council or, as is more likely, a committee of the council, it indicates at any rate that the group was made up of delegates chosen on a principle of proportion, as in the council of the city-state and in the Boeotian Confederacy of the period 447–386 B.C. About one other feature we learn from the literary sources. The Arcadian Confederacy had at its head a single general, corresponding somewhat to the *archon* of the contemporary Boeotian organization. However, there was a difference: the Boeotian *archon* is known only from the inscriptions as an eponymous magistrate and may have been a civil administrator of little importance; the *strategos* of the Arcadians was the outstanding personality in the Confederacy. One of the two *strategoi* known to us was Lycomedes of Mantinea (Diod. 15.62.2, 67.2), the virtual founder of the Confederacy. This is among the earliest examples known of what was to become common in federal states, a single extremely influential official as the head of the confederacy. The usual title, *strategos*, of course means general, and he was the commander-in-chief in war, but his position was such that he could well be called the president.

Just how this government functioned is not known to us. It is easy to guess that the primary assembly did not meet as often as in a city-state and, therefore, that much of the work fell to the *boule*, but it is clear that the primary assembly was the sovereign body of the state. On the method of voting we lack all information except what can be deduced from other Greek institutions. E. A. Freeman remarked in an obscure spot in a footnote that to give each city a distinct vote would be "more consonant with Greek Federal practice" than to count by heads.[11] It is true that for Hellenistic times there is evidence that the vote in the primary assemblies of a number of federal states was taken by cities, but for this earlier period such a practice is unlikely. The example of the city-state suggests representation in proportion to population in the council, but the vote counted by heads in the primary assembly.

It has been said that the government of the Arcadian Confederacy recalls democracy. Whether it actually was a democracy is another question and depends on whether there was a property qualification or some other limiting qualification for voting. Our answer, in turn, depends on how literally we take the word *myrioi*, "ten thousand," as applied to the body of voters of the primary assembly. If the body of voters was actually thought of as numbering approximately 10,000, this would correspond roughly to the number of hoplites in Arcadia and so would point to a property qualification.[12] *Myrioi* may, however, mean an indefinitely large number, and it is legitimate to doubt whether such numbers as ten thousand or five thousand when used in Greek as names for political bodies are ever to be considered even approximately exact. On the other hand, Arcadia was a land of soldiers and farmers, and a hoplite census would not be inappropriate. Even so, the adoption of a primary assembly may well have been based on the democratic argument for the superiority of the collective judgment of the masses. At any rate, there is no doubt about the existence of the primary assembly.

Of all federal states to be considered for this period, the most important is the Achaean Confederacy. The early confederacy mentioned in the preceding chapter need not be considered at any length. We know practically nothing about its form of government. We do know that as early as the first part of the fourth century before Christ it had begun to overstep the ethnic boundary and to incorporate non-Achaeans. Thus, when Aratus of Sicyon about 250 B.C. brought his Doric home city into the Achaean Confederacy and thus initiated an era of growth and expansion, the measure was not an innovation but a revival of an old practice. For the history of federalism as a force in Greek history this may be more important than details of forms of government—but at the moment the subject under consideration is institutions.

The Achaean Confederacy was, after some years of interruption, refounded in 280 B.C. Around its government has centered the controversy concerning the extent to which the ancient Greeks possessed representative government. The key words in the debate are, from the point of view of those who have followed earlier Greek institutions, newcomers. They are *synodos* and *synkletos*. Of these, *synodos* is used frequently in the accounts of Polybius of meetings in the Achaean Confederacy, and it also occurs in a couple of inscriptions of the second century; *synkletos* is used once in Polybius (29.24.6) about a meeting of Achaeans, and occurs in this sense also in an inscription of the second century B.C. (*SIG*³, 675), in which a *synkletos* follows a *synodos*. On the basis of this inscription it was not unnatural to take the two words as official names for two types of assemblies or meetings. It was recognized that *synkletos* was used for an extraordinary meeting of all active citizens called to deal with a question of war or alliance and later, also, with a written communication from the Roman senate. The main part of the work of the government and administration fell to the body which met at the regular *synodoi,* and on the composition of this depended the solution of our problem of representative government. Naturally the question has been much debated. For some time it was becoming more and more common to regard the *synodos* as a representative body or a meeting of such a body and consequently to consider the government of the Achaean Confederacy essentially a representative government.

All this was changed in 1938 with the publication of André Aymard's detailed and acute study of the Achaean assemblies,[13] in which he argued that the *synodos* was always a primary assembly. Seldom has any work had a greater impact on scholarship. Thus F. W. Walbank, who once had thought that a *synodos* was to be equated with "a meeting of the Boule or League Council,"[14] in his review accepted Aymard's interpretation almost without reservations.[15] Similarly Tarn, in his *Hellenistic Civilization* (66 f.) published in 1927, had referred to the *synkletos* as "a mass referendum," had described the *synodos* as "composed of delegations from the several cities in proportion to population," and had remarked that "so far then as the system could be called representation, the Achaean League had advanced much further than any other Greek state." The third edition of the same work remarks concerning the *synodos* that "the most probable reconstruction makes it a primary assembly" and then cites Aymard.[16] Naturally there was some dissent, for instance in reviews by M. Cary and myself,[17] but the dissenters also, while disagreeing on this point, recognized the importance and merit of Aymard's work.

It may be well to confess that among the statements which sought to demonstrate that the Achaean *synodos* was a representative assembly was one by myself.[18] This has not been published, but a copy of it was sent to Professor Aymard before he completed his own book, and he has courteously cited it on a number of points. After going over the evidence again, I now conclude that a *synodos* commonly was a meeting of a primary assembly down to 217 B.C., but that after 200 at the latest a *synodos* was normally a meeting of only the *boule* and magistrates, while the primary assembly no longer met except on special call for extraordinary meetings. This interpretation starts from the demonstration by Aymard (415-421) that the *synkletos* was first differentiated from the *synodos* shortly before 200 B.C. by means of a rule reserving action on certain questions for extraordinary meetings. It also owes much to his careful and acute analysis of the evidence. It differs from his approach, however, on one important question, the interpretation of *boule*.

Aymard argues that *boule* in Polybius—our chief source for Achaean institutions—means simply "a deliberative assembly" (*assemblée délibérante*) and could be applied to a primary assembly (155 and n. 4; cf. 67-75). He goes so far that when Polybius (2.37.10) speaks of the Achaeans as having "the same [i.e., federal] magistrates, *bouleutai*, and dicasts," he thinks that *bouleutai* refers not to the council but to the legislative assembly (157-159), and this he takes to be a primary assembly. But does not the very wording of this passage imply that *bouleutai*, like the other two nouns, denotes a body of men which is not identical with the citizen body but which serves it or acts for it? This one passage should be enough to establish that there existed a federal council which could be called a *boule*. Moreover, it is necessary to insist against Aymard that *boule* is used so regularly about a smaller council in opposition to a primary assembly that we must believe that this is its meaning also in Polybius. It is a question not of etymology but of usage. From Homer[19] through classical Greek, Hellenistic, and Roman times the word appears to have been used regularly for a council. We are less certain about *bouleuterion*, of which the normal meaning is "council chamber." Since assemblies commonly were poorly attended, what was theoretically a meeting of a primary assembly might at times be held in a council chamber. This, however, will not seriously affect our argument.

This disagreement about the meaning of a simple word makes it necessary to survey the reports of meetings in some detail. The argument should not be too difficult to follow since it turns largely on accepting the meaning of "council" for *boule* and "primary assembly" for *ekklesia*. On the other hand, *synodos* will be taken to mean a meeting rather than a council or assembly. Hence a *synodos* can be a meeting either of a *boule* or of an *ekklesia* or of both. Once this simple approach is taken, a large part of the mystery connected with reports of meetings will disappear and it will be seen that the statements of Polybius about Achaean institutions are much more simple and direct than they have often been considered, and his language more technical and accurate.

Synodos certainly could be used as the name for an assembly. It is so used by Diodorus (15.59.1), who applies it to the Ten Thousand of the Arcadian Confederacy. But the word has a great variety of meanings and "meeting" is a very common one. Thus it has already been seen that Thucydides (1.96, 97, and 119) uses it about meetings of the assemblies of the Peloponnesian and Delian leagues, and that it is used in a document about the meetings of the *synedrion* of the Hellenic League (*IG* IV², 1, 68. 70). It could also be used about a meeting of the Amphictions (Aeschines 2.115) and of meetings of both the *boule* and *ekklesia* at Athens (Arist. *Const. Aths.* 4.3). Polybius himself, when writing about the Aetolian Confederacy, uses *synodos* for the primary assembly but also, once, about a conference of Aetolian officials.[20] Thus it is clear that he can well have used the word with "meeting" as its primary meaning and that it is by itself no guide to the composition of the body attending the meeting.

Let us now turn to the meetings of the Achaean Confederacy from its refounding in 280 B.C. to 217 B.C. Since accounts of earlier meetings are not available, the period actually covered will be from 229 to 217. This is the time of the war of the Achaeans against Sparta and her reforming king, Cleomenes, of the entente of the Achaeans with Antigonus Doson of Macedonia and the resulting founding of a new Hellenic League, and of the Social War (220–217), that is, the war of the Aetolian Confederacy against Philip V, the new king of Macedonia, and his Greek allies. Not even all of these meetings will be discussed here. For the others see the Appendix.

For 229 Polybius (2.46.6) reports what appears to be an extraordinary meeting of both the *boule* and the *ekklesia*. The officials are said to have gathered the Achaeans and to have made the decision "together with the *boule*" to take up openly the war against Sparta. The wording suggests a meeting of the assembly at which the *boule* played a special part. Probably it acted as a probouleutic body.[21] The meeting appears to be an extraordinary meeting, but it is not called *synkletos.* Other extraordinary meetings are reported for 225. We learn from Plutarch (*Cleom.* 15.3, 17.1; *Aratus* 39.1) that the Achaeans invited Cleomenes of Sparta to attend a meeting of the *ekklesia,* that he proved unable to come at the time, and that he was to have attended a later meeting at Argos. The one specific mention of the earlier meeting places it at Lerna, but it has been conjectured that it too was to have been held at Argos.[22] Both meetings were called for negotiations with Cleomenes. Later in the year the *ekklesia* met at Sicyon and elected Aratus *strategos autokrator,* general with final authority (Plut. *Arat.* 41.1). All three undoubtedly were extraordinary meetings (Aymard, 310–313). Though we may not be able to rely on the terminology of Plutarch, it is interesting to note that he uses *ekklesia* twice but does not call any of the meetings *synkletos.*

For regular meetings, the accounts of those of 220 B.C. are most illuminating. For this year there are four *synodoi* implied or recorded (Aymard, 263 f.). An earlier electoral *synodos* is implied by the information given in connection with the next *synodos* that Aratus had already been elected general but had not yet entered his office. In this period, when the *synodoi* were meetings of the primary assembly, it is likely that the elections were held at a regular *synodos.* Aymard (253 and n. 6) places this particular meeting about April 15, though in 218 the election is known to have been held earlier.

The second *synodos* came just before the newly elected general took office (Pol. 4.7). Aymard (263) places it in the middle of May. The language used by Polybius implies that the meeting was a regular fixed *synodos* required by law.[23] The Achaeans, therefore, gathered in their *ekklesia* and voted to give military aid to the Messenians and to mobilize the army, adding the proviso that whatever the men under arms should decide was to be valid. In spite of the mention of the *ekklesia,* this has been taken as an example of a meeting at which the *synodos* was incompetent to make the final decision, but referred the question to the army instead of a *synkletos*. It is much better to follow the natural and simple interpretation of the language and conclude that the *ekklesia,* the primary assembly, was present at the meeting and that it made the decision on the main issue but referred future decisions on detail to the army, which thus was given special authority for the occasion (cf. Aymard, 222 f.). In virtue of this authorization a meeting of the men under arms was later held at Megalopolis and took up for consideration the appeal from Messene for aid and for admission into the Hellenic League. The answer given was that the Achaeans could not by themselves admit the Messenians into the Hellenic League, but that they would send aid if the latter would supply hostages. It was also decided to send an ultimatum to the Aetolians, who had been harassing the Messenians and were the cause of all the trouble (Pol. 4.9.1–5).

The third *synodos* of 220 was held at the very end of the Olympic year (Pol. 4.14.9). Apparently this was in midsummer, though no one seems able to date it precisely. The meeting followed a singularly unsuccessful campaign conducted by Aratus against the Aetolian force then in the Peloponnesus. A few days after the defeat at Caphyae the mass (*plethos*) of the Achaeans was gathered at a regular *synodos*.[24] At this meeting Aratus was criticized, but defended himself and regained the confidence of the majority. It was then voted to send ambassadors to the Epirotes, Boeotians, Phocians, and Acarnanians, and to Philip to report on the conduct of the Aetolians and to ask for help. It was voted, furthermore, that the general was to select 5,000 foot and 500 horse and was to support the Messenians in case the Aetolians should appear again. He was also to arrange with the Messenians and the Spartans about the forces to be raised by them for the same purpose (Pol. 4.14.1–15.4). Thus the meeting made decisions of the kind which in the second century were reserved for extraordinary meetings of the *ekklesia,* but in contrast to these later meetings did not deal exclusively with a single question, but with a variety of questions. At the time, the *synodos* must have been a meeting of a primary assembly competent to deal with questions of any magnitude whatsoever.

The fourth *synodos* was held near the time of the autumn equinox and appears to have been a regular meeting (Pol. 4.26.7). At this meeting the decree of the Hellenic League declaring war against Aetolia was ratified and raids against the Aetolians were authorized. Philip V came to Aegium at the time and addressed the *boule* (Pol. 4.26.8). The decrees reported must have been passed by the assembly, and since the issue involved was war we must presuppose the presence of the *ekklesia,* but the address of the king was delivered before the *boule.* Aymard (67) insists that here *boule* and *synodos* are identical, and this, in turn, is part of the demonstration that the term *boule* can be applied to any deliberative body, even a primary assembly. It is better, however, to take *synodos* to mean the meeting or entire assembly and *boule* to mean the council. It is possible that actually few besides the members of the *boule* attended the *synodos.* Moreover, if the meeting of the *boule* was not secret—and there is no indication that it was,—the others who attended the *synodos* might be present as listeners. Then, too, the narrative of Polybius implies that the king arrived after the war resolution had been passed, and it is possible that the meeting of the *ekklesia* had already been completed.

To summarize, there were at least four meetings in the year 220 and all four seem to have been regular *synodoi.* Two came within the term of office of one general, and two within the term of his successor, but this makes no difference to the conclusion which can be drawn, namely, that at the time there were at least four regular *synodoi* each year. At these, decisions of the kind later reserved for extraordinary meetings of the *ekklesia* could be made. The four came relatively close together: April, May, summer, and early autumn. This may in part be the reason why the Confederacy soon consciously shifted to representative government. When it included only Achaea, it may have been possible to secure good attendance at all meetings, but after much of the rest of the Peloponnesus had been admitted this proved impossible.

For 217 it is reported that Eperatus, the general of the year, laid down his office at the beginning of the summer, and that the Achaeans elected the elder Aratus (Pol. 5.30.7). Thus the time of the election seems to correspond to the time of the second meeting of 220 or probably was even a little later. It looks as if Eperatus had failed to call a meeting at the normal time of the elections and so called one at the very end of his term of office, and that his successor was elected at this meeting and took office immediately.[25] It can be taken for granted that even for regular meetings announcements and summonses must have been sent out, and it is possible that in a period of confusion the magistrates sometimes failed to do so. Consequently, in a difficult year such as this one, all the meetings required by law may not have been held. Other meetings are reported for the year, but less is to be learned from them.

This survey of meetings in the Achaean Confederacy down to and including 217 B.C. indicates that decisions on questions of war and alliances—questions which later were reserved for extraordinary meetings of the primary assembly—were made in this period at the regular *synodoi*. This may be seen most clearly from the vote taken at the fourth *synodos* of 220 ratifying the declaration of war by the Hellenic League against the Aetolians. By this vote the Achaeans pledged themselves to active participation in the Social War, the war of Philip and his Greek allies against the Aetolians. It is almost equally clear in the decision about military aid to the Messenians taken at the second *synodos* of the same year.[26] A few years earlier the recognition of Antigonus Doson as "hegemon of the allies," that is, the adherence of the Achaeans to the Hellenic League, was the work of a *synodos*.[27] Where primary assemblies existed, the Greeks tended to reserve for them decisions such as these three, and in the Achaean Confederacy, even after the activities of its primary assembly had been considerably reduced, they were reserved for extraordinary meetings of that body. The fact that such decisions were made at the *synodoi* is proof enough that these were meetings of the primary assembly.

As a proof of the presence of the *ekklesia* at *synodoi* in this period we have not only the nature of the decisions made, but also the word of Polybius. For the second *synodos* of 220 he says (4.7.1) that the Achaeans gathered in the *ekklesia*. Though we can place less reliance on Plutarch, we may notice that he mentions the *ekklesia* (*Aratus* 42.2) in connection with the meeting of 224 which voted to surrender the Acrocorinthus to Antigonus Doson, a meeting which in all likelihood was a *synodos*. Finally, the proviso of the later law that the *ekklesia* could be summoned only to extraordinary meetings implies that there was a time at which it had other meetings and these can have been nothing but the regular *synodoi*. Thus the presence of the *ekklesia* at the *synodoi* of the time seems amply demonstrated.

There is evidence also for the presence of the *boule*. The clearest evidence is for the fourth *synodos* of 220, at which the war vote of the Hellenic League was ratified, and at which Philip V addressed the *boule*. The vote on the question of war must have been taken in the *ekklesia* even if the *boule* may have discussed the question first, but the address of the king was delivered before the latter body. The *boule* is mentioned also in connection with the meeting of 229 at which it was decided to take up the war against Cleomenes. Again the decision must have been made by the *ekklesia*, with the *boule* probably acting as a probouleutic body. In addition to the meetings at which both the *boule* and *ekklesia* were present, the *boule* may—and one can almost say, must—have had other meetings of its own. We may have one such meeting reported for 222, but since the conclusion depends on the evidence of Plutarch this is not too certain.

Apparently all the meetings actually called *synodoi* by Polybius were regular meetings. Judging by the accounts of the meetings of 220, there were four such meetings a year, and this can be accepted with the reservation that complete certainty is impossible. These four meetings seem to have been attended by both the *boule* and the *ekklesia*. In the *boule* the examples of the city-state, the early Boeotian Confederacy, the Aetolian Confederacy, and the Arcadian Confederacy indicate that the cities were represented in proportion to their population. Any other arrangement would have been a retrograde movement. For the *ekklesia* we know that in the second century in the extraordinary meetings—the only meetings of the *ekklesia* at the time—the vote was taken by cities. In the earlier period, however, it is possible and even likely that the vote was taken by heads. There is no direct evidence on the point, though the manner in which the assemblies functioned in the Aetolian Confederacy and the Boeotian Confederacy after 379 suggests that this method was used in their assemblies. Thus it is likely that the Achaean Confederacy after 280 B.C. at first followed the model of the city-state in having both a *boule* with representation in proportion to population and an *ekklesia* in which votes were counted by heads.[28] The latter method may have worked well as long as the Confederacy included only Achaea itself. In addition to the regular meetings it is clear that there also were extraordinary meetings.

The governments of the federal states sketched above show a marked retreat from the earlier promising beginnings in the use of representative government in federal states. This retreat may have begun in the Aetolian Confederacy as early as the last part of the fifth century, although the retention of a primary assembly by that confederacy may be due to local conditions rather than to a conscious theory of government. It is different with the revived Boeotian Confederacy and the Arcadian Confederacy. They show that, in contrast to the oligarchic authors of the constitution of the early Boeotian Confederacy, the constitution makers of the fourth century, when they drew up constitutions for federal states, followed the democratic pattern with a *boule* and a primary assembly. The Achaean Confederacy, reorganized in 280, shows that this pattern was still being followed in the first part of the third century.

It is difficult to say just how successfully the primary assembly functioned in federal states. Instead of several regular meetings a month, we hear of two a year in the Aetolian Confederacy and four a year in the Achaean Confederacy. Whether the meetings were more frequent in other federal states, we do not know. Yet it is safe to say that more must have been left to the *boule* and committees than in the city-state. In the Boeotian Confederacy most of the routine of government probably fell under the supervision of the Boeotarchs. In the Aetolian Confederacy, diplomacy and the details of foreign affairs and the conduct of wars were in large part left not to the council proper but to the smaller body of *apokletoi*. Yet the Aetolian primary assembly continued to the end to make vital decisions and to have real influence on the policies of the state. This government seems to have suited the Aetolians admirably. Of the states discussed in the present chapter, it apparently was the Achaean Confederacy which first found government by primary assembly unsatisfactory and consequently for all intents and purposes adopted representative government.

V

The Introduction of Representative Government in Hellenistic Federal States

THE MOST important part of the demonstration of the general adoption of primary assemblies in federal states was the proof that it was used in the Achaean Confederacy down to 217 B.C. Similarly the most important part of the demonstration of the return to representative government will be the proof that it was adopted in the main by the Achaean Confederacy as early as 200 B.C. and actually, in all likelihood, in the autumn of 217 B.C. It is true that even after this the Achaeans rendered lip service to direct government by reserving decisions on questions of war and alliance for the primary assembly in extraordinary meetings. Aside from these meetings the primary assembly had ceased to exist. Otherwise the government was left to the magistrates and the representative council, the *boule*. Hence it can be said that the Achaean League essentially adopted a representative government with a proviso for referendum on a few vital questions. There were other federal states which adopted representative government, but some of them, notably Thessaly and the four Macedonian republics organized in 167 B.C., did so at a later date. Another, Lycia, was in Asia Minor. Moreover, of the two leading federal states of the Hellenistic Age, one, the Aetolian Confederacy, retained its primary assembly. Therefore it becomes particularly important to prove that the other adopted representative government. For that reason the Achaean Confederacy will be taken up first. Then will follow a few words about other federal states and the manner in which the development of federalism is reflected in the language and thought of Polybius.

When we turn to the Achaean Confederacy, the discussion will again largely center round the words *boule* and *ekklesia,* which occur frequently in statements in our sources. They are particularly prominent in statements concerning the law or laws by means of which its constitution was transformed. After this reform the Confederacy had two kinds of meetings, regular meetings which were open only to the *boule* and the magistrates, and extraordinary meetings of the *ekklesia.* In addition, there may occasionally have been extraordinary meetings of the *boule* also.

The two types of meetings resulting from the reforms are most clearly differentiated in an account by Polybius (29.23–25) of two meetings held in 168 B.C. The first was a *synodos* held at Corinth, at which an appeal from the Ptolemies for military aid against Antiochus IV was discussed. Those favoring the sending of aid seem to have had the best of it until an opponent blocked proceedings by objecting that it was against the laws to take counsel about military aid in the meeting.[1] Later the subject was reconsidered after there had been gathered at Sicyon a *synkletos,* in which it so happened that not only the *boule* gathered, but all citizens over thirty years of age.[2] This is the passage which has been the mainstay of those who have argued that the *synodos* was the *boule* or a meeting of the *boule,* and that the *synkletos* was open to all citizens over thirty.[3] Their interpretations, however, suffered from the weakness that they did not take into account the expression "it so happened." Aymard pointed out that this does not indicate permission or right to attend. He himself took the expression as part of a periphrasis merely indicating that they did attend.[4] The sentence, so interpreted, except for mentioning the age qualification of thirty years, tells nothing about who were qualified to attend, but merely records the fact that the attendance was much better at the *synkletos* than at the *synodos.* Aymard has certainly put his finger on a weak point in the exposition of his predecessors; but there are some considerations which make his own interpretation unlikely. If Polybius had wished merely to report that the second meeting was better attended than the first, there would have been no point in mentioning the age qualification. Moreover, the statement that all attended would have been absurd. There are so many better

ways of indicating a good attendance than by use of so obvious an
exaggeration. An illustration is found in his statement about a
meeting, in 146, that it was attended by an unprecedented number
of artisans and workingmen (Pol. 38.12.5). To make sense, it is
necessary to take both the "thirty years" and "all" as parts of the
qualification for attendance. Obviously the meeting to which all
over thirty were admitted was the *synkletos,* and the meeting attended exclusively by the *boule*—and, of course, the chief federal
magistrates—was the *synodos.*

This conclusion seems only to bring us back to where we were
before Aymard wrote his criticism; but it should not do so. The
statement that the *synkletos* was one at which it happened that not
only the *boule* but also others were present must have a meaning
and must differentiate it from other meetings. This meaning must
be that the *synkletos* was of the kind which was not attended exclusively by the *boule* but was open to all citizens over thirty. The
implication is that there was another kind of *synkletos* which was
attended exclusively by the *boule.* This should not seem too strange,
for why should not the *boule* also have an extraordinary meeting
now and then? Apparently such a meeting is actually reported for
170 B.C. (Pol. 28.3.10); it will be discussed below. But to resume. So
interpreted, the report of the two meetings of 168 suggests that there
were two kinds of *synkletoi:* one attended exclusively by the *boule,*
and one open also to all citizens over thirty. It also shows that the
boule is still functioning and implies that the *synodos* reported was
a meeting exclusively of the *boule.* Other evidence that a *synodos*
normally was a meeting of the *boule* alone, except for the magistrates, will be presented below.

Synodos and *synkletos* also appear as designations for two different assemblies in a decree of Oropus of about 154 B.C. honoring
an Achaean who had befriended Oropian magistrates before a
synodos at Corinth and later before a *synkletos* at Argos (*SIG*³,
675). The latter meeting was called as the result of a decree of the
synodos referring to it a question of military aid. A decree of
Oropus does not carry quite as much weight as an Achaean decree
would,[5] but the document does give the impression that both

synodos and *synkletos* were technical terms. *Synodos* occurs also in another inscription.⁶ These two inscriptions and the account of Polybius discussed above are the cause of the emphasis on *synodos* and *synkletos* in discussions of the Achaean institutions. A result has been a tendency to overlook or disregard the fact that Achaean law placed the emphasis on a distinction between the functions and duties of their *boule* and their *ekklesia.*

Information about Achaean constitutional law is contained in accounts of the visits of Roman ambassadors. In 185, when Caecilius Metellus asked Achaean officials to gather "the many" in an *ekklesia,* the officials asked for his written instructions from the Roman senate (*synkletos*); when Caecilius remained silent, the officials refused to assemble the *ekklesia,* for the laws forbade them to do so unless the Roman representative brought written instructions from the senate (Pol. 22.10.10–12). Here *ekklesia* is used once for the assembly attending the kind of extraordinary meetings of the Achaeans which we are accustomed to call *synkletoi* and once for the meeting itself. So also in the account of the defense of their magistrates made by Achaean ambassadors before the Roman senate. The ambassadors stated that their officials did not deserve to be censured for their refusal to assemble the *ekklesia.* The Achaeans had a law forbidding the summoning of "the many" except when it was necessary to act on a question of alliance or war or unless someone brought a letter from the (Roman) senate. Therefore the magistrates had quite properly consulted about calling together the Achaeans to an *ekklesia,* but had been prevented by the laws because he (Caecilius) neither brought letters from the senate nor was willing to turn over his written instructions to the magistrates (Pol. 22.12.5–7). Livy's account agrees in the main, which need hardly surprise us since it is obviously based on Polybius and so can have no independent value as evidence.⁷ Livy, in fact, regularly gets his information about Achaean affairs and institutions from Polybius.

If Polybius ever gives technical statements about the primary assembly of the Achaeans, it is in the passages just discussed. It is important to remember that in them he is quoting an Achaean law or laws, and it is very unlikely that he should speak of *ekklesia* if the word used by the law was *synkletos*. Hence we learn that the usual word for the Achaean primary assembly or a meeting of that body continued to be *ekklesia*. This conclusion is supported by his use of the word in other passages.[8] Apparently when the word has the definite article it means the primary assembly itself; when it is used without an article, it means a meeting of such an assembly. Similarly, we can speak of "the *ekklesia*" and "an *ekklesia*" in the case of Athens. Thus we learn from these statements of Polybius that there was a law or laws to the effect that the *ekklesia* could be summoned only to deal with questions of alliance or war. The reference to written communications from the Roman senate looks like a later addition to the original Achaean law. Whatever the date of the original law, this clause cannot antedate 198 B.C., the year in which the Achaeans broke with Macedonia and the Hellenic League and aligned themselves with Rome, and may actually result from the treaty of alliance concluded a few years later.[9] The earlier law must have specified merely that the *ekklesia* could not be summoned except to act on questions of alliance and war. All other meetings, regular and extraordinary, were to be meetings of the *boule* alone. In other words, by this legislation, except for the special mass meetings, the Achaean League transformed its government from what was in theory a direct government, with a primary assembly as the last resort for all important issues, into a representative government. This may well have been done because so few citizens had been attending the regular meetings of the *ekklesia* that it seemed advisable to discontinue them. Thereafter the *ekklesia* was to be summoned only from time to time to special meetings to deal with subjects of unusual importance and interest.

If this interpretation of the change is correct, we should accept as correct also the statements made by the Achaeans to the Romans to the effect that it was forbidden to summon the *ekklesia* except to deal with certain specific questions. Aymard has argued plausibly that these statements are a conscious distortion of the facts, and that the law contained no such prohibition but merely reserved the final decision on certain questions for the *synkletos*.[10] Action by the Achaean officials of the kind ascribed to them by Aymard would be natural enough. Yet a consideration of the circumstances of the reform as sketched above gives another impression. The reform meant the conscious abandonment of a system under which the primary assembly had met as often as four times a year. If experience had shown that direct government by a primary assembly in a state as large as the Achaean Confederacy was a farce, it was natural to take measures to prevent the cheapening of the extraordinary meetings of the *ekklesia* by too frequent use.

The fact that the law limiting the summoning of the *ekklesia* was an amendment of existing laws and institutions explains another contradiction discussed by Aymard (189 ff.). At Corinth in 168 the assertion was made that according to the laws a decision on military aid could not be made at a *synodos*, that is, a meeting of the *boule* alone.[11] At first glance this law limiting the competence of the *boule* and reserving certain questions for the *ekklesia* seems a contradiction of the law prohibiting excessive use of the *ekklesia*, but on second thought it is not. In the earlier days, when the *ekklesia* met four or more times a year, there still must have been times when the *boule* met by itself, and there must have been a number of details on which the *boule* acted without referring them to the *ekklesia*. Under the circumstances, nothing would have been more natural or more in accord with normal Greek political practice than a law or laws reserving to the *ekklesia* final action on certain important questions. Undoubtedly these laws remained in force, and the new law took the form of prohibiting the summoning of the *ekklesia* except when it was needed for a decision on one of these questions.

The Achaean primary assembly, even when it met only in extraordinary meetings, seems to have retained the name *ekklesia*. A natural name for an extraordinary meeting would be *ekklesia synkletos*, a term actually used at Athens (Dem. 18.37; *SIG*³, 651. 5), or merely *synkletos*. This term *may* have been used extensively for such meetings, but it is not so used by Polybius; the explanation probably is his frequent use of the word to signify the Roman senate,[12] a practice which seems to have been normal.[13] Nevertheless, where no ambiguity was involved, it is possible that *synkletos* was used as the name for the extraordinary meetings of the Achaean *ekklesia*, the only kind of meetings convoked by that body in the second century. Yet the one time it is used in the text of Polybius (29.24.6) as we now have it, this is not the meaning, for the author found it necessary to describe the nature of this particular *synkletos*, the implication being that there were *synkletoi* of another kind. Hence the only evidence which can be used to support the claim that *synkletos* was a technical term for an extraordinary meeting of the primary assembly is the decree of Oropus mentioned above (*SIG*³, 675), which after all is not an Achaean document. There is more evidence for *synodos,* which is used frequently by Polybius, though not always with the same meaning. Yet it is exceedingly convenient to use *synkletos* as a name for an extraordinary meeting of the *ekklesia,* and *synodos* for other meetings, and for this reason the words will occasionally be so used in what follows.

When we turn to the question of the date of the reform, it will be remembered that much of the evidence comes from accounts of events in 185 B.C., but it is clear that meetings in 200 and 198 B.C. reported by Livy were *synkletoi.*[14] Thus the reform—except for the special clause about the Roman senate—must be earlier than 200 B.C. Can it be dated more precisely? Not with absolute certainty, though the autumn of 217 seems the most likely date. This is said in the belief that the change is to be linked with the transfer of the election of the general from spring to autumn. Is it not likely that the two great reforms which by circumstantial evidence are placed about the same time belong together? It would seem that the changes must have been sponsored by a statesman with considerable insight. They also seem to belong in a period of optimism and reconstruction such as Polybius (5.106) tells us was experienced in the Peloponnesus at the end of the Social War. At that time Aratus, who had been the leading statesman for almost a generation, was in a strong position. He had got the Confederacy on its feet again after the disastrous year of Eperatus. The last year of the Social War had gone not too badly for the Achaeans. Moreover, for the change in the term of the general, it was almost necessary to have in office at the time one who was willing to have his own term of office shortened. By 217 Aratus had enough prestige and enough of a career behind him to gain rather than lose by such a step. Then, too, he was able to transmit the office to a trusted political ally. Finally, to turn to the evidence, Polybius (5.106.1) implies that Timoxenus was elected general in the autumn of 217, probably at the regular autumn *synodos,* and this in turn makes it practically certain that the change in the term of the general was introduced at that time.[15] Thereafter the general seems to have been elected at the last *synodos* of the year and to have taken office immediately. Is it being too bold to suggest that the law limiting the meetings of the *ekklesia* to extraordinary sessions to deal with questions of alliance or war was also passed at the same time? If so, all that can be said is that the reform came before 200, and it may be best to be satisfied with this more cautious conclusion. There seems to be no further evidence for fixing the date. Meetings are reported for 209 and 208, but they help little. One appears to be an extraordinary meeting, but it is impossible to determine from the report whether it was held under the old or the new dispensation.

The theory about the nature of the Achaean assemblies after 200 B.C. so far formulated has been tested in a survey of all meetings from 209 to 146 B.C. of which reports have been preserved, and it has stood the test.[16] Sometimes it may be difficult to determine the nature of the meeting reported, and sometimes the law may be stretched one way or the other. A *synodos* may at times have exceeded its authority and officials may at times have called extraordinary meetings of the *ekklesia* when it was not warranted, but such deviations are to be expected. Only once do the terms used cause difficulty. This is in connection with a meeting or meetings in 170 B.C. in the account of which scholars have thought that Polybius has used *ekklesia* and *boule* about the same meeting.[17] Here it seems that we—I have been guilty myself—have misinterpreted Polybius because his report is so simple and straightforward that we have failed to take it literally; this often happens with authors who acquire the reputation of having an artificial or indirect style. He reports that Roman ambassadors had planned to have the *ekklesia* of the Achaeans gathered and to accuse Lycortas, Archon, and Polybius, but they gave up the plan and instead, when the *boule* had been summoned to Aegium to confer with them, merely addressed words of greeting and exhortation to it and departed. The extraordinary meeting of the *ekklesia* neither was called nor took place, but was only a part of the plans or thoughts attributed to the ambassadors in the gossip of the time. Instead, the *boule* actually was summoned to what appears to have been an extraordinary meeting of that body.[18] Except for the point that the particular meeting of the *ekklesia* referred to existed only in the plans of the ambassadors, this interpretation is not new, but it has not been widely accepted and one or two of those who have arrived at the interpretation seem to have been afraid of it.[19]

Two typical *synkletoi* were held in 200 and 198 B.C. respectively. They are the earliest such meetings which can be so designated with certainty and are extremely useful for depicting the procedure of an extraordinary meeting dealing with a single problem announced in advance and giving three days to it. In 200 a meeting was held at Argos to deal with the war against Nabis of Sparta (Livy 31.25). In the course of the meeting Philip V of Macedonia appeared and offered to take over the war himself in return for having Achaean garrisons sent to several cities outside the Confederacy. The Achaean general, who presided, ruled this out of order on the grounds that it was contrary to law to take up any subject except the one for which the meeting had been called. In 198 a meeting was held at Sicyon at which Pergamene, Rhodian, and Athenian ambassadors were present. This was the meeting at which it was decided to break with Philip and the Hellenic League, to enter into alliance with Pergamum and Rhodes, and to go over to the side of Rome (Livy 32.19–23). The last was the real issue, and the alliances with Pergamum and Rhodes were mere corollaries. Thus again there was one and only one subject and it had been announced in advance. The account gives us the best picture we have of the procedure during the three days of an extraordinary meeting and shows us that the vote was taken by cities.

In contrast to the extraordinary meetings of the *ekklesia*, the normal *synodoi* exhibit a less rigid procedure and show several topics handled at the same meeting. An excellent illustration is a *synodos* held at Megalopolis in 185. There were present ambassadors from Ptolemy to renew an alliance, ambassadors from Eumenes to renew an alliance and to offer a gift of 120 talents which were to be invested and the interest used for paying "the *boule* of the Achaeans at the federal *synodoi*," ambassadors from Seleucus to renew friendship and offer a gift of ten "long ships," and, in addition, an Achaean ambassador back from Rome. The report of the Achaean ambassador was heard first, but no action was taken. The alliance with Eumenes was renewed, but the offer of money was declined. Next to be discussed was the question of the alliance with Ptolemy. The Achaean general of the time, Aristaenus, asked which treaty was being renewed and showed that there existed several old treaties. When no one could give a satisfactory answer, action was postponed. The friendship with Seleucus was renewed, but it was voted to decline for the time being the gift of ships (Pol. 22.7–9). This report, besides showing how much business and how varied could be handled at a single meeting, also helps to demonstrate that routine matters of foreign policy, including renewals of treaties of alliance, could be handled at a *synodos*. Probably all foreign ambassadors were normally heard at a *synodos* unless it was anticipated that action on their appeal might involve a question of war. Also, the rejection of the gift of Eumenes is interesting. Apparently what he offered was not money to relieve the budget of the state, but an endowment or foundation to supply money for gifts or favors to be handed to the members of the *boule* at the meetings in the style of other donations in Hellenistic and Roman times. The members almost certainly were unpaid and remained unpaid.[20]

The reports do not give any too much information concerning the composition of the *boule* and the procedure at its meetings. It can be inferred from indirect evidence that it was a large council. The *boule* or *synedrion*—both names are used—of the Aetolian Confederacy was so large that, according to the report of one in-

cident, there were members left after 550 had been put to death
(Livy 45.28.7). The Achaean *boule* should, if anything, have been
still larger. The fact that it was large is suggested also by the sum
of 120 talents offered by Eumenes so that the interest from the
money could be used for supplying pay to the members for attendance at the meetings (Pol. 22.7.3). To be sure, efforts to estimate the
numbers on the basis of the sum are useless. We do not know for
how many days the members met, nor the rate at which they were
to be paid, nor the income that could be realized from the capital.
Moreover, the money to be handed out probably was not pay so
much as favors, but a sum as large as 120 talents or 720,000
drachmas was a huge sum for such purposes. Thus, a similar dona-
tion to the Lycian Confederacy at a considerably later date consisted of 55,000 and another of 110,000 denarii.[21] The one fact that
it would be safe to deduce is that the number of the members was
much larger than the number of the cities belonging to the Confederacy. Even without direct evidence, such as we have for the
Aetolian *boule,* this suggests representation in proportion to population.[22] Nor can the Achaeans well have adopted any other plan.
The principle of proportion in representation was so firmly en-
trenched in the *boule* of cities and federal states, including the
Aetolian and Arcadian confederacies, that, after the accolade of
adoption even in the Hellenic League, its use in the Achaean Confederacy can be taken for granted. The system of taking the votes
in the *ekklesia* by cities must have been influenced by the system
used in the *boule.* The obvious purpose was to assure that the few
voters who came in from the more distant towns should not be
swamped by voters who were residents of near-by towns and of
the city in which the meeting was held. It would be most surprising if the system of proportion was not applied also to this vote,
in order that the vote of Corinth or Megalopolis, for instance,
might count for more than that of some petty town.

   With the reduction of the work of the *ekklesia* the importance
of the *boule* had been greatly increased, but it also lost its real
probouleutic function. This seems to have received scant notice,
but to have caused considerable trouble in the interpretation of

Achaean institutions. It is so easy to think that a *boule* must involve probouleutic activity. This normally meant that a *boule* not only considered in advance the subjects to be dealt with in the meetings of the assembly, but actually drew up the bills to be voted on by the assembly. The latter body might amend or change, but it started with a definite bill completely ready to be passed. This was the practice also in the Arcadian Confederacy, for which we have the record of a vote by the *boule* and the Ten Thousand. For the Achaean Confederacy there are indications that in the period before 217 both the *boule* and the *ekklesia* met at the *synodoi* and that the *boule* functioned as a normal probouleutic body. In this period, with at least four regular meetings a year, the *ekklesia* must have handled a variety of business and the meetings may have been something like that meeting of the *boule* in 185 for which we have a record of several questions taken up one after another. Under those conditions, much of the business must have been handled rapidly, and often the *ekklesia* may have done little but approve measures formulated by the *boule*. It certainly cannot have given three days to a single problem as it did in the extraordinary meetings of the second century. At that time too the *boule* did occasionally consider in advance the problem later to be presented to the *ekklesia* at an extraordinary meeting, but it did not formulate the resolution or bill to be passed. Nor was a preliminary consideration by the *boule* necessary. When the *ekklesia* met, whether foreign ambassadors were heard or whether only Achaean magistrates spoke, the first day was given over to a presentation of the problem or a statement of the case. The second day was taken up with formulation of motions and with debate. On the third day, the vote was taken by cities.[23] This procedure leaves no room for a preliminary formulation of a motion. It was in use as early as 200 B.C. and thus seems to have been adopted at the time the meetings of the *ekklesia* were curtailed and limited to extraordinary sessions.[24] This radical change in procedure shows that the Achaean statesmen of the time were well aware of the importance of the reform. When the number of meetings of the *ekklesia* was limited, every effort was made to give additional dignity to the few meet-

ings that were to be held. The voters were even told to formulate
their own bills at the meetings. In practice this seems to have meant
that, when the political leaders agreed, they presented their pro-
gram and had it approved; when they disagreed, the voters chose
between the proposals of rival leaders.

Another result of the limiting of the activities of the *ekklesia*
was that the election of the general, the hipparch, and undoubtedly
the other chief magistrates, now fell to the *boule*. Before the reform
it had been conducted at a regular *synodos,* and after the reform
this practice seems to have been retained. Certainly elections are
not included among the activities for which the *ekklesia* could be
called. Election by a representative assembly should not be considered impossible. Aristotle (*Politics* 1318b23), refers to the delegation of elections. There is also the example of the Lycian
Confederacy in which elections were conducted by a representative
assembly. Finally, there is the statement of Polybius (38.15.1) with
reference to the death of Critolaus in 146, that if a general died his
predecessors took over until the next regular *synodos* of the
Achaeans. The implication is that the elections were conducted at
a *synodos* and that when a vacancy occurred, instead of waiting for
the usual time of elections, it was filled at the next regular meeting.

One result of the change may at first seem paradoxical. For the
period before the reform there are recorded in our sources more
regular meetings than extraordinary ones. For the period after the
reform, when there probably were four regular meetings of the
boule a year, and the *ekklesia* was to be called only occasionally for
extraordinary meetings, a larger number of extraordinary than of
regular meetings is recorded. The reason is that the routine work
of the *boule* is passed over in silence by historians, who fill their
narratives with wars and plans for wars and alliances. In the period
before 217, when the regular meetings were qualified to deal with
such problems and came fairly close together in the spring, summer, and autumn, there seldom was any need of extraordinary
assemblies. Later, when only such assemblies could decide questions of war and alliance, the meetings became frequent. The rule
that they could be called on the presentation of written communica-

tions from the Roman senate caused them to be still more frequent. Nor should it be overlooked that the Achaean magistrates, when feelings ran high, may have stretched the law and called extraordinary meetings when there was no real need of them.

It may seem strange that questions of war were specifically reserved for the relatively cumbersome procedure of the extraordinary assembly. Even in urgent situations it must have taken several days to send out the summonses and gather the voters, and when they were gathered, the meeting itself lasted three days. The explanation is in part that the Greeks could do a great deal of fighting without going to war. It was not necessary to have a declaration of war in order to repel the raids of pirates coming by sea or land, or even to authorize retaliatory raids. In 220 B.C., before the outbreak of the Social War, it was still possible, after a good deal of fighting between the Achaeans and Aetolians, to debate whether peace was to be maintained or war declared.[25] Since a federal army seems to have been made up of contingents from the various cities within a confederacy, it is natural to believe that the commanders of the troops of a community could mobilize the local forces in case of a raid without thereby involving the federal government. There is an illustration of this in events of about the same period involving the Lycian Confederacy in southwestern Asia Minor. These are known from a decree passed by the city of Araxa honoring one of her citizens for his services.[26] Araxa, a town situated near the northern border of Lycia, seems to have been engaged in a regular war against the neighboring city of Bubon and an influential local magnate, Moagetes. When a settlement had been made, Moagetes sent out raiders and carried off prisoners. Araxa as a consequence became involved in hostilities with the more powerful neighbor, Cibyra. Thereupon Araxa appealed to the federal government, and it intervened diplomatically but apparently sent no other help. The explanation must be that these raids were treated as mere border incidents in which each city must look after itself. Probably the federal government did not, as a matter of fact, consider it worth while to become involved in war merely for the sake of Araxa. On the other hand, when attempts were made to establish tyranny in two larger and more central cities, the Confederacy went to war. From nearer by comes a treaty of alliance of about 262 B.C. between the Aetolian and Acarnanian confederacies (*IG* IX² 1, 3A). If aid was needed, it could be sent on a large scale by either of the two, though both possessed primary assemblies, without consulting the assembly. Such an act merely involved giving aid to an ally, not committing one's own state to a war. Judging by such practices as these, the need of action by an extraordinary meeting of the *ekklesia* in order to declare formal war did not prevent the officials from acting rapidly in emergencies.

After the reform in the Achaean Confederacy discussed above, the federal states of the Greek world fall into two groups, those that retained primary assemblies or even adopted new constitutions which provided for such assemblies, and those that had representative government. Primary assemblies were retained after 200 B.C. by the Aetolian, Boeotian, and Acarnanian confederacies. Of these the Boeotians had adopted the system of taking the vote by cities at least as early as 197 B.C. (Livy 33.2.6). The Acarnanians had for some time been subject to Epirus and had regained their independence about 230 B.C., which may, then, be considered the date of their constitution also.[27] Hence it is an example of the inclusion of a primary assembly in a new federal constitution of a relatively late date. On the other hand, there is evidence for the taking of votes by cities in the assembly as early as the last part of the third century, which suggests that the procedure was a part of the new constitution of about 230 B.C. This appears to be the earliest evidence we have. It suggests that federal states adopted this innovation earlier than the return to representative government. A new constitution with a primary assembly even later is that of the Magnesian Confederacy as reorganized in 167 B.C.[28] In this there is no indication that the vote was taken by cities. Probably there was a return to the old-fashioned method of counting by heads, in which case, of course, the Confederacy was almost completely under the control of the capital, Demetrias. It may well be that the desire to produce this control determined the choice of form of government. The influence of near-by Aetolia may also have made itself felt. In both the Acarnanian and Magnesian confederacies the formulas used in the decrees indicate the existence of a *boule* and a primary assembly. If these constitutions represent a genuine devotion to the cause of direct government, their proponents were fighting a losing battle.

To turn to the other side of the question, the transformation of the Achaean Confederacy was in fact a victory for representative government, and, as far as we can judge from Polybius, was so regarded, even though the Confederacy continued to express formal allegiance to direct government by reserving certain questions for decision at extraordinary meetings of the otherwise defunct primary assembly. It appears to have been the earliest such victory in Hellenistic Greece, but not necessarily in the Greek world as a whole. Here the vexed problem of the relative contributions of the Greeks on the two sides of the Aegean enters in. The Lycian Confederacy is a clear example of representative government with representation in proportion to population, though according to a rather rigid formula.[29] The Confederacy had both a federal *boule* and a federal *ekklesia,* but both were representative assemblies. Our chief literary source, Strabo, tells that there were three classes of cities having one, two, and three votes each respectively. The most plausible conjecture is that these numbers are the numbers of representatives in the *boule,* while the cities were represented in the same proportion but with a larger number of representatives in the *ekklesia.* Even this would make the *boule* a rather small council, but the Lycians had learned much in the hard school of experience which warfare provides, and may well have become aware that a small and efficient council was necessary. The fact that the larger of the two bodies is called an *ekklesia* suggests that it once must have been a primary assembly, and this, in turn, indicates also for Lycia a change from direct to representative government. The details of the change differed from that adopted by the Achaeans. While the latter retained their primary assembly and restricted its use to a minimum, the Lycians retained the name *ekklesia,* but transformed the assembly into a representative body.

Which change came first, it is impossible to say for certain, but it was probably the Achaean reform. All that can be said with fair assurance about the date of the Lycian reform is that it came before 100 B.C., the approximate date of the work of Artemidorus of Ephesus, from whom Strabo derived his own description. It is interesting to observe that while the Lycians retained the terms *boule* and *ekklesia*—or, to be more precise, *archaresiake* (electoral) *ekklesia*—even under the Roman Empire, Strabo and probably Artemidorus before him wrote of their *synedrion*. This was a word becoming more and more common as a name for the representative council or assembly of a federal state. If, as in the Aetolian Confederacy, there were both a council and a primary assembly, the body to which it was applied was the council. The use of the old terms in the Lycian Confederacy suggests a relatively early date for the origin of the federal government but gives no clue to the date of the transformation of the *ekklesia,* that is, to the date of the introduction of representative government.

In Greece proper, representative government was adopted in Thessaly in 194 B.C. Its introduction was part of the reorganization of Greece under Roman supervision after the Second Macedonian War, but, though Romans were in the background, there is not the slightest doubt that the government established was Greek—specifically, Hellenistic Greek. In the cities of the Confederacy there was a property qualification for holding office (Livy 34.51.6). The same qualification must have applied also to federal offices, and hence the government was aristocratic or timocratic. The chief organ of government was a *synedrion,* which in the time of Tiberius had 334 members. This is known from a record of a vote by secret ballot in which there were 298 votes on one side, 31 on the other, and 5 invalid votes (*IG* IX, 2, 261). Though this record is late, there is reason to believe in the continuity of institutions; we may therefore conclude that the *synedrion* of this document originated when the Confederacy was organized in 194. The number of representatives is considerably larger than the number of cities, and from what we know of Greek institutions in general this must mean representation in proportion to population. The record of the vote and its secrecy shows that the members voted as individuals and not by delegations. The absence of any information about a primary assembly suggests that the Thessalian Confederacy adopted representative government more completely than the Achaeans and without any reservations whatsoever. The examples of the Achaean and Lycian confederacies should show us that it is no longer necessary to imagine that a federal primary assembly must have existed at least to conduct elections. There is no reason why the delegates to the federal representative assembly could not elect the magistrates.[30]

The case for the adoption of representative government is even clearer for the four federal republics into which Macedonia was divided in 167 b.c.[31] Our information is derived from Polybius through Livy, in other words, from a contemporary deeply involved as an Achaean politician in the intrigues of the period and personally acquainted with Aemilius Paulus, the Roman commander who supervised the establishment of the new order. Livy does not give many details about the form of government, but he does tell us that each of the four republics was to have a *synedrion* as the chief organ of government. His statement that they were to elect senators "whom they call *synedri*" shows that the name *synedrion* for the council, or *synedroi* for its members, occurs in the account of Polybius. The latter word occurs also in Polybius (31.17.2) in an account of some later events in Macedonia. It looks as if *synedrion* was becoming the common name for the council or representative assembly of a federal state. There is no further evidence about the composition of the councils of the four republics, such as about the number of representatives from each city. There is one statement which may seem to indicate an equality of representation: ten dignitaries from each city were invited to the convention at which the new order was proclaimed (Livy 45.29.1). Yet the procedure followed here is no indication of the form of government adopted. Certainty is impossible, but the influence of Greek tradition is likely to have produced representation in proportion to population.

Some details of interpretation given above may be doubtful, but the general picture of the advance of representative government is proved correct by an expression used by Polybius (31.2.12) in a report on civil strife among the Macedonians a few years later. He remarks that the Macedonians were unaccustomed to "democratical and representative government," to quote a nineteenth-century interpretation of the expression *demokratike kai synedriake politeia.*[32] This must mean a form of government which is democratic and which has a *synedrion* or representative assembly as the chief organ of government. Thus the old translation by Bishop Thirlwall is correct, and *synedriake politeia,* government by a *synedrion,* seems to be Polybius' name for representative government. Moreover, the tone of the passage implies that the Macedonians with their lack of experience of such government are rather low creatures. He could hardly have written as he did unless he considered the government of the Achaean Confederacy a representative government and unless he considered this form of government as standard for federal states. The reference to democracy, on the other hand, should not be interpreted too closely. By this time, any republican state, no matter how oligarchic, could call itself a democracy.

This one expression used by Polybius is enough to show that the Hellenistic Greeks, at least in the second century before Christ, had a name for representative government. Furthermore, the slur directed against the Macedonians implies that Polybius was proud of the Achaean use of this form of government. Otherwise he gives us no theory of representative government. The reason seems to be that Greek formal political theory was so dominated by the city-state that even a laudation of a federal state took the form of a claim that it was almost a *polis.* Consequently, after he has remarked about the phenomenal growth of the Achaean nation (*ethnos*), he states that the union was closer than mere alliance and friendship; that its members used the same laws, weights, measures, and coins; had the same magistrates, councilors, and judges; and that the entire Peloponnesus scarcely differed from a *polis* except in not having a single fortified center for all.[33] In other words, there were several towns within the state instead of only one. The emphasis on the common councilors or the federal *boule* fits with the adoption of representative government. Otherwise, probably the most remarkable aspect of the passage is the implication that the expansion of the Confederacy meant the growth of a nation. Achaeans, Dorians, and Arcadians were being molded into a single nation. This is reflected in the normal mode of referring to the citizens of the state. Polybius himself, who came from an Arcadian city, was Polybius an Achaean from Megalopolis.

To return from theory to fact, the examples of the Achaean, Lycian, Thessalian, and four Macedonian confederacies show that in 200 B.C., at the latest, representative government began to be a standard form of government for federal states. Both in the Achaean and the Lycian confederacies the change came when the governments were still real governments with important decisions to make. This is true of the Achaean Confederacy even if the change did not come in 217 B.C. but only a short time before 200 B.C., while the Lycian government must have remained active well into the first century B.C. even if not to A.D. 43, the year of the loss of independence. Some account of the manner in which many such confederacies continued as instruments for local government even under the Roman Empire will have to be given in the next chapter. The same is true of the fact that the primary assemblies ultimately disappeared in all or most of those confederacies which retained them during the period of real independence.

VI
Federal States and
Commonalities in the Hellenistic
Provinces of the Roman Empire

To SPEAK of federal states within the Roman Empire may seem strange. The justification is that the Empire was in a sense a conglomerate of small states united under the supremacy of Rome. The relations of these states to Rome were governed largely according to principles of what once had been international law. The theoretical independence of these communities and their actual independence at an earlier date were never quite forgotten. Most of them were muncipalities, that is, city-states which had lost their real independence. Rome, however, did not enforce complete uniformity, and so in a number of places preserved federal states as instruments for local government. In Greece, she also gave new prominence to the ancient Amphictionic League and created new agencies for furthering Panhellenism both within and without Greece. Similar associations of cities were numerous also in Asia Minor. To those associations of cities or other political organisms which are not close or intimate enough to rank as sympolities or federal states the name "commonality" has been given. The Greek word *koinon* (plu. *koina*) was used both for these and for federal states.

The subject is complicated and the source material is not easily mastered. Some information is derived from literary sources, but most comes from inscriptions, and for Asia Minor these have not yet been collected in a corpus, but remain scattered in special publications and periodicals. The task of keeping in touch with new material is greatly lightened by special reports,[1] but even so it is not easy, and at times the crucial evidence may be an inscription published a century ago and consistently neglected ever since. Under the circumstances it is not surprising that there have been neither many special studies nor many works of broad interpretation in recent years. Some attention has been given to part of the material in studies on the so-called provincial assemblies[2] and, to a less extent, in works on emperor worship.[3] The result is none too satisfactory. Many of the organizations to be considered are not provincial organizations at all except in the sense that they existed in the Roman Empire outside of Italy; some have little or no connection with imperial cults; "provincial assemblies" is an unhappy term which places the emphasis on the assemblies rather than on the organizations represented by the assemblies; and the discussion under "provincial assemblies" of eastern *koina,* that is, federal states and commonalities, tends to obscure their importance as the connecting link between earlier Greek institutions and the institutions of the Roman Empire. The title of the present chapter suggests that the institutions of the eastern provinces remained largely Hellenistic, but that does not mean that they did not influence the West. Hellenistic or not, these *koina* deserve further study and anyone with the time and patience to gather and examine all the scattered and varied evidence is likely to find the work rewarding. I had hoped to do so myself, but have found the task too big when taken together with the other material necessary for the present study. Hence, what will be presented here cannot claim to be based on an exhaustive study of the available material and literature.

To begin in Greece, it is necessary to try to exorcise a false idea which still seems common, namely, that Rome dissolved all the federal states of Greece after the destruction of Corinth in 146 B.C.[4] This is nothing but a facile repetition of a statement by Pausanias (7.16.9–10), the author of a description of Greece written in the second century after Christ. Whatever else Pausanias was, he was not a great historian. Moreover, no statements are more likely to be inaccurate than such sweeping generalizations as some of those made by Pausanias in his description of the reorganization of Greece by the Romans in 145 B.C. The reorganization of all states would have been a complicated task, and it would have been most surprising if the Romans had bothered to make any detailed changes in the make-up of states which had been friendly to her.

Therefore, every probability favors the conclusion that only those federal states which had opposed Rome in the war were dissolved.[5] Hence it should have been no surprise when evidence for the survival of various confederacies began to appear. To be sure, those who must believe in the account of Pausanias can argue that he states that confederacies were soon reconstituted again. It is much more likely that several were left intact in the first place.

Those who believe that Rome after the Fourth Macedonian War (149–148) and the Achaean War (146) suddenly reduced all Greece to a subject status and imposed tribute upon it fail to reckon with Rome's tendency to cling stubbornly to a policy once adopted. The policy of what might be called "directed freedom" had been adopted for Greece at least as early as 200 b.c., when the states of Greece were invited to join with Rome in a fight against Macedonia for the freedom of Greece. Though Rome conquered much in the Second Macedonian War which followed, the policy of freedom was implemented in the settlement after the war, and Roman troops withdrew from Greece in 194. Even so, the Greeks must have been made to feel from the outset that their freedom did not mean the right to pursue an entirely independent foreign policy. Thus, the Achaeans had been made the protectors of the maritime cities detached from Sparta. When Nabis of Sparta besieged Gythium in the autumn of 193, the Achaeans protested to Nabis, aided Gythium, and dispatched an embassy to Rome to report (Livy 35.13.1–3). The next spring, though Nabis had raided their territory, the Achaeans at first hesitated to go to war before they heard from Rome (Livy 35.25). There was a party which felt that they had a right to act more independently in local Peloponnesian affairs, though in those affairs only, but this point of view was the beginning of great evils for the Achaeans. Equally significant is a statement made the next year by one of the citizens of Chalcis on the island of Euboea when Antiochus III and the Aetolians appeared before the gates. After elaborating on the freedom of the Greeks, the speaker closed with the remark that the Chalcidians would contract no treaty of alliance without the approval of the Romans (Livy 35.46.9–13). This, then, is the measure of the amount of freedom Greece possessed⁶ and, to some degree, retained. Thereafter the states which caused trouble were punished, but usually not even the federal states were dissolved. Thus the Aetolian Confederacy was not dissolved as punishment for its invitation of 192 B.C. to Antiochus the Great to come to Greece to liberate the country from the Romans. Instead, some Aetolian territory was detached, the Aetolians were forced to pay an indemnity, and a treaty was imposed on them which informed them clearly that they could have no independent foreign policy of their own. Similarly Epirus, even after seventy settled places had been destroyed and 150,000 people had been sold into slavery, was allowed to retain a federal state of a kind. Most surprising of all is the fact that the four Macedonian republics established in 167 B.C. were not dissolved after the rebellion of 149, but remained in existence at least to the time of the Flavian emperors. The evidence for this consists of an inscription and a reference in the Acts of the Apostles (16: 12), though this point cannot be seen clearly in the translations or the commonly accepted text of the Acts.⁷ One of the four republics, at least, seems to have continued to coin silver tetradrachms⁸—the coin which was the standard Greek coin for the transaction of business on a moderately large scale. The Achaean Confederacy, on the other hand, seems to have exhausted the patience of the Romans and was dissolved after the destruction of Corinth, but a smaller confederacy was reconstituted a few years later. Probably other confederacies which had taken part in the war against Rome were also suspended for a few years.

Federal states continued under the Empire as an important instrument for local government. In a sense they must have been a convenience, for it was simpler to deal with a few federal states than with many cities, nor were any of them strong enough to be dangerous. Naturally there continued to be a number of cities which were not members of federal states, but undoubtedly the larger part of Greece was incorporated in such states, while Macedonia proper constituted four federal states, though these did not include the entire province.⁹ The prominence of confederacies in Greece is indicated by their efforts to combine in a sort of new

Hellenic league, which can probably best be called by one of the contemporary names, the Panachaean League. This can be traced from about 34 B.C. to the reign of Nero and beyond. The membership seems to have fluctuated but did include at some time or other the Achaean, Boeotian, Phocian, Euboean, Locrian, and Dorian confederacies.[10] It must have been a special favor when an emperor at times allowed himself to be elected general of one of these confederacies, as Augustus did in the Thessalian and Claudius in the Magnesian Confederacy.[11] Since Augustus served in Thessaly in 27/6 B.C., at the time when the provinces of Achaea and Macedonia were being formed, the act may have a special significance. After the humiliation of the Aetolian and Achaean confederacies, the Thessalian Confederacy may well have become the strongest surviving state in Greece. Moreover, during the Roman civil wars from 48 to 31 B.C., Thessaly had been not only the scene of one important battle but also a source of men and supplies, and from Augustus' point of view it is likely that more had been furnished to the wrong than to the right contenders.[12] Therefore, the act of Augustus in allowing himself to be elected general is probably a part of the official recognition of Thessaly and of the permission to the Confederacy to continue to function. Moreover, Augustus also increased considerably the territory of the Confederacy, allowed it to rank as a free state,[13] and assigned it to a privileged position in the Amphictionic League. Is it too much to imagine the Thessalians during the year of the generalship of Augustus boasting that their state had the same head as Rome or, in the language of a later generation, was united to Rome by a personal union?

If we now turn from the federal states which were continued as instruments of local government to larger organizations, the most important, at least from Augustus to Hadrian, was the Amphictionic League. As with local government, so also with Panhellenic organizations, Augustus preserved and encouraged the old. This is shown in his own chief foundation in Greece. Nicopolis, the city of victory, which was founded to commemorate the battle of Actium, was definitely a Greek city and ranked as a *civitas foederata,* an allied city.[14] Its territory was as large as that of some federal states. In the reorganization of the Amphictionic League the city was given a privileged position with six votes in the council, which was enlarged so that there were now thirty instead of the earlier twenty-four votes. Of these thirty, besides Nicopolis, Thessaly and Macedonia also had six votes each, while all the rest of Greece had only twelve. This, at least, is the most plausible reconstruction of what little evidence we have,[15] and it fits with what else is known concerning the plans of Augustus for Greece and Macedonia. The prominence of Nicopolis, Thessaly, and Macedonia seems to belong to the general plan for the Balkans at the time when Macedonia was the most northerly province in that region and when not only the defense of the frontier but also campaigns for expansion were conducted by its governor. Under the circumstances it was natural for an emperor who posed as a favorite of the Greek god Apollo to try to strengthen the Greek states nearest to the northern frontier. Certainly, whatever was the policy of Augustus in other parts of the Empire, the man who celebrated his victory by founding a Greek city, Nicopolis, and by establishing Actian games in honor of Apollo, who included in his plans for Greece a reorganization of the Amphictionic League, and who gave prominence to both Nicopolis and Thessaly by assigning to them an unusually large representation in the Amphictionic League, did not appear in Greece as a defender of Roman and Western traditions against things Eastern. He must rather have posed as a patron of Hellenism and as a leader under the special protection of Apollo. This, incidentally, suggests that the Macedonia given prominence in the Amphictionic League was not a province distinct from the province of Achaea, but rather a Greek state or states. The boundaries of Hellenism did not coincide with the boundaries of Roman provinces.

The policy of Augustus in Greece and Macedonia was such that he cannot have demanded official deification or encouraged the formation of a provincial organization that was in large part devoted to this cult. To the Greeks he did not wish to be a god, but to be regarded as the favorite of Apollo. It is no surprise, therefore, that under Augustus and his immediate successors there are no indications of provincial cults and assemblies in Achaea and Macedonia, and that it is even doubtful if they existed later. That does not mean that there were not eventually imperial cults and high priests enough also in these provinces, but only that they developed later and that the organizations maintaining the cults may never have embraced the entire provinces.

For the province of Achaea the nearest approach to a provincial assembly seems to have developed from the Panachaean League already mentioned. As late as the reign of Gaius this appears to have been an exclusively secular and political organization, its officers and *synedrion* making arrangements for sending ambassadors to congratulate the emperor on his accession. In the entire group of documents connected with this event (*IG* VII, 2711; cf. 2712) there is no reference to divine honors or cults on the part of the League itself or its component parts. Instead the emperor's letter mentions that the members had performed sacrifices for his safety. They did not pray to the emperor, but to the gods on behalf of the emperor. The organization, consisting as it did of a group of federal states, recalls the symmachies of earlier days. Each of the confederacies belonging to the League was represented on the embassy to Rome at its own expense—or rather, probably, at the personal expense of the ambassador. Similarly all the members obviously sent delegates to the *synedrion*. The head of the League was probably at first called *strategos* but later acquired the title of Helladarch. Though the League at the outset does not seem to have maintained an imperial cult, it was only a question of time until it acquired one, apparently in the form of a cult of the *domus Augusta*. It seems to have been established between the accession of Gaius in A.D. 37 and A.D. 55. It is heard of first in connection with the record of C. Julius Spartiaticus, who probably was the first high priest.[16] Later it became common for one person to be high priest and Helladarch at the same time, but the two offices seem to have remained distinct. It is interesting to note that all known high priests, judging by their names, were Roman citizens. Among them were C. Julius Spartiaticus, already mentioned, who belonged to a famous family from Sparta and had served as a magistrate at

Corinth, and Cn. Cornelius Pulcher, also of Corinth. Sparta was a free city, and Corinth a Roman colony. Thus there can have been no city which ranked too high to belong to the Panachaean League. The impression is that of a League which began as a purely political organization in order to be able to appeal to Rome more successfully than the individual states could do, which was recognized as such by Gaius and given permission to continue (*IG* VII, 2711. 29), and which later, like so many other public organisms, voluntarily established an imperial cult.

The connection with the Amphictionic League makes it likely that also the *koinon* of Macedonians,[17] probably best named the Macedonian League, originally was a political organization which later established an imperial cult and thereafter numbered a high priest among its officials. The reference to the "parts," the technical name for the four republics of 167 B.C., in a document recording the action of the larger organization, suggests that the latter was a union of the four republics. If so, it supplied the organ for Macedonian union and nationalism denied to the country when these were first organized. Coins show that the League existed as early as the reign of Claudius, but it is natural to believe that it goes back to Augustus if not earlier, and that it was this Macedonian League which sent representatives to the Amphictionic League. Since the four republics had had some political tasks to perform, for instance in connection with the payment of taxes to Rome, it is possible that the four had been allowed to get together in a sort of symmachy even earlier. The prominence given the organization in the Amphictionic League by Augustus would, then, be a recognition and encouragement similar to that given to Thessaly, as well as a gentle hint that Macedonia was to be a representative and champion of Hellenism. Though most records of the League are those of honors bestowed upon individuals, one such record shows a continued political activity. Licinius Rufinus, a man of consular rank, was honored for pleading the cause of the League in connection with the inclusion of the Thessalians in the payment of contributions or taxes.[18] Apparently when Thessaly was transferred from the province of Achaea to that of Macedonia it was incorporated into the Macedonian League, which thus continued to be an organization of the Greeks of the province.

The interpretation given above suggesting that the Macedonian League consisted of the four republics organized in 167 B.C., later augmented by the addition of Thessaly, may seem contradicted by the use of the word *eparcheia,* which is equivalent to the Latin *provincia,* to designate the organization. This may seem to imply that it was a League covering the entire province under the governor of Macedonia. The answer to this objection is that "province" is a very elastic word with a variety of meanings. The word originally meant the sphere of activity or task of an official, and hence could just as well be applied to the task of a treasury official or an administrator of justice as to that of a governor. It was also used frequently for the territory administered by an official, but even then it remained elastic. Thus Sicily might at the same time be one province from the point of view of the praetor who governed the island, but two provinces from the point of view of the quaestors, one stationed at Syracuse and one at Lilybaeum, who administered the finances. Similarly, when the province of a governor fell into several more or less well-defined districts, as some of those in Asia Minor did, it could be viewed as one province or several provinces. Likewise Crete and Cyrene could be viewed as one province or two provinces, and either of the two component parts could be considered a province.[19] It would not be surprising if in the same manner the Macedonian part of the province of its governor should be considered a province distinct from that of the Illyrian part. After all, the two parts had been organized separately in 167 B.C. by two distinct officials each aided by a staff of emissaries from the Roman senate,[20] and it would not be unnatural that this division should continue to be recognized even after the two districts were placed under one governor.

For the Macedonian League a *synedrion,* a secretary, the high priest, and Macedoniarchs are known. The members of the *synedrion,* the *synedroi,* are referred to in such a way that it is clear that they were representatives. The prominence of the high priest in the records may seem to contradict the reconstruction of the history of the organization as a secular organization at the outset, but it may be noted that our documents are relatively late, the earliest record of a high priest apparently coming from the reign of Nerva. Before this there had been time for development. Then there are the Macedoniarchs, who clearly were secular officials and probably secular heads of the League. They were elected by the *synedrion,* which on at least one occasion even passed a decree honoring a defeated candidate.[21] We have one reference to a daughter of a Macedoniarch and a high priestess.[22] Since the high priestess must have acquired her title as wife of a high priest, this seems a curious way of indicating that the father bore both titles, that is, Macedoniarch and high priest. This in turn suggests that either the two offices were held concurrently or that they were titles for the secular and religious aspects of the same office. Helladarch and high priest seem to have been two offices, but that is no clue to the state of affairs in Macedonia. These offices were highly prized, to judge by the records of the unsuccessful candidate already mentioned and of a woman who had been high priestess five times and whose husband consequently must have been high priest five times.[23] Another indication of the value placed on the office is that the tenants regularly seem to have been Roman citizens.[24]

The sketches of the Panachaean and especially the Macedonian leagues given above may be even more tentative than usual and more subject to revision through the discovery of new evidence and through detailed investigations. Yet some additional evidence can be cited in support of the general conclusion that the two leagues originally were secular and only later established imperial cults. This is the work of Hadrian, who not only was responsible for a reform in representation in the Amphictionic League, but also organized the Panhellenion with headquarters at Athens as a new instrument for Panhellenic unity.[25] This was an organization in which Greeks not only of Greece and Macedonia but also of Asia and Africa were represented. The assembly, of course, was a *synedrion* or representative council, and the head of the organization bore the simple title of *archon*. With it is coupled, commonly but not always, the title of priest of Hadrianos Panhellenios, and this seems to have been retained after Hadrian's death.[26] Thus this is not a normal imperial cult, not an expression of loyalty to the ruling emperor; it is rather a cult expressing gratitude to the founder. An inscription recently discovered has shown that some member, apparently Cyrene, was represented in the assembly by two *synedroi.* This, in turn, combined with other evidence, has indicated that also in the Panhellenion representation was on a basis of proportion, not equality. Hadrian, by reducing the representation in the Amphictionic League of at least one of the units with six votes and increasing that of Sparta and Athens, was shifting the balance away from the northern frontier of Greece. In the Panhellenion he went farther in an effort to consolidate the Greeks on all sides of the eastern Mediterranean, reviving at the same time the prestige of Athens. The headship of the Panhellenion ranked above that of the Panachaean League,[27] and was probably the highest office attainable outside the service of the Roman government.

The adjustment of representation in the Amphictionic League by Augustus and Hadrian and the introduction of representation on the basis of proportion by Hadrian in the Panhellenion indicates continued preoccupation with just representation. This should prepare us for finding the principle of representation in proportion to population applied also in other parts of the Hellenistic East and particularly in Asia Minor, from which most of our other evidence comes. Otherwise the early adoption of deification in Asia Minor and the confused and varied history of the country should also prepare us for a somewhat different picture. Asia Minor rather than Greece took the lead in emperor worship. In fact an important study of the Commonality of Asia took as a starting point the assertion that the imperial cult spread from Asia to the rest of the Empire.[28]

The two eastern *koina* which are best known are the Lycian Confederacy and the Asianic Commonality. They are also representatives of the two chief types. The Lycian Confederacy is an old federal state which continued as an instrument for local government much like the Thessalian Confederacy and the Macedonian republics. The Asianic Commonality is a larger organization somewhat resembling the Panachaean and Macedonian leagues but apparently less political and more specifically devoted to the imperial cult; hence it may best be called a commonality, to use a name which is a fairly adequate translation of the Greek *koinon* and the Latin *commune*. The adjective used in the name "Asianic" will be used with reference to Asia Minor and particularly the Roman province of Asia in order to avoid confusion with "Asiatic" in the broader sense of that word. The two organizations were the object of special studies in the last part of the nineteenth century, when a great deal of work was being done on the subjects of provincial assemblies and emperor worship by French scholars.[29] What has been done and discovered later down through 1947 is summarized and interpreted with full bibliographical information by Professor Magie in his monumental work, *Roman Rule in Asia Minor.*[30] This will remain as a whole indispensable for a long time—but it will soon be out of date on a number of points. Much work is being done in Asia Minor and reports of new discoveries and studies follow each other rapidly. Among those busy in the field is L. Robert, and new material of importance is quickly noted in the *Bulletin épigraphique* of J. and L. Robert. Thus it is possible to speak with some assurance about the institutions of federations and commonalities in Asia Minor, though it may be noted that a number of the most important questions remain matters of dispute. For anything outside Asia Minor any statements will be even more haphazard.

It may be well to start with the observation that the Hellenistic provinces of the Roman Empire developed a mania for titles and dignities of all sorts. That is probably to be seen best in the province of Asia and the Asianic Commonality. The Asians were not content with one temple for the imperial cult of the Commonality, but there were temples in several cities. This appears sometimes in the titles of high priests. The exact significance does not seem to be known. There were also other ways in which a city was honored, as by bestowal of the title *neokoros,* which Magie (636 and *passim*) renders as "temple-warden." Naturally also, prominent individuals were overloaded with titles. It has already been noted

in the discussion of the Panachaean League that those who had
served as high priests afterward bore the title of high priest for life,
and similar titles were undoubtedly used in many if not all parts
of the Hellenistic world. Naturally, the system was not always the
same. According to a very plausible theory, in the Lycian Confederacy in imperial times high priest and Lyciarch were titles of
the same official, high priest being the title employed during the
year of office and Lyciarch the one retained for life. It must be
admitted, however, that Professor Magie, who knows Asianic institutions better than anyone else, believes that the two offices were
distinct.[31] The group of titles which cause most trouble are those
of the type of Helladarch, Macedoniarch, and Lyciarch. The largest group is the Asiarchs, who have the distinction of being mentioned by Strabo (14.649), who wrote under Augustus and Tiberius, and in the Acts of the Apostles (19: 31), where it is stated that
the apostle Paul, when he was at Ephesus, had several friends
among the Asiarchs. Similar titles are found in many parts of the
Near East.[32] All that it may be safe to conclude from the prevalence
of such titles is that they were very popular and that each title of
the kind had some connection with a confederacy or commonality.[33]
Nevertheless, a solution will be suggested.

It may be observed that the titles of the kind sometimes represent
officials of organizations the boundaries of which may have coincided with those of a province, as for example the Commonality
of Asia. But in other organizations they cannot have coincided;
an obvious example is Lycia, a part of the province of Lycia and
Pamphylia—for the other part we have records of a few Pam-
phyliarchs. For Bithynia and Pontus there similarly are records of
Bithyniarchs and Pontarchs. Of the two parts, Bithynia is remarkable for the absence of any records in inscriptions of high priests
of the Commonality. Though there was a cult of some kind, and
though a record of a high priest may turn up at any time, this suggests that the organization primarily was active politically. This is
further suggested by a rescript addressed by Severus Alexander to
the *koinon* of the Hellenes in Bithynia (*Digest* 49.1.25). Aside
from Asia, the one commonality of the peninsula which corre-

sponded approximately to a governor's province and for which
there are officials of this type is Galatia, where there are records
both of Galatarchs and high priests. Outside of Asia Minor, a
Thracian commonality is known by a few documents including
a rescript from Antoninus Pius, and some references to Thracarchs.[34]
In one dedication it appears that the organization called itself "the
koinon of the Hellenes in Thrace."

High priests on the one hand, and Asiarchs, Lyciarchs, Bithyniarchs, Galatarchs, etc., on the other, represent the two sides of the
activities of the organizations, the religious and the secular. The
relation of the two sets of officials to each other, or even whether
there were two sets or whether the high priests and secular heads
of the state were the same men under different titles, remains a
matter of dispute. Probably the view most widely held at present
is that the Asiarchs, and the like, were the high priests or that
titles of this kind were retained for life while the title of high priest
was the one used during the year of office. That fits fairly well with
the statement quoted from the jurist Modestinus of the first half
of the third century to the effect that service as high priest of a
nation, such as Asiarch, Bithyniarch, Cappadociarch, carried with
it exemption from service as guardian, *that is, as long as one held
office.*[35] This statement clearly implies that the names belonged to
the high priests both during their term of office and afterward,
that is, that such titles were retained for life. This statement can
probably be accepted as true in general but not as giving all the
details about every organization. Moreover, in the days of Modestinus there may have been more uniformity than there had been
a century earlier. Thus, to give one example, for the Panachaean
League it was suggested above that the high priest and Helladarch
originally were separate offices; by the third century they may well
have been merged. There is evidence that titles of the kind were
used by holders of the office, and the aorist participle of the corresponding verb is used to indicate that someone has served, for instance, as Lyciarch or Asiarch.[36] There are also records of repeated
tenure of such offices. In spite of this, the individuals undoubtedly
still bore the title after their term of office was over. This would

make it possible for Paul or others to find several Asiarchs in some prominent city such as Ephesus, where there might be living several former high priests from the city as well as others who might have been attracted to the metropolis. Nevertheless, during the term of office the title most commonly used was that of high priest. This was the title which was used both in the Asianic Commonality and the Lycian Confederacy as that of the eponymous head of the organization.[37] In any case, the office or offices were annual. There is evidence of this for so many organizations that it can almost be assumed where evidence is lacking. If evidence to the contrary should turn up for some particular confederacy or commonality, it will be safe to regard it as an exception. The evidence consists largely of the use of the high priests as eponymous magistrates, though there also is other evidence—which cannot, however, be discussed here.

The question of assemblies must be handled in much the same manner, and this statement applies to all Hellenistic provinces including Greece. It can be taken for granted that any primary assemblies which may have been retained in late Hellenistic confederacies were abandoned at the latest under the early Roman Empire, and that any new organizations were formed without primary assemblies. Thus all confederacies, leagues, and commonalities of the period possessed only representative assemblies, and it is very unlikely that there were exceptions. The evidence cannot be surveyed in detail. It may be enough to observe that there is no evidence, as far as I know, for a primary assembly under the Empire in any confederacy or commonality. One of the names applied to assemblies in Asia suggests an interesting evolution. It has already been mentioned that the Lycians had a federal representative assembly which was named *archairesiake ekklesia,* or electoral assembly. Similarly a meeting of the assembly of the Asianic Commonality, or the assembly itself, is once called *ekklesia archairetike.*[38] In the discussion of Lycia, it was stated that the name suggested a development from a time when the Lycians actually did have a primary assembly. This can hardly be suggested for the Asianic Commonality. All that can be asserted is that the latter

organization was consciously following the model of federal organisms as they had been developing in Asia Minor. No explanation can be offered here for the fact that we find electoral assemblies
passing honorary decrees and thus performing business which has
no particular connection with elections. The solution is probably
to be found in the study of the governments of the cities in Asia
Minor and on the coasts of the Black Sea.[39]

As for the composition of the representative assemblies, it is
almost certain that some system of representation in proportion to
population was normal if not universal. Thessaly and Lycia have
been discussed earlier. In the present chapter, evidence for adjustment of representation in the Amphictionic League by Augustus
and Hadrian and the recently discovered evidence for proportion
in the representation in Hadrian's Panhellenion have been noticed.
To this can be added the fact that a document already once referred to indicates that in 4 B.C. the assembly of the Asianic Commonality counted 150 members (*Inscr. Sardis* 8, doc. 7). This is
almost certainly more than the number of cities of the Commonality. There is also a rescript of Antoninus Pius to the *koinon* of
Asia (*Digest* 27.1.6.2) in which the cities are grouped in three
classes. This and the example of Lycia suggest three representatives
each for the large cities, two for the medium-sized, and one for the
small.[40]

It is likely that the same classification supplied the basis for the
contributions of the cities to the treasury of the commonality or
confederation. It will be remembered that the principle of contributions in proportion to representation was applied in the early
Boeotian Confederacy and in the Aetolian Confederacy. It was apparently very common. Strabo (14.665) says it was used by the
Lycians. Obviously even the loosest commonality had expenses connected with honors bestowed, festivals celebrated, and embassies
sent to Rome. For these expenses a central treasury and income
were necessary, and it is pretty clear that the income took the form
of contributions from the cities in proportion to their representation. For the Asianic Commonality we actually possess evidence
which indicates that the cities contributed and that the contribu-

tions of all cities were not the same. Dio Chrysostom (35.17), when addressing the people of Apamea in Phrygia, remarked that their city contributed just as much to the expense of the temples of Asia as the cities in which those temples stood. This clearly means that the contributions of cities differed and that Apamea was among those making the largest contributions. Yet such is the fate of evidence when glanced at superficially that this has been used as evidence for equal contributions.[41]

The two chief activities attributed to provincial assemblies are, in general, the maintenance of the imperial cult and some supervision of the record of the governors of the provinces. To begin with the imperial cult, there can be no doubt about the prominence of cults of Rome and the emperor and other prominent Romans in the Hellenistic provinces, though less in Greece and Macedonia than in Asia Minor. It has long been known that a temple of Roma was built in Smyrna as early as 195 B.C., and it has been noted above that there now is evidence for a cult of Roma on the part of the Lycian Confederacy almost as early. These are only examples of the manner in which Hellenistic states, following habits of long standing, attempted to curry favor and express friendship or loyalty by means of deification. How much religion there was in this cannot be discussed here. This Hellenistic habit Augustus seems to have tolerated rather than encouraged (Magie, *Asia,* 447). In Greece he preferred to be considered a human being under the special protection of Apollo, and even in Asia Minor the cult of Roma and Augustus, the one usually associated with provincial assemblies, does not seem to have been maintained by all commonalities and confederacies. One difficulty in trying to determine the nature of the cult is that in the records of most high priests the deities are not listed. There seems to be no doubt about the Asianic Commonality, though at the outset it appears definitely to have made the second god of the pair Augustus personally as the son of the deified Caesar, rather than the emperor in office at the time (*Inscr. Sardis* 8). The case seems clear also for the Galatian Commonality, for which we have the inscription on a temple dedicated to Augustus and Roma (*OGIS* 533). For the Bithynians, for whom we lack records of high priests, the evidence is indecisive. Early in his reign Augustus is reported to have permitted the Asians to dedicate a precinct to himself in Pergamum, and the Bithynians one in Nicomedia (Dio Cassius 51.20.7), but this does not necessarily mean that the cults of the two groups were the same. Apparently the evidence of Suetonius (*Aug.* 52) to the effect that Augustus did not allow the dedication of temples to himself in any province except in conjunction with Roma is supposed to settle the question. Such general statements, however, have little value as evidence. It is almost unthinkable that Augustus should have issued an edict on the subject applicable to the entire Empire. His ruling must have taken the form of replies to particular requests or decisions on specific problems. In all likelihood Suetonius had seen a number of such documents and had made his own generalization. If so, it is dangerous to argue back from his generalization to a specific cult. Therefore, it is best to leave unsolved the problem of the nature of the cult maintained by the Bithynian Commonality. For the Lycian Confederacy, on the other hand, we know that their high priests were high priests of the Sebastoi, that is, the Augusti. However, it seems that also the old cult of Roma was retained (*IGR* III, 490), and hence that the Lycians expressed their loyalty by separate cults of this goddess and of the imperial family. We cannot go into further detail. Though much is uncertain, and though this survey is superficial, it does lead to the conclusion that no systematic ruler cult was imposed upon the Hellenistic provinces during the early Principate. Rather, the cults were allowed to develop. Ultimately there probably were no cities and no groupings of cities which did not maintain some sort of cult.

Of the other activities of the provincial assemblies, the one which has attracted most attention is that of the prosecution of governors.[42] After a governor's term of office was over, the assembly of a confederation or commonality surveyed his record and commonly voted him honors, but not infrequently decided to prosecute him for extortion. Much of our information consists of brief notices by Tacitus of trials from the reign of Tiberius to that of Nero and a fuller account by the younger Pliny of trials before the senate in the reign of Trajan at which he served as an attorney for the defense or the prosecution. These accounts show that the commonalities of Asia and Bithynia were among the most active; Bithynia was probably the more active of the two.[48] This impression may not be entirely correct, for Bithynia had the advantage that Pliny took part in two trials and so has described them at some length. Nevertheless, it is remarkable that we have so much activity on the part of so small a commonality. It may be well to emphasize that the accusations definitely were brought by the Bithynian Commonality, and not by the province of Pontus and Bithynia. Also in the province of Crete and Cyrene, another province with two distinct parts or provinces, accusations were brought by each of the two.[44] These activities seem to have been encouraged by the Roman government, which welcomed aid in keeping administrators in line. It is significant that the one rescript of Severus Alexander to the Bithynian Commonality from which an excerpt has been preserved (*Digest* 49.1.25) fulminates against governors and other officials who use force to prevent appeals to the emperor. These appeals, of course, concern lawsuits in general rather than accusations of governors. It seems strange to us to have the central government communicate criticisms of governors to organisms serving as instruments for joint action on the part of their subjects. By the time of Severus Alexander we are approaching the spirit of suspicion and espionage of the complicated bureaucracy of the Late Empire, but even earlier the activities of the various commonalities seem to have been encouraged.

Other activities of the commonalities and confederacies cannot be discussed. They naturally varied from organization to organization, and what we know depends on the accident of the preservation of evidence. One form of evidence little used in the present discussion is that of coins. In the Hellenistic provinces many of the *koina* minted money or at least were honored by having their names on coins. This at times included silver and not merely the small change which frequently was minted even by cities. This and the other activities encouraged something in the nature of nationalism within the Roman Empire, at least on the part of privileged groups, the Hellenes of Asia, the Hellenes of Bithynia, the Macedonians, and the like. Possibly the sort of spirit encouraged by the continuation of the Thessalian and Lycian confederacies can best be compared to a vigorous interest in states' rights or a local patriotism within a larger unity. For the encouragement of Hellenism in the broadest sense there were the Amphictionic League and the Panhellenion of Hadrian. These efforts seem to have been rather successful in the confederacies. In the Lycian and Thessalian confederacies there was competition for office and pride in service to the state,[45] and the bestowing of honors upon the candidate who failed to be elected Macedoniarch suggests the same for Macedonia. There was nothing anti-Roman in this budding nationalism and local pride. The various organizations regularly expressed their loyalty through imperial cults. Moreover, the greatest local dignitaries often attained even greater heights in the imperial service. If there was glory to be attained in the services of Thessaly or Hellenism, there was even greater glory to be attained in the service of Rome. Hence, the higher the dignity the greater the likelihood that the incumbent was a Roman citizen. Many of the heads of the Thessalian and Lycian confederacies were men without Roman citizenship, while the high priests of the Panachaean and Macedonian leagues and Asiatic Commonality normally were citizens. It is doubtful, however, that citizenship was required.[46]

VII

The Provincial Assemblies in the Western Provinces of the Roman Empire

THE WESTERN provinces means the Latin provinces. For our purposes, that signifies the provinces in which the business of the assemblies was conducted in Latin and the officials bore Latin titles. No one doubts that these assemblies were representative assemblies in the sense that primary assemblies did not exist. The name for an assembly was *concilium*. The title of the annual head was *flamen* or *sacerdos*. Thus the head was definitely a priest connected with an imperial cult, and there is here no problem of the relation to each other of the religious and civil authorities. There may be a question of the extent of the political and other nonreligious activities of an assembly or the commonality represented by the assembly, but that is another matter. This commonality was usually called simply a "province," for the commonalities and provinces normally coincided. Thus we get the titles *flamen provinciae* and *sacerdos provinciae* and more rarely *concilium provinciae*. There was at least one important assembly for which these titles did not fit, namely, that of the Three Gauls. Yet, if there was a Latin word in use for the corporation represented by the assembly, I do not know what it was unless it was *commune,* the translation of the Greek *koinon*. This was employed in the Latin version of the names of the Lycian Confederation and the commonalities of Asia and Sicily,[1] but there seems to be no evidence for its use in the Latin provinces. Sicily was more Greek than Latin and so cannot be cited as an example of a Latin province. In mentions of the Three Gauls, where "province" would not do, we find such expressions as "treasury of the Gauls," or "priest of the altar at the confluence of the Saône and the Rhone."

Even so, there remain problems enough. Thus there is the problem of the policy of the emperor and the central government. Sometimes the initiative came from above. But always? And were assemblies imposed on all provinces at the very beginning of the Principate, or was there also in the West as in the East some room for local initiative? How were the assemblies made up? Did they consist of representatives, or of dignitaries who belonged in virtue of their attainments? If the members were representatives, was there one representative or vote for each city, or were the cities represented in proportion to their size? Were the assemblies and the entire system merely borrowed from the Hellenistic East, or was there a genuine Latin or Western tradition behind them? Did the assemblies owe anything to local institutions and traditions? Specifically, was the assembly of the Three Gauls more Gallic and Celtic than Graeco-Roman?

The question of Greek borrowing or Western origin is more than a mere question of detail. It involves the choice between two different systems. In Greek cities the council consisted of members chosen by lot or otherwise to serve for a short term, usually a year. In Rome and Italy and the Latinized provinces, on the other hand, councils made up of dignitaries serving for life were normal. The best-known example is the senate of Rome itself, made up as it was—in large part—of former magistrates. Also the city councils of the Latinized cities throughout the West, though smaller, were constituted in much the same way. This is illustrated by the *album* of the council of the city of Canusium in the early third century (*CIL* IX, 338; Dessau, 6121), in which, after the patrons, the regular members are listed by groups in order of seniority, according to the highest office they had held or the highest dignity to which they had been elevated. If the provincial assemblies were to follow this model, they might consist of the senior ex-magistrates of the various cities or the leading members of the councils of the cities, which would amount to much the same thing. It may be said in advance that the assemblies actually consisted of delegates combined with a group of former high priests who had been given life membership. Thus the result is, as it were, a hybrid institution, half Hellenistic and half Roman. Yet it cannot be said for certain that the use of delegates was exclusively due to the Hellenistic influence. There may well have been a Roman or Latin tradition for the use of delegates in similar organizations, though Rome's Italic allies had no league and no federal assembly.

The Romans came early into contact with Greek federal institutions. Probably the first direct contact was in 228 B.C., when a Roman consul at the end of the First Illyrian War sent ambassadors to the Aetolian and Achaean confederacies to explain the actions of the Romans (Pol. 2.12.4). It will be remembered that about a generation later the Thessalian Confederacy was reconstituted under Roman supervision and that it was not long before other federal states were organized under similar auspices. The first transfer of these institutions to the West came with the organization of the Sicilian Commonality soon after the reduction of Syracuse in 212 if not before. The organization was known as the *Commune Siciliae;* it celebrated games in honor of Marcellus, the conqueror of Syracuse; it could vote honors; and the cities contributed to the expenses of the Commonality in proportion to their share in its affairs. Verres, of course, had the games changed by substituting *Verria* for *Marcellia.* The assembly of the Commonality, during the governorship of Verres, seems to have sent two petitions to Rome, one requesting from the senate a ruling on a point of legal procedure and one asking for the adoption of a rule that statues should not be promised to anyone until after he had left the province. The reference to the actions of the *legationes,* the embassies of the various cities, indicates that the assembly was a representative assembly. The references to the collection of funds indicate that they were collected when needed, but the statement that the Syracusans contributed *pro parte* suggests that the size of the contributions was regulated according to some scale or rule. The details may be uncertain, but there can be no doubt about the existence of the organization.[2] There is also something that comes near to being contemporary evidence for its existence in 200 B.C. A Macedonian orator is represented by Livy (31.29.8–9) as addressing the Aetolians and contrasting the freedom of their meetings with that of Sicilian meetings at Syracuse, Messana, or Lilybaeum held in the presence of the Roman praetor. Livy's source is almost certainly Polybius, and the latter is likely to have reported what actually was said. That the meetings were held in conjunction with sessions of the governor's court does not prove that no commonality existed. Sicily was Rome's first conquest outside of Italy, and she may well have allowed institutions there which she at first did not permit in other provinces. Thus Greek federal institutions established a very weak bridgehead in the West, but this particular organization may not have had much effect on later developments in the Latin provinces. The opposite process, the extension of Latin institutions in Sicily by the transformation of the *boulai* of the cities into miniature senates consisting of life members appointed by censors, began almost at once. By the time of Cicero and Verres, and probably even earlier, the system was universal.[3] Thus Sicily furnished a good example of the interaction of the two sets of institutions on each other. It is probably significant that it was in the governments of the cities that the Roman influence made itself most felt. If the cities adopted a form of government which placed the control in the hands of a small group of men of property, then the society of the provinces was safely dominated by the best people. If that was done, there was no harm in permitting these cities to elect delegates to assemblies of federal states and commonalities.

It is uncertain whether from the days of the Latin League there was left in Italy any tradition making for the creation of federal organizations, but it is clear that at least in the first century B.C. there was serious discussion of representative government on federal lines. In fact, this discussion should lend credence to the report that the opponents of Rome in the Marsic War adopted a government in which a representative council of five hundred members was given full powers. The evidence for the discussion of representative government is found in Livy. He reports that in 340 B.C. the Latins demanded that one consul and half the senate be Latin; that after Cannae it was suggested that two men from each Latin city be given citizenship and admitted to the senate; and that, according to some annalists, the Campanians demanded that one consul should be Campanian. The last incident Livy himself hesitated to accept as historical.[4] This reference to earlier writers shows that the discussion did not originate with Livy, but had been going on for some time. Apparently, since there was talk of membership in the senate, the proposal was to give permanent membership to dignitaries from the various cities rather than to have delegates elected for short terms. If so, the result might have been an admirable representative assembly for a group of cities aristocratically governed and desiring representation only of the aristocracy. It was approximately the type of assembly which was used in the Late Empire, but it was not the type adopted in the western provinces under the Principate.

Two assemblies, those of the Three Gauls and of Narbonensis, will be taken as a starting point, and most of the discussion will center around them. Of the two, the assembly of the Three Gauls represented approximately the part of Gaul conquered by Caesar; that of Narbonensis, the older and more Romanized province of Narbonese Gaul. Thus the two are closely associated, but their institutions differed somewhat, as is indicated by the fact that the high priest of the Three Gauls was called *sacerdos,* and the high priest of Narbonensis, *flamen.* They also provide a key to the solution of a number of problems including whether newly conquered and Romanized provinces were treated alike—a matter which depends largely on the dates of the establishment of the two cults.[5] The assembly of the Three Gauls is known from literary sources to have been established in 12 B.C. by Drusus, who summoned the leading Gauls to Lugdunum.[6] This means that the initiative came from above, and if it be taken for granted that Drusus acted in accordance with the plans of Augustus, the Commonality of the Three Gauls (if we can use that term) illustrates his policy toward a newly conquered district. As will be seen, he desired loyalty, but again, as in Greece, he encouraged a local nationalism. That the cult and assembly of Narbonensis, on the other hand, were established considerably later has been proved by an Athenian inscription published a few years ago.[7] This is one of a group of inscriptions honoring Q. Trebellius Rufus, who had been the first high

priest of Narbonensis and later served as eponymous archon of
Athens sometime between A.D. 85/6 and 94/5. This brings to a
conclusion a protracted argument, not without its humorous aspects, concerning the origin of the cult of Narbonensis. Earlier
attempts to place it usually took the form of attempting to date the
charter of the provincial assembly of the province.[8] Efforts to date
this on epigraphical grounds proved inconclusive, but Krascheninn-
nikoff, in an article published in 1894, recognized that the solution
would depend largely on the career of Trebellius, that is, provided
that Trebellius was the earliest *flamen* of the province. On that
basis he argued that the cult originated under Vespasian. The same
conclusion has been reached more recently by Gagé. Kornemann
(*RE* 4, 811 f.) accepted this date for the inscription, but argued
that the cult originated under Nero. Others, however, maintained
that in what was then the key inscription (*IG* II², 4193) Trebellius
Rufus was not represented as the earliest high priest, but as high
priest and a leading man of the province. Thus the question of the
date of the establishment of the imperial cult in Narbonensis and,
as a consequence, the interpretation of an important phase of the
policy of Augustus and Tiberius, seemed to depend upon the
meaning of πρῶτος in an Athenian inscription. Did it mean "first"
in the chronological sense, or was it used as a substantive, meaning
a leading or outstanding man, "first in the province"? Those who
adopted the latter meaning failed to analyze the document with
sufficient care or to take into consideration that both meanings are
common. There are many examples to show that the word and
its derivatives have been used to emphasize prominence, but it is
also clear that it was common to boast of such things as being "first
of all time" to attain a certain dignity. Hence either meaning is
possible, and the meaning in any particular case can be determined
only by analysis of the document in which it occurs. This should
have given the meaning "first" in the chronological sense. However, since this was not the opinion of all, it was very important
that a document entirely clear on the particular point should be
discovered. The inscription in question is very fragmentary, but
even so it is clear that a letter from the assembly of Narbonensis

to the Areopagus and the council of six hundred (as it was at this time) at Athens contained a reference to "our first high priest" in such a way that it can mean only first in time.

It is hardly stretching the evidence too much to say that this disposes of another theory, namely, that the cult described in the charter may have been preceded by an earlier imperial cult. In the charter, the high priest is called *flamen*. Earlier there may have been a cult in another form in which he was called *sacerdos*. This was the theory of Camille Jullian, the brilliant historian of Roman Gaul, who held that *flamen* was a higher and more dignified title than *sacerdos*. Augustus had at first permitted the province to have a cult headed by a priest with the less dignified title of *sacerdos*.[9] Against this theory is the lack of evidence of change from *sacerdos* to *flamen*. Changes rather went the other way. Even if the example of Sardinia is not too certain,[10] it is known that *sacerdos* became the normal title in the Late Empire, and it was not the style of that period to abandon more dignified titles in favor of less dignified ones. In any case, as far as Narbonensis is concerned, the Athenian inscriptions, in which *archiereus* is used, dispose of the theory. Trebellius Rufus was the first high priest, whatever Latin title was used.

The two Gallic assemblies thus show one established in 12 B.C. on the initiative of an adopted son of Augustus, and another established considerably later. Since the assembly of the Three Gauls belonged to a district conquered only a little more than a generation earlier, it may well be that the organization was intended to serve as an instrument for Romanization. It is a plausible conjecture that the cult at the Ara Ubiorum on the site of modern Cologne was to serve as a similar instrument for the Romanization of Germany, but everybody knows that nothing came of this. The reason for not establishing an assembly of the kind in Narbonensis might well be that this more Romanized province was in no need of such an instrument. Even so, Augustus does not seem to have had any plan for using provincial cults systematically as instruments for Romanization. In Spain, Hither Spain was less Romanized than Further Spain. For this province an anecdote suggests that there may have been a municipal cult at Tarraco within the lifetime of Augustus. Quintilian (6.3.77) states that when the people of Tarraco reported to Augustus that a palm tree had sprouted on his altar, he retorted that this showed how often they sacrificed to him. This certainly supplies no evidence for a provincial cult. Instead, we learn that in A.D. 15 Tiberius in reply to a request granted the Spaniards permission to erect a temple to Augustus at Tarraco, and, adds Tacitus (*Ann.* 1.78.1), an example was thereby given to all the provinces (*datumque in omnes provincias exemplum*). A permission to build a temple to Augustus was granted. That is all. The statement about the example to the provinces is added by Tacitus, and he does not suggest that it represents a pronouncement of policy by Tiberius. To try to deduce from these words information about the policy of Augustus or Tiberius, as some have done, is a gratuitous waste of time. There is much that we do not know. Naturally, no one can prove that the temple was not preceded by an altar, and naturally—and equally so—no one can prove that it was. A temple to Augustus in A.D. 15 sounds like a cult of *Divus Augustus*. If this was the forerunner of the later provincial cult, there must have been modifications introduced at a later date, for the title of the high priest was *flamen Romae divorum et Augustorum provinciae Hispaniae citerioris* or something of the kind.[21] Thus, all we know is that, about twenty-seven years after the founding of the assembly of the Three Gauls, the province of Hither Spain was permitted to build a temple to Augustus, and that the cult established did not at the time take the form of the later provincial cult. It looks as if Augustus encouraged the imperial cult in Gaul and possibly in Germany as an instrument for Romanization and for attaching the people of the districts to himself. Otherwise the development of cults and assemblies seems to have followed somewhat the same haphazard lines as in the Hellenistic provinces. A question which cannot be answered is whether provincial assemblies at times antedated the cults. Since Augustus seems to have encouraged rather than discouraged local patriotism, the formation of assemblies may have been encouraged. On the other hand, some of the cities in the provinces were capable of appealing to Rome individually, and thus it is hard to tell whether the appeal from Hither Spain, to use this as an example, came from the province as a whole or from a group of cities. It may be well to recall that the Panachaean League seems to have resulted from the combining of small confederacies for concerted action in approaching the emperor. Of the ultimate existence of assemblies and imperial cults in all, or practically all, the western provinces, there can be little doubt.

In spite of the differences in their history and origins, the general impression is that the assemblies were much alike. Possibly this is a false impression resulting from lack of evidence, for the evidence we have, largely records of high priests, shows one striking difference. In some provinces the high priests are named *sacerdos*, in some *flamen*. To begin with Gaul, the high priest of the Three Gauls was a *sacerdos;* that of Narbonensis, a *flamen*. The term of office of these priests, whatever their title, was a year. This is suggested by the example of the eastern commonalities and the common practice in the priesthoods of muncipal cults.[12] The annual term is attested for Narbonensis by the charter, which, in a statement of the honors of a former *flamen,* provides that the year of his priesthood is to be inscribed on the base of his statue. It is attested likewise for Africa, where the year of the priesthood of the provincial *sacerdos* was indicated according to an era beginning early in the reign of Vespasian.[13] It is also implied by a reference in Tacitus (*Ann.* 1.57.2) to the year in which Segimundus was elected that the term of office of the high priest at the Ara Ubiorum was annual. Where the evidence is so scattered, this is enough to indicate that the usual term was one year. It is particularly significant that some of our best evidence comes from Narbonensis, where the title was *flamen* and where the priesthood was modeled on that of the *flamen Dialis,* for the Roman model suggests life tenure. Hence there must be a reason for the short term. From the point of view of Rome, the purpose must have been to have as many as possible of the most prominent men of the province conduct rituals which expressed loyalty to Rome and the emperor; from the point of view of the provincials, it must have been to open the highest dignity within the gift of the provincials to a greater number of persons. The short term of the high priest is proof enough that the real purpose served by the cults and assemblies was political.

The statement just made referring to the high priesthood as an office within the gift of the provincials naturally begs the question, but is nevertheless warranted. A short term of office of the kind calls for election or appointment, and the entire spirit of the assemblies implies election. It would make little sense to have the head of an organization which was to pass upon the record of a governor appointed by that governor or his successor or even by the emperor. There is also a certain amount of more direct evidence. The term *creatus* used by Livy (*Epitome* 139) in connection with the first high priest of the Three Gauls, Gaius Julius Vercondaridubnus, and by Tacitus (*Ann.* 1.57.2) about Segimundus at the Ara Ubiorum, though not completely unambiguous, is best taken to mean election. It is used also in an inscription with reference to the *sacerdos* of the Three Gauls (Dessau, 5163.16). More direct evidence is derived from a few inscriptions referring to the election of particular individuals. A good example is that of a provincial *flamen* of Baetica or Further Spain on whose monument the following words were inscribed: *hic provinciae Baeticae consensu flaminis munus est consequuutus* (*CIL* II, 2344), that is, he had attained to his dignity through the consensus of opinion of the province. Apparently this is meant to indicate a unanimous vote at his election. For the Three Gauls there are two inscriptions, for Narbonensis one, all three fragmentary but clearly indicating election.[14] Indirect evidence for election comes also from literary sources. The younger Pliny (*Ep.* 2.13.4) in recommending a man of equestrian rank mentions that he has recently been *flamen* of Hither Spain and adds, parenthetically, *scis, quod iudicium provinciae illius, quanta sit gravitas*. This statement, which, strictly speaking, is untranslatable, can be rendered, freely, "You know how much the judgment of that province counts, and how great its dignity is." Thus Pliny writes as if the election to the flaminate of the province was a highly prized honor. Finally there is the evidence of Paulus (*Sent.* 5.30A), who, writing early in the third century, discusses the punishment to be meted out to those who cause riots in connection with the election of the high priest of a province. Thus there is no doubt about the election of the high priests, and election means election by the representative assembly, for primary assemblies did not exist and popular elections of the modern type were out of the question. With the poor communications of ancient times, they would have been completely impossible unless public opinion had been aroused to an unusual degree.[15] One suggestion that has been made is that the post of high priest was passed around in such a way that the real election took place in the home community of the man to be elected, in which case the election would be conducted by the local *curia* or city council. From Sardinia there is some slight evidence pointing in this direction, but it is doubtful whether the system was commonly so rigid. Certainly no community, unless it should be in a province with a single large city, was allowed to have a monopoly on the position.[16] For the Three Gauls we have a double set of inscriptions, one from the altar area outside of Lugdunum, which was the center of the cult, and one of local inscriptions. In this manner we know of some twenty-seven high priests coming from fifteen of the sixty or more Gallic tribes represented in the assembly.[17] Of these twenty-seven, eighteen are known from inscriptions in the altar area and thirteen from local inscriptions, some being listed in both places. The addition of one priest from a literary source brings the total up to twenty-eight. Of these, not more than three are from any single tribe. These numbers may, of course, be upset at any moment by new discoveries. The evidence, such as it is, indicates a wide distribution. For Narbonensis we have nothing corresponding to the set of inscriptions from the altar area, but only the evidence of local inscriptions and of two inscriptions found outside the province. From these sources we know of ten high priests, four from Nemausus, one each from five other cities, and one from an unknown city.[18] Of these ten, eight are known from local inscriptions from within the province. At first glance this may give the impression that Nemausus was in a favored position, but a comparison with the Three Gauls dispels this feeling and shows that it is only the accident of local finds which is behind this impression. Yet, after all, four for one city is only one more than the three known from several tribes in the larger organization, and for one city all three are recorded in local inscriptions. Moreover, eight known from local inscriptions is rather a higher average than the thirteen known similarly for the larger area of the Three Gauls.

The inscriptions indicate what kind of men were elected high priests. Their records commonly contain some such phrase as *omnibus honoribus apud suos functus,* which indicates that the incumbent has already filled all local or municipal offices. The examples of this are so numerous and so easily accessible that it is not necessary to cite the evidence. In fact, it is possible to work the other way. The presence of some such phrase as the one just cited is a sure sign that the person honored has risen from local offices to higher spheres. Thus, if it occurs in one of the tribes of the Three Gauls in conjunction with *sacerdos* or *sacerdotium,* even if everything else is lost, it is pretty clear that we have the record of one who has been high priest. The same is true for Narbonensis, except that there the title was *flamen,* and so also for the other provinces. For Narbonensis we learn another rather surprising fact. From the clause in the charter providing for the course to be taken if the *flamen* loses his Roman citizenship, it is clear that Roman citizenship was required. This is somewhat startling in a provincial organization which existed in part to serve as an instrument for the expression of the will of the provincials and in part to pledge their loyalty to the Empire. So far as loyalty was concerned, it might seem desirable to make the organization as inclusive as possible. On the other hand, Roman institutions were largely based on privilege, and it is possible that the high priesthood was from the outset reserved for privileged groups. If citizenship was regularly required, it would seem that already Augustus must have wished to have the provincials feel that Roman citizenship was a goal attainable by the best of them. From that point of view, the requirement of citizenship may have been a subtle way of inspiring loyalty by making even the highest local positions open only to Roman citizens and thus inducing the provincials to strive to gain this status.

This requirement may have been common in the western provinces. The case is not entirely certain for the Three Gauls. The names of the high priests are regularly of the Roman type with *praenomen, nomen,* and *cognomen.* This is true even of the first of them all, Gaius Julius Vercondaridubnus, with his strange un-Roman *cognomen.* Yet, since usually no Roman tribal name is given, it is not entirely certain that all actually were citizens, and, even if they were, this would not constitute proof that citizenship was required.

The assembly was naturally made up of members of much the same kind as the high priests, though exactly how far they had got in their career when they were first elected to serve in the assembly is not known. As to form of representation, there is evidence for the Three Gauls which points to proportion. In the amphitheater in the altar precinct near Lugdunum there are names of Gallic tribes inscribed upon the seats. The seats so marked must have been reserved for the delegates of the respective tribes. The name of one tribe occurs six times, the name of another twice. Little as this is, it is enough to indicate that some of the tribes had several delegates and that the number varied. Another indication is the record of a delegate who had been elected by his home community together with others (*CIL* XIII, 3162). When this is viewed in the light of what is known about the tradition of representation in the Hellenistic world, it should be enough to indicate that in all likelihood the western provinces also adopted the principle of representation in proportion to population. To treat the cases of Gaul, Lycia, and Thessaly as exceptions, as once was done, for instance by Guiraud (p. 65), has now become absurd. We must judge by the evidence we have instead of by the evidence we do not have. On the question of election of delegates by their home community, we have very little evidence. Since the delegate referred to just above was called a *legatus,* there has been a tendency to apply to these delegates the regulations in imperial edicts and municipal charters concerning ambassadors. It is very unlikely that this procedure is legitimate. However, on account of the prominence of the municipal councils in local affairs, it is likely that the delegates were normally chosen by the councils rather than by popular elections.

An assembly made up of delegates elected by communities on the basis of representation in proportion to size is an out-and-out Hellenistic type of assembly. But that is not the whole story. The former high priests retained life membership in the assembly. This is clearest for the assembly of Narbonensis, in which, according to its charter, one of the prerogatives of a former high priest was the *sententiae dicendae signandique ius* in the assembly. The first part of this privilege is perfectly clear. It was the right to speak in the assembly and submit proposals. *Signandi ius* is more troublesome, but, without going into details, it can be said that indirect evidence makes it reasonably certain that the phrase meant the former high priest's right, when absent, to send in a written proposal or statement.[19] In any case, it is clear that he acted as an individual and that the procedure followed at the meetings was modeled on that of the Roman senate. This, in turn, indicates that also the elected members voted as individuals and that the delegations from cities did not vote as units. There is not equally direct evidence for the inclusion of former high priests in other assemblies, but it is the impression that this was normal and that former high priests, *sacerdotales* or *flaminales* as the case might be, formed a class apart.[20] Thus a western provincial assembly, with a group of former high priests superimposed upon the elected delegates, became a hybrid organization, partly a Hellenistic representative assembly and partly a council of dignitaries of the Roman type. In large organizations, as in that of the Three Gauls, the elected delegates must have far outnumbered the life members. Whether the prestige of the latter caused them to exert great influence on the activity of the assembly cannot be stated, for lack of evidence. We have a report of a meeting of the assembly of the Three Gauls early in the third century at which a member, a Viducassian named Titus Sennius Sollemnis, exerted great influence, but he was one of the elected delegates.[21] As will be seen later, so far as provincial assemblies are concerned, the change from Principate to Late Empire took the form of a complete swing to the Roman type of a council of dignitaries.

It has already been suggested that the procedure at the meetings was modeled on that of the Roman senate. A century ago there was a lively controversy over the question of procedure; traces of this are still to be found in the literature on the assemblies, but it is best forgotten. It was argued both that delegates received mandatory instructions from their home communities, and that they possessed the *liberum veto,* so that a single member could veto a proposal. The arguments were based on the story of the action of Sollemnis just mentioned. A former governor of Lugdunensis wrote in a letter that his predecessor was being attacked in the assembly at the instigation of individuals who wished to have an accusation lodged against him as though it represented the unanimous opinion of the province. Sollemnis opposed the attempt and stated that he had been given no instructions on lodging an accusation. On the contrary, praise had been expressed. As the result of his intervention, proceedings against the former governor were dropped. The instructions mentioned by Sollemnis were cited as proof for mandatory instructions, and the effectiveness of his intervention as proof for the *liberum veto.* The incident can, however, best be taken as showing a procedure under which delegates could change their minds and debate could therefore be effective. Certain individuals wished to initiate proceedings but desisted after Sollemnis objected. It is likely that an accusation to be effective needed to be backed by a unanimous vote, and that the objection of Sollemnis was therefore extremely important. If that was the situation, it was possible for a member to disagree with a decision but to allow his disagreement to be disregarded in order that the assembly might present a unanimous vote and a united front to the outside world. But it was also possible to persist in one's objection in such a way that the dissenting vote would have to be recorded and would thus produce the effect of a minority report. The objection of Sollemnis must have been of the latter kind. If so, it was natural to appeal to the public opinion of his constituents, whether he had any formal instructions or not. At any rate, for Narbonensis mandatory instructions are excluded by the proviso in the charter for a secret vote taken under oath.

In most assemblies the unit of representation was the city. In the
Three Gauls it was the Gallic tribe. The number of these was sixty
or about sixty. The exact number is not known for certain, nor is
it clear whether only Gallic or also German and Iberian tribes were
represented. Strabo (4.192) tells us that the names of sixty tribes
were inscribed upon the altar; Tacitus (*Ann.* 3.44) gives the number of Gallic states as sixty-four in A.D. 21. It is possible that Strabo
gives a round number, Tacitus the exact number. It is also possible
that the higher number represents an increase brought about by the
subdivision of some of the larger tribes or in some other way. On
these points, one man's guess is as good as another's. An enumeration of tribes known by records of high priests and other officials
to have been members does not help, for less than half of the
required sixty or sixty-four have been placed in this way. Such an
enumeration apparently cannot even settle whether only Gallic
tribes, or others also, were represented. Scholars seem to have been
able to fill up the required number with or without non-Gallic
tribes.[22] Nor does it solve the question to insist, even if this is correct, that the assembly was an organ for Gallic nationalism within
the Empire. Even so, the Iberians might have been included in an
effort to merge them with the Gauls. On the other hand, if the
Ara Ubiorum was intended as the center for German nationalism,
it is unlikely that German tribes were included with the Gauls
before the conquest of Germany had been definitely abandoned. In
fact, an addition of German tribes might account for an increase
from sixty to sixty-four members, if there was such an increase.

The nature of the constituencies represented in the assembly is
proof enough that some consideration was given to local institutions, and it is likely that this was not the only point on which
thought was given to Gallic institutions. Some scholars, to be sure,
have formulated excessive claims for the Gallic nature of everything. Thus, in Ireland, festivals were celebrated on August 1 in
honor of the god Lug. It was claimed that the name of this god is to
be found in the name Lugdunum, that he was the Gallic god
identified with Mercury, and that Augustus in Gaul was identified
with Mercury. Thus the festival celebrated annually at the altar

area near Lugdunum on August 1 was nothing but a continuation of a native festival in honor of Lug.[23] There is probably not a point involved in this theory which has not been attacked, and there were reasons enough to choose August 1 as the date for a festival to Augustus without regard for Gallic usages. Yet the likelihood that the name of Lugdunum is derived from that of a god Lug,[24] and the possibility that there was a festival in his honor on August 1, remain. The theory appeals to me on general grounds much more than it did when I first came upon it, but I shall leave the question to the specialists. The emperor who made such efforts to be regarded as a Hellene in Greece might well attempt corresponding concessions to local nationalism in Gaul.

It is also likely that the union of the Three Gauls was built on traditions of a national union and aspirations. Farther, judging by what we know about pre-Roman conditions, the Gallic influence did not go, at least not to the extent of modifying what was created. There was both a political and a religious tradition of unity. On the political side, it is clear that the Gauls of Caesar's times were acquainted with the use of assemblies to deal with inter-tribal affairs.[25] The meetings reported might be meetings of all Gaul or of a part. For 58 B.C. there is a report of a *concilium totius Galliae,* a meeting of an assembly representing all Gaul, held before Caesar's campaign against Ariovistus (Caesar *B.G.* 1.30); for 57, of a meeting of the Belgic Gauls (*B.G.* 2.4). Both give the impression that there was a recognized way for calling meetings at irregular intervals to deal with questions of mutual concern. Apparently only chiefs and nobles took part, and the proceedings were supposed to be confidential. Meetings of this sort were further utilized in connection with the revolt of Vercingetorix. Caesar himself seems to have built on this tradition, and, when interrupted by the revolt of Vercingetorix, to have developed a regular system of autumn and spring meetings.[26] Thus in organizing an assembly for the Gauls Augustus could build upon both Gallic practices and the policy of Caesar.

The other influence which may have made for Gallic unity was Druidism. Without making too clear the relations of this to political institutions, Caesar (*B.G.* 6.13) reports that the Druids held annual meetings in the territory of the Carnutes, that is, near modern Chartres. At the head of the organization was a sort of pope who served for life. Apparently others than Druids attended, for the people came from far and near to have their quarrels settled, and the controversies in question are said to have been of a public as well as of a private nature. The organization, however, cannot have constituted a federal state any more than the system of meetings discussed above. Yet, though Druidism may have contributed its bit to the movement toward Gallic unity, it may be more important to notice that the Druidic high priest did not serve as a model for the high priest who presided over the festival in honor of Roma and Augustus celebrated by the Three Gauls and who served as chairman of their assembly. The high priest of the Druids served for life, the *sacerdos* of the Three Gauls for a year.

This brief survey of Gallic elements leads to the conclusion that they may have been decisive both in determining the nature of the units represented in the assembly and in producing a single large organization for the Three Gauls. They may also have influenced the choice of date for the annual festival. Yet in spite of this the assembly as such does not seem to have differed in the slightest from what it would have been if there had been no Gallic tradition. It was a combination of an assembly of delegates in the Greek manner and an assembly of dignitaries sitting for life in the Roman manner. Thus if anything was typically Graeco-Roman it was this particular assembly. This makes one inclined to believe that in other provinces also the assemblies remained or became Graeco-Roman. Undoubtedly, consideration was given to local conditions in other provinces, but this is not likely to have modified the general picture.

Other activities of the assembly cannot be discussed. For the Three Gauls we have evidence of the existence of a group of officials connected with the treasury,[27] but they are not easy to interpret and add little to our knowledge of the finances of the organization. A reference to money in the charter of Narbonensis also points to the existence of a treasury. In the prosecution of governors the western provinces do not seem to have been as active as the eastern.

More important, however, is their role in the Romanization of the West and indirectly in the formation of the modern Romance nations. As Professor Adcock has remarked, Rome offered the Gauls "a sense of national unity within the Empire" (*CAH* X, 585).

To conclude, the provincial assemblies of the western provinces did little governing, but contributed to the development of the parts of the Empire in which they existed. It has been maintained above that the encouragement of nationalism within the Empire, as in Greece and Macedonia, did not tend to disrupt it. The same can be said for the western assemblies. On the other hand, though they stimulated loyalty to Rome and all took Rome for granted, they do not seem to have produced an effective pan-Roman public opinion. This, however, is probably not to be held against the assemblies as such. Undoubtedly there was a tendency to look to the central government as a protector and a dispenser of favors and punishment rather than as a common responsibility, but it is difficult to assess the blame for this situation. Other things aside, it must have been impossible, because of the ancient lack of means of rapid communication, to have created an effective public opinion over an area as large as the Roman Empire. Augustus and his successors seem to have tried it, but to have tried to do so piecemeal, as it were, and one of the instruments was the provincial assemblies.

VIII

The Transformed Assemblies
of the Late Roman Empire —
Conclusion

THE STORIES of the assemblies of the Principate and
of the Late Empire are the same in several respects. The assemblies
under the Principate were interesting primarily for the study of the
evolution of institutions. Except for those Hellenistic federal states
which continued as instruments for local government, they had
little governing to do. They were encouraged to function particularly as an aid to the central government in supervising local administration, but they had little real administering of their own to
perform. Nevertheless, they did supply all parts of the Empire with
potential instruments for representative government. For the Empire as a whole there was no such instrument. The assemblies of
the Late Empire, which can be traced back as far as to Constantine
the Great, are also interesting largely for the evolution of institutions and therewith as symbols of the transformation of society.
They too had little governing to do, though they were assigned
a more important role than many students of the period realize.
Like those of the earlier period, they supplied all parts of the Empire with potential instruments for government through assemblies, though it is a question whether the resulting government
could have been called representative government. They likewise
failed to supply such an instrument for the Empire as a whole. In
fact, except for an occasional diocesan assembly, an assembly acting for a group of provinces, the assemblies represented the smaller
provinces of the Late Empire and so did less to create unity in the
Empire than the assemblies of the earlier period.

The assemblies of the later period were so different from those
of the earlier that it is difficult to recognize any continuity. Whether

they were assemblies of provinces or of dioceses, they now consisted exclusively of dignitaries. The old provinces had been so subdivided that when assemblies appeared in the new, smaller, provinces, it is difficult to look upon any single one as the continuation of a particular assembly of the earlier period. Even the sources of our knowledge are different. Aside from a few references in the literary sources, most information for the earlier period is derived from inscriptions. For the Late Empire the information comes largely from edicts of the emperors. Most of these are found in the Theodosian Code.[1] This may give the impression that the assemblies of the earlier period disappeared in the confusion of the third century and that the later assemblies are due to a completely new start and independent initiative. This may be true literally, but there still are factors which indicate a continuity of development.

There would be little object in mustering evidence to show how late the commonalities and assemblies of the earlier period survived or to show how early there is evidence for the assemblies of the Late Empire. Whatever we do, a gap remains. A decree by its *synedrion* in honor of the Emperor Carinus (*SIG*[3], 896) shows that the Magnesian Confederacy was still in existence in A.D. 283, while the existence of a number of others is attested beyond the middle of the century.[2] For the later assemblies, however, we do not seem to have any record earlier than A.D. 315. This, however, is a relatively early date, for the first entry in the Theodosian Code dates from 313.[3] Since the early entries do not imply that the assemblies were new at the time, it is impossible to say when they originated. Is their organization or revival to be credited to Constantine, or were they in existence already under Diocletian? At present it is impossible to say.

The evidence for continuity is to be found particularly in the nature of some of the communications by emperors to eastern *koina*. The assemblies of the Late Empire not only continued the practice of bringing charges against governors, but also served as organs for the publication of laws. Naturally these were largely edicts of the kind that governors could not be trusted to publish since the edicts concerned them too intimately. This practice is so contrary to what one normally expects in an empire governed by an absolute monarch through a bureaucracy that it is likely to be received with some suspicion. It will be discussed more fully below. Meanwhile it may be noted that the practice of making important rulings on points of law in communications to confederacies and commonalities began as early as in the late second century. There were not yet, so far as is known, edicts addressed *ad provinciales* and sent to all assemblies of the Empire as in the later period, but there were a few communications, addressed to individual organizations, which dealt with points so important that the rulings became known and became a part of the recognized law of the Empire. Two jurists quote from a rescript addressed to the *koinon* of the Thessalians the ruling that in case of a trial involving questions both of the use of force and of property, the verdict on the question of the use of force was to be given first. Callistratus (*Dig.* 5.1.37) attributed it to Hadrian; Marcianus (*Dig.* 48.6.5.1) quoted it in a slightly fuller form as from Antoninus Pius.⁴ The rescript had been written in Greek but is quoted by both in a Latin translation. Ulpian (*Dig.* 49.1.1.1) quoted a rescript of Antoninus Pius to the *koinon* of the Thracians to the effect that even after the emperor has ruled on a subject an appeal is permitted if the statement originally sent in was false. This is given in the original Greek. Both of these rescripts contain rulings on general points of legal procedure and might just as well have been sent to a governor as to a commonality, but the fact that the second was sent to such a body gives us grounds for some interesting conclusions. Ulpian cites the rescript in connection with remarks about the fallibility of magistrates. Since a rescript is a ruling on a particular appeal or query, this must mean that an appeal had been sent in from the authorities of the Thracian Commonality charging the governor with misrepresentation. The emperor obviously had made a ruling against the governor in a rescript addressed to the Commonality. Even more striking is a rescript of Severus Alexander addressed to the *koinon* of the Hellenes in Bithynia quoted by Paulus in the original Greek (*Dig.* 49.1.25). In this the emperor forbade governors and procurators to use compulsion and soldiers in order to prevent appeals. Such documents show what was going on. Nevertheless, the cure attempted is also important. Instead of merely being allowed to bring charges against governors after their term of office was over, commonalities were now permitted to appeal against their decisions while the governors were still in office, and communications from the emperor on the subject of the conduct of governors were sent directly to the commonalities. This must mean that the commonalities had some kind of executives, at least a secretary, who functioned between meetings of the assembly. The activity implied in these documents foreshadowed the role assigned to the assemblies in the Late Empire.

Turning to the Late Empire, the nature of the evidence suggests that, after the reconstituting of the Empire, they probably were organized by an edict laying down rules for the assemblies of the Empire as a whole. These were so different from those of the Early Empire that, in spite of the continuity of development, direct survival seems impossible. In the second place, the areas represented by them were decidedly different from those of the earlier period. It looks as if, when provinces were subdivided, assemblies were organized for each of the new provinces. In Africa there is evidence for Tripolitana, Byzacena, Proconsularis, Numidia, and Mauretania Sitifensis. Among the Gallic provinces for which we have evidence are two, Lugdunensis III and IV, which were not formed before late in the fourth century.[5] There is specific evidence for the assemblies of only a few of the many provinces, but their presence in such provinces as some of those cited above suggests that they were universal throughout the Empire and that as soon as a province was formed an assembly was organized or was supposed to be organized. The same is implied by the practice of issuing edicts addressed to the provincials (*ad provinciales*), which undoubtedly were published through the provincial assemblies. There were also assemblies for certain of the dioceses. The one such organization concerning which we have much information is that of Viennensis, known from an edict of Honorius of A.D. 418.[6] Since the history of the provincial assemblies seems to imply first an order or a grant of permission to organize, later encouragement, and finally compulsion, it is possible that some provinces omitted setting up assemblies until compulsion was applied, and even then some omissions are possible. It is an old story that the enforcement of general laws applicable to the entire Empire was not always the same in all its parts.

The change from less positive measures to compulsion needs a little further consideration. It is difficult to see how edicts addressed *ad universos provinciales* were published unless they were transmitted to the provincial assemblies. They cannot well have been addressed to the governors. Therefore an edict addressed in this manner can normally be considered proof of the existence of assemblies. Still, there must have been a first time. If provisions for the establishment of assemblies in all provinces were contained in an edict, it would be natural that it too should be addressed *ad universos provinciales.* Thus some officials must have been entrusted with the task of calling the first meetings and getting the machinery under way. It is barely possible that this task was entrusted to the governors, though the latter were not likely to welcome the new measures. Therefore, it is more likely that it was assigned to the pretorian prefects and the *comites provinciarum,* who already in Constantine's edict of 331 *ad universos provinciales* appear as agents to receive communications from the provincials and transmit them to the emperor. Mommsen, in fact, held that the general ordinance was a part of this particular edict.[7] In this connection it may be well to recall that the Theodosian Code does not quote edicts in their entirety, but only excerpts under various headings. The fact that no excerpt on this particular subject has been preserved does not prove that the edict did not deal with it. More important is a quotation from an edict of 325 addressed *ad universos provinciales (Cod. Th.* 9.1.4). Thus a general ordinance must have been issued at least as early as this. Since some assemblies may have been revived before it was issued, it is less certain that it must be placed before 315, the year of an edict *ad Afros (Cod. Th.* 8.4.2). Since the assemblies of the Late Empire did not contain elected delegates of the old style, it would be relatively easy to formulate in a single edict rules to be applied in all provinces by simply stating what groups of dignitaries had a right to attend the meetings. These rules could then be applied to new provinces as well as to the old. Thus there would be no difficulty in getting new assemblies under way when provinces were subdivided. In the light of later measures it is likely that the first general ordinance called for assemblies in all provinces but did not impose penalties for nonattendance.

It is obvious that the assemblies did not function equally well in all parts of the Empire. Among those which proved particularly active were the African assemblies; in fact they proved so active that some officials apparently tried to restrain them. Therefore, in 355 Constantius and Constans issued an edict addressed to the pretorian prefect, Taurus, to the effect that in all the African provinces the assemblies were to have the unimpeded right to formulate all their decrees on the basis of an agreement reached concerning their own feeling, to consult about what they considered their own advantage, to formulate statements about their conclusions in decrees, and to transmit these through ambassadors. No one must interfere with either the meetings or the consultation.[8] The language of the document and the fact that it is addressed to the pretorian prefect show that this is not an edict which grants new rights to the provinces, but one which seeks to check interference by officials. The double emphasis on the right of the assemblies to express themselves freely in decrees indicates that pressure had been brought to bear on them to modify their statements. There is an implication of interference from governors also in an edict of Gratian (382) addressed *ad provinciales,* in its prohibition against interference by governors with diocesan or provincial meetings. The holding of a meeting does not require authorization from a governor, vicar, or pretorian prefect. The edict further provides for placing the public post at the disposal of ambassadors from diocesan assemblies or ambassadors sent by provincial assemblies separately (*Cod. Th.* 12.12.9). The implication seems to be that all provinces have assemblies and that these are free to do as they wish about acting separately or combining and acting through a diocesan assembly.[9] The admonition not to send unnecessary appeals implies that some provinces overdid this activity. That, however, appears to have been the exception.

The examples mentioned show that assemblies might be hampered by meddlesome bureaucrats. Probably a greater handicap was the inertia and lack of interest of the members of the assemblies. This at least is implied by the provisions for compulsory attendance contained in an edict of Theodosius I and his sons, of 392. In this the emperors state that they wish all *primates*—let us for the moment say, men of high rank—except *praefectorii* to gather at the provincial assemblies. The *praefectorii,* former pretorian prefects, are to be consulted at their homes.[10] It is this edict which usually is considered as indicating compulsion, and undoubtedly an expression of imperial will was meant to have the effect of compulsion. That it was meant to do so, and that it was taken by others in this sense, is implied by an edict issued later the same year giving all *honorati* or former imperial office holders the choice between attending or being represented by proxies (*Cod. Th.* 12.12.13). It is noticeable, however, that no penalties are indicated for nonattendance. This naturally raises the question of how strictly attendance was enforced.

The last two documents cited also contain information about the membership. The second insists that meetings are to be public. This seems to indicate some sort of check upon the membership by public opinion, but undoubtedly real membership was limited to those who were ordered to attend. In the first of the two edicts these are defined as *cuncti ... qui primatum honorantur insignibus* (*Cod. Th.* 12.12.12.1). Hence all the men of the province who rank as *primates* are required to attend. The reference to *insignia* implies that they have been officially designated in some way, but the term *primates* does not give too much help in determining the basis of classification, for the word (cf. Berger) apparently could be used about the leading men in various organizations or groups. The first of our two edicts, by granting a special position to former pretorian prefects, shows that they were included. The second, by granting privileges to all *honorati,* implies that they were only a part of those required to attend. Who were the other *primates?*

In view of the connection of cities with provincial assemblies, they can hardly have been anything but the leading men of the cities. Another document actually refers to the *primates* of cities, villages, and forts.[11] These are to be notified that all provincials are authorized to help seize deserters. Such an edict naturally was to be given the widest publicity possible. The villages and forts must have been smaller civil and military settlements with some sort of corporate organization, but it is likely that only the cities as such were represented in the provincial assembly. Ammianus Marcellinus (14.7.1) too uses *urbium primates* as a designation for a class ranking between *honorati* and *plebei*. Consequently it is likely that the *primates*, the leading men of the province, who were to attend the assembly included the *honorati*, former imperial office holders living in the province, and the *primates* or leading men of the cities within the province. The latter undoubtedly were the leading members of the *curia* or *ordo*, the city council, the members of which by this time formed a hereditary petty aristocracy. How many members of each council were included it is difficult to say.

To turn to the members from the cities, the conclusion that they constituted one part of the membership of the provincial assembly is confirmed by the edict of Honorius of A.D. 418 concerning the diocesan assembly of Viennensis (see n. 6). Attendance at this assembly was made compulsory. Each governor who failed to appear on time was to pay a fine of five pounds of gold, and each of the *honorati* and *curiales*, three pounds. Thus, aside from the governors, who would hardly figure in the provincial assemblies, the members were *honorati* and *curiales*, the latter being members of the councils of the cities within the diocese. It seems safe to transfer the latter name also to provincial assemblies and to say that their members consisted of *honorati* and *curiales*. Since the average city council contained a hundred members, it is clear, however, that not all these members were expected to attend. To return to the term *primates*, it is clear that only the leading members of each *curia* were required to attend. How large the group was cannot be said for certain. In an earlier study I argued somewhat hesitatingly for five from each *curia*,[12] and it is doubtful that further study would add anything of value. Representation in proportion to population seems to have been definitely abandoned. There is also evidence for *sacerdotales,* former high priests, during the Late Empire.[13] Undoubtedly, all former high priests had a right to participate in the meetings, but it is noticeable that they have not been mentioned in any of the documents concerned with attendance at the meetings. The reason probably is that there were no former high priests who were not members either as *curiales* or as *honorati.* Thus they did not form a group apart. By this time the entire assembly consisted of willing and unwilling dignitaries who were members in virtue of the position they had attained. The high priests, therefore, retain interest mostly for the problem of the reconciliation of Christian and pagan elements. As late as A.D. 413 *sacerdotales* used to flock to Carthage for festivals. This represents a problem which cannot be considered here. If the connection of Constantine the Great and Theodosius the Great with organizations headed by high priests of the relics of imperial cults seems strange, it may be well to recall that the apostle Paul had friends among the Asiarchs at Ephesus and that Constantine himself was deified after his death.[14] The existence of *sacerdotes* and *sacerdotales,* however, is itself another proof that the assemblies were regarded as a continuation of those of the Principate.

One term applied to members of the assemblies throws further light on their social and economic position. In the edict of Honorius concerning the assembly of the diocese of Viennensis the members are once referred to as *honorati, possessores,* and *iudices* in such a way that *possessores* clearly refers to *curiales.* With this can be compared an edict of 409 addressed to the *honorati et possessores per Africam (Cod. Th.* 11.28.5). Here the two terms must refer to the two groups in the provincial assembly. Thus, with reference to their economic interests, the *curiales* are described as *possessores* or landholders. This must not be taken to mean that the *honorati* were not landholders. If there is anything we know about the society of the Late Empire, it is that the senatorial class, the clarissimate, to which the *honorati* belonged, consisted of a landed nobility. Thus the membership consisted of the greater and some of the lesser landlords of the province. This means that there was no representation of urban or commercial interests in opposition to rural or agrarian ones. The only economic conflict that there could be within the membership was between the big and the little. The *honorati* probably were largely engaged in the creation of large estates; some of the *curiales* were busy trying to prevent their own land from being absorbed into these estates. If we start with the *honorati* as former office holders, we come to a similar conclusion. Also those *curiales* who actually served in the assembly were former office holders even if, commonly, only of the municipalities. They simply had not attained to offices as high as those formerly held by the *honorati*. The governors on whose work they were asked to report were themselves members of the land-holding aristocracy.

It can be taken for granted that the type of assembly consisting exclusively of an aggregation of dignitaries goes back as far as to the first general ordinance on the subject of provincial assemblies and probably farther. Nor did the change come suddenly. If the evolution of the institutions of cities, leagues, eastern commonalities and western provincial assemblies is considered as a whole, the transformation began when the first changes were introduced under Roman influence in the governments of the cities of Sicily, and it continued when Roman influences and even enactments introduced similar changes in the cities of Asia and Bithynia. The manner in which the Romans seemed to take over what they found, but still succeeded in transforming it, is one of the most interesting and difficult problems in history. It is likely that the influences which caused the governments of Hellenistic cities to approach closer and closer to the Roman or Western type also affected the confederacies. Thus in Lycia, in the second century after Christ, members of the councils of cities served for life, and it has been conjectured that the federal *bouleutai* also held office for life and that the former high priests were included among them. The evidence on the last point consists of the fact that, while an earlier document refers to a distribution of a largess to *bouleutai*, electors, and former federal magistrates, later provisions for largesses omit the former magistrates. In the second century such an omission would be surprising, and so the conclusion must be that the former magistrates are included in one of the other groups. If so, the group must be the councilors rather than the electors, who clearly were the elected representatives of the cities.[15] In that manner, with life membership in the *boule* and a group of elected delegates in the *ekklesia,* the government of the Lycian Confederacy was approaching the type of the western provincial assemblies. This is a development we should expect, and it is likely that Lycia was not unique in that respect. In the western provinces themselves, though for the Three Gauls we have evidence that delegates continued active far into the third century, we can imagine rather than trace an increase in the influence of the life members. The one detail that is obvious is that when the assemblies were first founded, it must have taken some time to accumulate a sizable group of former high priests. When that had been done, it is easy to imagine that they exerted considerable influence on issues in which they took an interest. In any case, the change from the old to the new type cannot have been sudden. It merely exemplified the general tendency to develop a society based on the principle of privilege.

Now as for the functions of the assemblies, it will be remembered that evidence has already been presented which shows that the assemblies were encouraged to express themselves freely and to communicate their views by means of embassies. The importance of these embassies is seen further in the fact that the public post was put at their disposal. The encouragement of the provincial assemblies is clearly coupled with a suspicion of governors, many of whom were considered corrupt. To give some citations from edicts *ad universos provinciales,* that of 325 encourages the lodging of information with the emperor concerning corrupt officials of many kinds (*Cod. Th.* 9.1.4). One of the excerpts from that of 331 begins: *Cessent iam nunc rapaces officialium manus, cessent, inquam,* "Lay off straightway ye rapacious hands of bureaucrats, lay off, I say" (*Cod. Th.* 1.16.7). The document goes on to encourage communications about abuses through the *comites provinciarum* or the pretorian prefect. Another excerpt makes similar suggestions concerning governors who do not administer justice honestly (*Cod. Th.* 1.16.6). Others deal with the right of appeal (*Cod. Th.* 11.30.16–17). These communications are directed to provincial assemblies but seem to encourage complaints from almost any source. The one which probably goes farthest of all is the edict of 403 which seems to give to anyone who wishes it the authority to seize deserters (*Cod. Th.* 7.18.13), though this was addressed not *ad provinciales* but to a pretorian prefect with instructions that it be made known to all provincials and brought to the attention of the leading men (*primates*) not only of the cities but also of villages and forts. This may be the key to the seeming liberal authorization of this document and others. Only the leading men of the communities, such men as those who met in the provincial assemblies and some of the other *decuriones* or members of the city councils, would have sufficient resources and a sufficient number of dependents under their control to be able to lay hands on deserters. It was only to such men, in all likelihood—certainly not to the *coloni,* virtual serfs on the large estates,—that the communications *ad provinciales* were addressed. Such men it was who were invited, urged, and later commanded to gather in assemblies, to watch the work of administrators, and to take action against the corrupt. In so doing, of course, they judged members of their own class. They may at times have been thoroughly devoted to justice and efficiency, but they must have viewed all problems exclusively from the point of view of the upper classes. Even so, the interest of the emperors in the assemblies is evidence of a genuine effort to improve administration. A part of this effort seems to have been the creation of a channel for communicating with the central government through *comites provinciarum* and pretorian prefects (*Cod. Th.* 1.16.6–7; cf. 7.18.13) and thus to bypass the governors.

This is not too cheerful a note on which to conclude a discussion of representative government. It is possible to argue that the assemblies of the Late Empire were in a sense representative assemblies. As society was constituted at the time, it was natural that such groups as the municipal aristocracies should desire to retain their outstanding members permanently as their representatives. It was also natural that all former officials of any importance should be asked for their advice. Yet the assemblies represented only an aristocracy, and, what was worse, an aristocracy of landowners more interested in securing and increasing their own wealth and power than in the welfare of the Empire. Both the *curiales* and the *honorati* were groups of landowners, but though the *curiales* undoubtedly outnumbered the *honorati,* it is likely that the wealthy members of the clarissimate dominated the assemblies. That would accord with the habit of deferring to wealth and position. Hence, when the emperors, in an effort to check corruption, encouraged the assemblies, they may unwittingly have helped to strengthen an element which was fully as disruptive as corrupt administration. The developments of the period were definitely the end of any hope that salvation might come to the ancient world through representative government.

◇   ◇   ◇

How had things come to such a pass? If any single explanation is to be suggested, it will have to be that from the time of Alexander the Great to Theodosius the Great and beyond, the world relied too exclusively on strong men for salvation. It may be true that such men as Alexander and Augustus did more to reform administration in antiquity than all democratic and republican activities combined. It may be true also that the combination of the ideas of the brotherhood of man and world monarchy is the nearest the ancient world came to giving practical application to those ideals which are represented in modern times by the League of Nations and the United Nations. Even so, reforms imposed from above do not produce self-government and may not even produce an effective public opinion. Moreover, the brotherhood of man under the direction of an absolute monarch is almost a contradiction in terms. To call the monarch a god and to deify him hardly improves matters. Whether the deification is sincere or not, it is likely to produce subservience.

In antiquity, genuine representative government was developed only in states so small that, compared in expanse to the ancient empires, they might almost as well have been city-states. It looks as if the first experiments with representative government were in cities. Then came the early Boeotian Confederacy and probably other contemporary confederacies. At this point the development of representative government was arrested at least in part through the victory of the democratic theory demanding the supremacy of the primary assembly. Of course, the dissolution of the Boeotian Confederacy in 386 B.C. was due to the King's Peace and Spartan policy, but, when it once had been dissolved, it was over a century and a half before representative government was introduced again in the Achaean Confederacy. Meanwhile the closest approach to representative government on a large scale was developed in the *symmachies* and particularly in the Hellenic League of Philip of Macedonia and his successors. This, in fact, looked as though it might have a chance to develop into a constitutional federal monarchy with representative government. Had this occurred, it would have meant representative government for most of Greece at least. Instead, the Hellenic League was overshadowed by Alexander's empire and, after various vicissitudes in the period of confusion following his death, finally disappeared.

Alexander's career, nevertheless, was not fatal to the causes of republicanism and federal government. In fact, the greatest development of representative government came later. He himself neither discontinued the Hellenic League nor broke up the federal states that existed at the time. In the period of weakened monarchies and conflicts between kings, it looks as if Greece actually would have had an opportunity to develop a strong power of her own if there had been a leader able to unite the country. Instead, local jealousies prevented any union or effective alliance of the more important states. The largest state to develop representative government was the Achaean Confederacy. If the date of 217 tentatively suggested above is correct, it must have been Aratus who brought about the development. In spite of all his faults, he is probably still to be rated as the greatest Achaean statesman, but he was utterly unsuccessful in building up a united leadership for Greece. He could neither defeat the Aetolians or Sparta nor cooperate with either. Again the most hopeful movement for unity was a revived Hellenic League, this time under the leadership of Antigonus Doson. The hopeful start came to little or nothing because of Doson's early death and the intervention of the Romans.

This intervention did not itself put an end to the development of representative government, which actually had its greatest expansion in the second century, in part under direct Roman patronage. Yet, even in the period beginning with the Second Macedonian War when Greece was in theory free, the federal states with representative governments were forced to limit their activities to local affairs, and the Roman authorities often gave directives about even local problems. Before Rome intervened, the more active Greek states, except Aetolia, were combined in the Hellenic League. Even if this cannot be said to have been a federal state, it did have a representative assembly for the discussion of interstate problems. After the Roman intervention, Greece was given no organization to replace this, though Rome did organize or supervise the organization of federal states. But she did not make any Greek state strong enough to act as her agent. Instead there was a flood of ambassadors and messages from the senate. The fact that the Romans meanwhile had permitted the formation of the Sicilian Commonality gives added significance to this state of affairs. It looks as if the group of senators responsible for the policy toward Greece deliberately, as it were, substituted the leadership of the Roman senate for the Hellenic League. Directives on larger problems were to come from the senate, while the Greek states were to be permitted to decide minor matters for themselves.

The contributions of Rome to the ultimate failure of representative government are difficult to assess. Rome seems to have flourished on anomalies. She allowed her allies less freedom than Athens and Sparta had done, but was infinitely more successful in winning their allegiance and in uniting Italy than any Greek state had been in uniting Greece. Yet this was accomplished without the aid of representative institutions. Her allies possessed no organ comparable to the assemblies of the Peloponnesian and Delian leagues. In the first century before Christ there was talk of representative gov-

ernment, but the only real experiment with it at the time was that
of Rome's revolting allies (90-88 B.C.). Rome's own remedy for their
discontent was not the establishment of representative government,
but the absorption of her former allies into the Roman citizen
body. Thereby the territory of the city of Rome became coextensive
with the peninsula of Italy, and there were also many citizens outside Italy. Yet Rome continued to be governed as a city-state with
primary assemblies meeting in Rome. The choice of this solution
and the rejection of representative government was in all likelihood
deliberate. The Italians were given the civil rights of Roman citizens, but since they had to go to Rome to vote they had little
influence on the government. In this manner the older Roman
citizens retained their control of the state, but at the same time
they ruined this state. By this time the city of Rome had become
so large that the honest use of the primary assemblies would put
them in the hands of the city mob. The need of devising means for
avoiding this undoubtedly contributed to the downfall of the
republic. Representative government might not have brought the
millennium, but at least it would have helped. As it turned out,
the remedy applied led to the development of monarchy. Augustus
personally may well have been willing to employ representative
institutions as an instrument. In addition to his general pretense of
the restoration of the republic, some experiments with elections can
be cited as evidence.[16] As it turned out, it was too late for such
measures. Instead, the emperor and his underlings soon took over
much of the administration of Rome and Italy.

In the provinces too, Augustus adopted a liberal and tolerant
policy, particularly in Greece and in Gaul. A part of this policy was
the permission and encouragement given to confederacies and commonalities. Yet such a policy could not well lead to any real blos-
soming of representative government on a large scale. After all,
the main role assigned to many of the organizations was that of
aiding the emperor in keeping his subordinates in order. Except
for the Three Gauls, there was no experiment with representative
assemblies for large territories, unless the Amphictionic League and
the Panhellenion of Hadrian can be brought in here. These ten-

dencies became even more pronounced in the Late Empire. The assemblies were given more encouragement than before to act against corrupt officials, but with the subdivision of provinces the area represented by the average provincial assembly became smaller. Even the assemblies of the dioceses, where they existed, did not represent an area as large as that of the Three Gauls. Finally, the tendency to have the assemblies stand only for the upper classes was accentuated.

The unsatisfactory character of the provincial assemblies of the Late Empire and their ultimate disappearance were the last stages of the failure of representative government in antiquity. This, in turn, was an important phase in the failure of free institutions and self-government. One cause can be said to be too much monarchy; but we are faced with a dilemma. Did free institutions fail because there was too much monarchy, or was there too much monarchy because free institutions had failed? To a considerable extent Roman history favors the latter solution. Yet one can easily argue that, in the light of the general tendency in ancient times toward monarchy, the little experiment with self-government in Greek and Roman history should be regarded almost as a miracle. Finally it is legitimate to ask, if representative government had been given a better trial, could it possibly have worked over an empire as large as that of Rome? In view of the lack of means of communication, could an adequate public opinion have been developed? Would it have been possible for representatives of Egypt, Syria, Asia Minor, the Balkans, Italy, Africa, Spain, Gaul, and Britain to discuss the policies of the Empire intelligently with each other? A solution might conceivably have been found in regional assemblies which in turn could have sent representatives to a central council. If there had been more organizations like that of the Three Gauls, with a central body over them, something might have been accomplished—but there is little object in speculating about what might have been.

One last word. It is easy to note failures. Yet, until we have done better ourselves, it is well to be charitable.

Appendix

The Meetings of the Assemblies
of the Achaean Confederacy

BELOW is given a survey of the meetings of the Achaean Confederacy from the refounding in 280 B.C. to the fall of Corinth in 146 B.C. Some of those listed have very little interest but are included for the sake of completeness. Even so, some have undoubtedly been overlooked. All those discussed in the text above will be taken up again even though usually a brief note will suffice. For others additional material will be given. The first year for which we have a report is 229 B.C. For the earlier period we can at best infer actions by assemblies. For convenience, *synkletos* will be used as a name for extraordinary meetings, *synodos* for regular meetings. The two words rarely occur in the accounts of meetings, though *synodos* is somewhat more frequent than *synkletos*. In Livy's accounts it is impossible to tell which, if either, of the two words was used by Polybius.

229.—Polybius (2.46.6) reports a meeting which above has been taken to be an extraordinary meeting of both the *ekklesia* and the *boule*. The Achaean leaders, after observing the hostile activities of Cleomenes, συναθροίσαντες τοὺς ᾿Αχαιοὺς ἔκριναν μετὰ τῆς βουλῆς ἀναλαμβάνειν φανερῶς τὴν πρὸς τοὺς Λακεδαιμονίους ἀπέχθειαν. The manner in which the meeting was called suggests an extraordinary meeting of the primary assembly. The decision to go to war or to recognize that a state of war existed is one of the kind which later were reserved for extraordinary meetings of the *ekklesia*. Therefore a meeting of a primary assembly can be taken for granted. The language, however, seems to imply that the decision was made by the leaders and the *boule* alone. But we know from other evidence that the Achaeans had both an *ekklesia* and a *boule*. Consequently it is best to take μετὰ τῆς βουλῆς as an indication that the *boule* played an important part at the meeting, probably as a probouleutic body. The reason for the form of the statement may be that the real decision was the result of a discus-

165

sion in the *boule,* and that the *ekklesia* approved this decision without much debate.

227.—There is reported a meeting at Aegium at which the Achaeans voted not to furnish supplies or mercenaries to Aratus (Plut. *Arat.* 37.5), who was general at the time. The meeting took place after the battle of Ladoceia, in which Lydiades was killed. There is no further information about it or the attendance. W. H. Porter, *Plutarch's Life of Aratus* (1937), in his commentary takes it to be the regular autumn *synodos.*

225.—Nothing need be added concerning the meetings held in connection with the negotiations with Cleomenes. The last was the one held at Sicyon at which Aratus was elected *strategos autokrator* (Plut. *Arat.* 41.1).

224.—Later, probably early in 224, the Achaeans gathered at Aegium in a meeting to which Aratus was summoned from Sicyon, then besieged by Cleomenes, to be present at the *ekklesia* which voted to turn the Acrocorinthus over to Antigonus Doson (Plut. *Arat.* 42; cf. *Cleom.* 19). Plutarch's two accounts do not agree about the order of events. The *Aratus* places the meeting after Sicyon has been besieged for three months; the *Cleomenes,* before the siege. The first account is supported by the statement of Polybius (2.52.5) that Cleomenes raised the siege after he had learned that the Achaeans had reached an agreement with Antigonus. The nature of the meeting is not too clear, but in all likelihood it was a regular *synodos.* On this supposition it is easiest to explain that the Achaeans, after they had gathered at Aegium, summoned Aratus from Sicyon as Plutarch (*Arat.* 42.1) implies. Both Plutarch's reference (*Arat.* 42.2) to the *ekklesia* and the nature of the decision taken indicate that it was a meeting of a primary assembly. Attempts have been made to reconcile Plutarch's two accounts by presupposing two meetings, one before the siege and one later, the first being a *synodos* not competent to make the decision, and the other a *synkletos* (Aldo Ferrabino, *Arato di Sicione* [1921] 266; Walbank, *Aratos,* 100 and 199), but neither of Plutarch's accounts suggests two meetings, and the interpretation of the two scholars is based on a differentiation between *synodos* and *synkletos* attested only for the second century. Tarn in his *CAH* account, in which he held that the *synodos* had two regular meetings, "one immediately after the autumn equinox, and one about April" (*CAH* VII, 737), took the meeting to be the spring meeting (p. 758).

223.—The agreement with Antigonus Doson referred to above brought him to Greece. Two *synodoi* at Aegium were attended by him. The first is probably to be placed about February, 223. Since it came at the end of a military campaign, and since Antigonus went into winter quarters after the meeting, it is natural to think of the autumn. However, since he seems to have remained in winter quarters only a short time before resuming campaigning in the spring, Aymard (268 n. 3) has suggested February as a possible date. At this *synodos* Antigonus was elected—or probably, rather, recognized—as *hegemon* of the allies (Pol. 2.54.3–4). By this term must be meant the position as permanent head of the new Hellenic League. This, therefore, must have been the meeting at which the Achaeans ratified the constitution of the Hellenic League and pledged their allegiance to it. Hence the conjecture is probably correct that delegates of the other allies had been invited to Aegium (Beloch, *Griechische Geschichte,* 2d ed., IV, 1, 712). Thus it looks as if something like a constitutional convention was held in connection with the *synodos*. In any case, the decision made by the Achaeans was an extremely important one concerning an alliance and thereby demonstrates that such decisions were not at the time reserved for extraordinary meetings. In all likelihood, the rule that they required action by the *ekklesia* was in force. Thus there is every reason for believing that this particular *synodos* was a meeting of the primary assembly.

At the end of the season's campaigning, in the autumn of 223, Antigonus again came to Aegium to attend the *synodos* of the Achaeans (Pol. 2.54.13). This seems to have been a regular meeting and is important chiefly as an additional proof that a regular *synodos* took place at this time of year.

222.—The next *synodos* reported must belong to the winter early in 222. After the autumn meeting of 223, Antigonus had sent his Macedonian troops home for the winter (Pol. 2.54.14). Cleomenes made use of the opportunity to conduct several operations and to capture Megalopolis. According to Plutarch (*Cleom.* 25.2), the Achaean *boule* was in session at Aegium at the time. When Aratus appeared on the *bema* and reported that the city had been lost, the *synodos* broke up. Possibly we should say that the meeting broke up and take this *synodos* as a meeting of the *boule* alone, but we can hardly trust Plutarch's language to be precise on such matters.

220.—The four meetings of this year have been treated fully above, pp. 79–81.

219.—In connection with the election of Aratus the younger as general, Polybius (4.37.1–2) states that at this time the Achaeans held their election near the rising of the Pleiades, that is, about May 22 (Aymard, 254). It looks as if this corresponds to the second of the *synodoi* reported for 220.

218.—The elections were preceded by a political campaign against Aratus conducted by the Macedonian, Apelles. Philip himself was present at Aegium. The result was the election of Eperatus and the defeat of Aratus' candidate (Pol. 4.82.7–8). On the basis of the narrative of Polybius, Aymard (251) has been able to place the elections at the end of February or, at the very latest, in the first part of March. The assumption of office by Eperatus is reported a little farther on, about the time of the rising of the Pleiades (Pol. 5.1.1–2). Thus, in this year there was a considerable interval between the election and the assumption of office.

Soon after Eperatus had taken office, Philip, through their magistrates, gathered the Achaeans in an *ekklesia* and the *plethos* met at Aegium κατὰ τοὺς νόμους (Pol. 5.1.6–7). Aymard (308 f.) argues correctly that νόμοι here means "tradition" rather than "law." This is supported by Livy's use of *mos* (38.30.3) about the practice of holding meetings at Aegium. Later the king persuaded the magistrates to transfer the *ekklesia* to Sicyon (Pol. 5.1.9). Clearly the entire story suggests an extraordinary meeting. That such meetings could be called at this time is implied also by the story that Apelles suggested that the king might gather the Achaeans and present a matter to them (4.85.3). The transfer of the meeting from one city to another suggests that the rigid procedure of the later *synkletos* known best from the meeting at Sicyon in 198 had not yet been adopted. After the *ekklesia* had been transferred to Sicyon, it voted money and supplies to Philip while operating in the Peloponnesus. Whether in later days this would have required an extraordinary meeting or not, it is hard to say, but at this time, to judge by the events of 220, the regular *synodoi* could handle questions of any magnitude. Obviously Philip was in a hurry for a decision, and this explains the extraordinary meeting.

217.—The first meeting reported for this year is the one at which Eperatus laid down his office and the elder Aratus was elected general (Pol. 5.30.7). As stated above, it seems to correspond to the second of the four meetings of 220. Soon after he had assumed office, Aratus assembled the Achaeans (Pol. 5.91.1 and 5) and secured measures for the military reorganization of the Confederacy. This undoubtedly was an extraordinary assembly.

A *synodos* is reported for the summer of the same year. This seems to belong early in June (Aymard, 266) and to correspond to the third meeting of 220. This obviously was a regular meeting, and the time of meeting was known to other Greeks, including the enemies of Achaea. The Aetolian, Euripidas, watched his opportunity to make a raid on Achaean territory at the time of the meeting, but suffered a defeat at the hands of the mercenaries of the Achaeans under the command of Lycus of Pharae (Pol. 5.94.1–6). By a careful analysis of this story and the following events, Aymard (88–95) has shown that in all likelihood the citizen soldiers had been dismissed or given a furlough for the *synodos,* with the result that Lycus had only mercenaries available. This seems strange, since the age qualification for voting was thirty years and many or probably most of the soldiers under arms must have been under thirty. Even so, this tendency to put aside everything else when the time for a *synodos* came around fits a primary better than a representative assembly.

A third *synodos* this year (Pol. 5.102.5) is mentioned in connection with events which came before the end of the Olympic year (Pol. 5.105.3), but there is no indication that the meeting itself came this early. In all likelihood it was the autumn meeting corresponding to the fourth and last meeting of 220 (Aymard, 267 n. 1). Thus the three *synodoi* of the year mentioned by Polybius correspond to the second, third, and fourth of those mentioned for 220 and tend to confirm the conclusion that there were four regular meetings a year. Nothing is reported concerning the actions taken at this last meeting. Indirect evidence suggests that at this time the elections were transferred from the spring to the autumn and that probably other reforms were introduced.

209.—This year,[1] at a conference between Philip and various ambassadors, it was decided to postpone action on peace to a meeting of the Achaeans (*in concilium Achaeorum*) and a place and date were set for the meeting (Livy 27.30.6). This sounds like an extraordinary meeting of the Achaeans. However, when Philip went to Aegium, he went *ad indictum multo ante sociorum concilium* (27.30.9), though both the Aetolian and other ambassadors had been invited *in concilium Achaeorum* (27.30.12). The confused account makes it difficult to determine the nature of the meeting. Probably it was, so to speak, a combination of an extraordinary meeting of an Achaean assembly and of the *synedrion* of the Hellenic League.

208.—Livy (28.7.17; 28.8.2–6) reports a *concilium* at Aegium, which probably was a *synodos*. This is the view of Aymard (41 n. 3) and Walbank (*Philip V*, 96). In any case, the meetings of 209 and 208 offer us no help in determining the date of the law restricting the meetings of the *ekklesia* to occasions on which a question of war or alliance was to be decided.

Probably in the autumn of the same year Philopoemen delivered an address before an assembly (Pol. 11.9) at what was probably the very autumn *synodos* at which he was elected general.[2] In the address he urged the Achaeans to pay less attention to their dress and more to their armor and their weapons. The listeners were so much impressed that when they left the *bouleuterion* they pointed their fingers at overdressed dandies and forced them to leave the *agora*. Aymard (95–102) has treated the meeting at length and has argued that it must have been a meeting of a primary assembly largely made up of men who themselves served as hoplites. Thus it is made to supply an additional proof that the *synodos* was a primary assembly. Certainly a hortatory address could be delivered more easily at a *synodos* than at the later type of *synkletos* at which only one subject could be taken up. Nor does the reference to the *bouleuterion* supply sure proof that the body present at the particular meeting was the *boule*. It does, however, suggest that the meeting was not too well attended. Otherwise there would not have been room for it in a council chamber. Philopoemen, no doubt, wished to reach as many as possible, but if the *boule* was the only body available he would have to deliver his address before it. The only bearing of this meeting on the present investigation is toward ascertaining the date of the law reducing the number of meetings of the *ekklesia*. If the *ekklesia* was present at a regular *synodos* in 208, the law had not yet been passed. On the other hand, if we could argue from *bouleuterion* to *boule,* the law had been passed. Unfortunately the nature of the meeting is too uncertain to warrant either conclusion.

200.—For this year we have a report of a meeting which is the earliest clear example of a *synkletos* or extraordinary meeting of the *ekklesia* of the type resulting from the law prohibiting the calling of the *ekklesia* except for certain special problems. Unfortunately we have only Livy's version (31.25) of Polybius' original report. The words attributed to the Achaean general, Cycliadas, *non licere legibus Achaeorum de aliis rebus referre, quam propter quas convocati essent* (31.25.9), are the most positive evidence we have to the effect that such meetings could act only on the subject announced in advance. At the same time these words indicate that the meeting must have been a *synkletos*. The meeting had been called to consider the war with Nabis. The occasion for the ruling of Cycliadas was that Philip V appeared and offered to take the war off the hands of the Achaeans, but in return demanded garrisons for Oreus, Chalcis, and Corinth.

198.—This was the year of the *synkletos* at Sicyon at which Roman, Pergamene, Rhodian, and Athenian ambassadors were present, and at which the Achaeans decided to break with Philip and the Hellenic League, to enter into alliance with Pergamum and Rhodes, and to go over to the side of Rome (Livy 32.19–23). This was the one and only issue presented (*concilio ad eam rem unam indicto* [Livy 32.20.4]). The occasion was the arrival of the ambassadors already mentioned, and so we find in Livy (32.19.5) an expression, *datum est iis concilium,* suggesting that the ambassadors had asked for a hearing and that the meeting accordingly was called. Such meetings, called to consider proposals submitted by ambassadors, are one of the commonest types of *synkletoi.* The account gives us the fullest description we have of the procedure during the three days of a *synkletos* and shows that the vote was taken by cities.

193.—The attack of Nabis on Gytheum, one of the Laconian maritime towns which had been placed under the protection of the Achaeans, must have occasioned action by them in a meeting, probably a *synodos.* The Achaeans sent ambassadors to Nabis to denounce his violation of his treaty with Rome, dispatched aid to Gytheum, and sent ambassadors to Rome to report (Livy 35.13.1–3). To send aid to an ally to help repel an attack was not itself an act of war. Therefore it is unlikely that a *synkletos* had to be called.

192.—This year a meeting, obviously a *synkletos,* was called at Sicyon to decide what to do about Nabis. Nabis had raided the territory of the Achaeans in retaliation for the help they had sent to Gytheum. Even so, the Achaean leaders hesitated to act until the ambassadors sent to Rome should return. When they did return, the meeting was called and ambassadors sent for advice to Flamininus, who had returned to Greece at the head of a Roman embassy. Though Flamininus sent a letter counseling the Achaeans to await the arrival of the Roman fleet, the Achaeans, on the suggestion of their general, Philopoemen, voted war. The details of time and method were left to his decision (Livy 35.25). The question considered, a decision on war, was one for which an *ekklesia* was required, and the report of the manner in which the meeting was called also indicates that it was an extraordinary meeting.

Later the same year another *synkletos* was called, this time at Aegium, to give a hearing to the ambassadors of Antiochus and the Aetolians in the presence of Flamininus (Livy 35.48.1). This is marked as an extraordinary meeting called to give a hearing to the ambassadors by the words *legatis . . . datum est concilium*. The Achaeans chose the side of Rome, voted to declare war on Antiochus and the Aetolians, and to send troops to Chalcis and Piraeus (35.50.2–3). The latter decision about the conduct of the war was supplementary to the main decision and thus not a violation of the rule that action could be taken only on the one question announced in advance.

191.—A meeting, obviously a *synkletos,* was called by the general Diophanes at the request of Flamininus (Livy 36.31.10). The assembly took up the question of the island of Zacynthus, which had just been acquired as an indirect result of the defeat of Antiochus. On the insistence of Flamininus it was voted to turn the island over to the Romans. Livy reports the decision both before and after the summary of a speech by Flamininus. The first report is to the effect that the decision was to be left to Flamininus (31.32.4); the second, that the island was to be turned over to the Romans (31.32.9). Aymard (394 f.) thinks the address was delivered after the normal business had been completed. If so, it may not throw light on the normal procedure. Flamininus, even if Achaean leaders did not always follow his advice, undoubtedly could take liberties that most people could not take.

Later in the year Flamininus and the Roman commander Acilius Glabrio attended a meeting at Aegium at which the questions of the membership of Elis in the Confederacy and of the restoration of exiles at Sparta were taken up. Both the Romans spoke in favor of the Spartan exiles (Plut. *Philop.* 17.6) and undoubtedly also on the subject of Elis. No decision was made on either question. The Achaeans are said to have wished themselves to have the credit for restoring the Spartan exiles, while the Eleans wished to negotiate directly with the Achaean Confederacy (Livy 36.35.7). Since two unrelated questions, neither involving directly a question of war or alliance, were taken up, the meeting must have been a regular *synodos.*

190.—On the arrival of an embassy from Eumenes, the Achaean "many" gathered in an *ekklesia* and voted to renew the alliance and to dispatch 1,000 foot and 100 horse under the command of Diophanes (Pol. 21.3b). The meeting was obviously a *synkletos* called to give a hearing to a foreign ambassador. The mere renewal of an alliance would not have necessitated a *synkletos,* as can be seen from the report of a *synodos* in 185. The same seems to have been true about ordinary military measures when a war was in progress. The sending of an expeditionary force to Asia might well be considered another matter. In any case, there may from time to time have been a certain looseness in the interpretation of the law.

189.—In the autumn, after Philopoemen, the general for 189/8, had assumed office,[3] there were two extraordinary meetings occasioned by the Spartan problem (Aymard, 236 f.). After Sparta had made an attack on Las, and after the coastal towns of Laconia and the Spartan exiles in them had sent a joint embassy to the Achaeans, Philopoemen called a meeting and it was voted to send an ultimatum demanding the surrender of those who were responsible for the attack (Livy 38.31.1–3). When the Spartans, instead of yielding, put to death thirty, voted to renounce membership in the Achaean Confederacy, and sent an embassy offering to surrender to the Romans (38.31.4–6)—that is, appealed for Roman support against the Achaeans,—the latter at another meeting, with the unanimous vote of all cities, voted to declare war on Sparta, though the winter made it impossible to begin major operations at once (38.32.1–2). Both meetings must have been *synkletoi.* The vote by cities in the second followed the usual procedure of such a meeting. The two suggest that extraordinary meetings could be summoned quite rapidly.

188.—The first meeting reported for this year appears to have been the first *synodos* of the year.[4] At that meeting a rule was adopted that thereafter *synodoi* were to be held in various cities of the Confederacy in rotation. Before this, it had been the custom to hold them regularly in Aegium. The meetings so far reported as held in other cities all seem to have been extraordinary meetings. Philopoemen not only advocated a law embodying the change, but fixed Argos as the place for the meeting, while the *damiourgoi* announced the meeting for Aegium. The people of this city ap-

pealed to the Roman proconsul, Fulvius Nobilior. When he came
to Aegium, he found that all had gone to Argos, and himself proceeded there, but found that the question had already been decided.
He consequently gave up advocacy of the cause of Aegium, but was
induced to intervene in favor of Sparta (Livy 38.30.1–6). No action
on the Spartan question is reported for this meeting. Since the
Spartans the preceding fall had voted to secede and the Achaeans
to make war on Sparta, the question may well have been considered
one which could be acted on only by the *ekklesia.*

At the request of Fulvius a *concilium* (*synkletos*) was called at
Elis and the Spartans were invited to present their case. There was
such disagreement that the best he could suggest was that they
abstain from war until the Roman senate could be consulted. Both
parties sent ambassadors (Livy 38.32.3–5).

When the ambassadors returned from Rome, it is almost certain
that another extraordinary meeting must have been held before
hostilities began, as they did at the beginning of the spring (Livy
38.33.1). The earliest any *synodos* is known to have met is February. If the meeting at Argos was in February, things must have
moved rapidly. The *synkletos* at Elis must have been called at the
earliest possible date after the *synodos,* the ambassadors must have
left immediately, and the senate must have received them as soon
as they reached Rome. In connection with the settlement at Sparta
later in the year, there is a reference to a decree concerning the
restoration of exiles passed at a federal assembly (*in concilio communi Achaeorum*) at Tegea (Livy 38.34.5). It is not quite clear
whether this was the *synkletos* held after the return of the ambassadors from Rome or a later meeting.

186.—In all likelihood a *synodos* this year received an embassy
sent by Ptolemy V to renew the existing alliance with the nation
of the Achaeans. The embassy came while Philopoemen was general (187/6). The assembly acted favorably on the proposal and
chose Lycortas and two others as ambassadors for the exchange of
oaths (Pol. 22.3.5–7).

185.—The *synodos* held at Megalopolis this year has been considered above as an example of the great amount of varied business

which could be handled at a single *synodos*. Ambassadors from Ptolemy, from Eumenes, and from the Seleucid court were presented. In addition, an Achaean ambassador back from Rome reported (Pol. 22.7–9).[5] The embassy from Ptolemy followed up the work of the preceding year, and Lycortas and his fellow ambassadors were now back from Alexandria. The confusion caused by the existence of many older treaties is important chiefly as evidence of the intense diplomatic activity of the Ptolemies in Greece. The embassy from Eumenes brought the famous offer of a gift of 120 talents to be invested and the interest used to supply pay for the federal *boule* at the *synodoi* (ἐφ' ᾧ, δανειζομένων τούτων, ἐκ τῶν τόκων μισθοδοτεῖσθαι τὴν βουλὴν τῶν Ἀχαιῶν ἐπὶ ταῖς κοιναῖς συνόδοις [Pol. 22.7.3]). The bearing of this on the question whether the *boule* was paid or unpaid has been discussed above. The passage, of course, has been used as a proof that the *synodoi* were meetings of the *boule*. One of the speakers in the debate was Cassandrus of Aegina, a city which then was subject to Eumenes. Aymard (102–120) argues that the presence of an Aeginetan at the meeting can best be explained by considering it a primary assembly. The Aeginetans had been Achaean citizens when their city belonged to the Confederacy, and those who lived outside the city may have retained their citizenship. Cassandrus spoke as an Aeginetan and cannot well have been a representative of another city. However, as Aymard points out, this is not enough by itself to prove that the *synodos* was a primary assembly. Another possible explanation—and, in my opinion, more likely—is that those Aeginetans who had escaped capture or had been ransomed afterward had been allowed to keep up a sort of corporation and to send delegates to the meetings. Certainly it seems that in ancient Greece groups of exiles could negotiate and act almost like states. Sometimes groups were given special treatment by other states, such as the granting of new homes in colonies.[6] Thus, not to mention their experience with Spartan exiles, the Achaeans themselves later granted privileges to the Delians expelled from the island after 166 B.C. The report of Polybius (32.7) implies that they moved to Achaea *en masse,* were enrolled as citizens, and continued to negotiate and act as a group.[7]

Later in the year Caecilius Metellus arrived and at a conference with Achaean magistrates asked to have "the many" gathered in an *ekklesia*. His request was refused on the ground that he did not bring a written statement from the senate (Pol. 22.10). The chief evidence for the Achaean law limiting the calling of the *ekklesia* is found in the account of this incident and the subsequent defense of the refusal before the senate by Achaean ambassadors.

184.—Two meetings are reported for this year. Of these, the first was probably a *synodos*. When the approach of Roman ambassadors was anticipated, Lycortas, the general of the year, called a meeting, as it were, to prepare for their arrival. At this the Spartan question was discussed. The only action reported was the condemnation to death *in absentia* of Areus and Alcibiades, two Spartan ambassadors to Rome. They were former exiles who had been restored by the Achaeans and consequently were regarded as ingrates. The condemnation seems to have been due to an impassioned speech by Lycortas, and the vote seems to have followed immediately upon the speech (Livy 39.35.5–8). It is this which is the chief reason for suggesting that the meeting was a *synodos*. The procedure required at a *synkletos* does not seem to have been followed. It is also true, as Aymard (205 f.) has pointed out, that the action reported concerned exclusively domestic affairs and so came within the competence of a *synodos*. This, however, is not decisive. Particularly when feeling ran high, officials may well at times have stretched the law. On the other hand, the report about the summoning of the meeting suggests an extraordinary meeting; but again, as Aymard has pointed out, this is not decisive. Summonses had to be issued also for *synodoi*.

The second meeting reported certainly was a *synkletos*. When the Roman ambassadors arrived, a meeting was called at Cleitor to give them a hearing (*his Clitore in Arcadia datum est concilium* [Livy 39.35.8]). When the ambassadors arrived, it was observed that the two condemned Spartans, Areus and Alcibiades, were in their party. Lycortas pleaded the cause of the Achaeans in vain, and the Achaeans are reported to have ended by requesting the Romans themselves to make what changes they wished in the status of

Sparta rather than force them to violate their oaths. The only action reported was the cancellation of the condemnation of Areus and Alcibiades (Livy 39.36–37).

182.—After the death of Philopoemen, Plutarch (*Philop.* 21.1) reports that the men of military age met together with the *probouloi* at Megalopolis, elected Lycortas general, and immediately invaded Messenia. This report is unusual and has been the subject of much debate. At first glance the meeting reported does not seem to conform to Achaean law as we know it. In fact, the election of the general by the army, largely consisting of men under thirty, seems in itself a violation of law. Moreover, for 146 B.C. we have a report that the law provided that when a general died his predecessor should take over until the next regular *synodos* (Pol. 38.15.1). As long as there is no evidence to the contrary, it is natural to believe that the same law was in force in 182. Now Archon, not Lycortas, was the predecessor of Philopoemen and so the one to take over after his death. The key to the riddle may be found in the *probouloi*. These may be the members of the *boule,* and, in spite of the language of Plutarch, they may have been the ones who theoretically were responsible for the election. Thus Archon may after all have taken over after the death of Philopoemen and may have summoned the *synodos* at Megalopolis, for even for fixed meetings it is clear that summonses were necessary. The language also implies a mobilization of troops in connection with the meeting, obviously in anticipation of the speedy invasion of Messenia. When the meeting came, it was natural to elect Lycortas, the right-hand man of Philopoemen. The role of the army in the election may actually have been confined to exerting influence. The demand for Lycortas may have been so strong that the *boule* would not have dared to go against public opinion. The conclusion that the meeting was a *synodos,* and specifically the first *synodos* of the year, finds some support in the statement that the settlement of the affairs of Messene after the campaign of Lycortas was made at the second *synodos* of the year, and that it too was held at Megalopolis (Pol. 23.16.12).

With regard to this second *synodos* Polybius reports that Lycortas left the general settlement to the nation (*ethnos*). By a fortunate coincidence it so happened that the Achaeans were gathering at Megalopolis for the second *synodos*. We learn thus that the settlement with or readmission of a revolting member could be handled by a *synodos,* that even such an important question apparently could be submitted without an advance announcement, and that in 182 there were still several regular *synodoi* a year.

Soon after the settlement with Messene, the general gathered "the many" at Sicyon—obviously a *synkletos*—and submitted the question of admitting Sparta into the Confederacy. The settlement was made and later recorded on a stele, and ambassadors were sent to Rome to report to the senate (Pol. 23.17–18).

Thus in one year two similar questions were submitted, one to a *synodos* and one to a *synkletos*. The *synodos* clearly was competent to negotiate the admission of a member (Aymard, 207–209). Thus it is the calling of a *synkletos* for the admission of Sparta which appears to have been irregular.

181.—Polybius (24.2.1–3) reports a meeting at which Spartan exiles presented a letter from the Roman senate to the Achaeans concerning their restoration. The Achaeans decided to postpone action until their own ambassadors should return. Next they approved of the agreement with the Messenians which was to be inscribed on a stele—undoubtedly the one which the meeting of the previous year had in mind. The settlement apparently was amended, and some concessions were made, including three years' exemption from federal taxes. The fact that at least two major questions were taken up shows that the meeting was a *synodos* (cf. Aymard, 207 n. 2). An additional proof is to be found in the presentation of a letter by the Spartan exiles. It is very unlikely that the Achaean authorities would have called an extraordinary meeting at their request.

When the Achaean ambassadors returned from Rome and reported, the Achaeans decided to make no change in the status of Sparta (Pol. 24.2.4–5). This must mean that an extraordinary assembly was called (Aymard, 342 n. 3). Thus again a *synkletos* was called to deal with a subject which fell within the competence of the *synodos*. The explanation probably is that the Spartan question aroused such a passion that it led to irregularities. Yet it is possible that the irregularities were not so numerous as they may seem. The real question of competence was not between regular and extraordinary meetings, but between *boule* and *ekklesia*. It is possible that some of the extraordinary meetings for which there are no indications of the nature of the body attending were meetings of the *boule*. In the present case ἔδοξε τοῖς 'Αχαιοῖς indicates merely that the decree passed was an official Achaean decree, not whether it was passed by a primary or a representative assembly. On the other hand, the reference to the summoning of "the many" to the meeting of the previous year (Pol. 23.17.5) indicates that the *ekklesia* was summoned.

The same year, ambassadors came from Ptolemy V to offer the Achaean nation (*ethnos*) a gift of 10 penteconters. The renewal of an alliance, which had been prevented in 185, had by this time. been completed during one of the generalships of Lycortas (Pol. 24.6.4). The Achaeans elected Lycortas, Polybius—though he was strictly below the legal age,—and Aratus of Sicyon, probably grandson of the great Aratus, to go as ambassadors to thank the king for previous gifts and to take over the ships. News of the king's death prevented the embassy from leaving (Pol. 24.6). The meeting at which this business was conducted was almost certainly a *synodos*. Since Lycortas was general in 182/1 and was elected to serve as an ambassador, the meeting must have come at the end of his term of office and must have been the autumn *synodos* at which the new general was elected.

Later in the autumn the new general, Hyperbatus, called a meeting to reconsider the letter from Rome on behalf of the Spartan exiles (Pol. 24.8). Aymard (*Rev. ét. anc.* 30 [1928] 59–61) points out that the letter in question must have been the same as the one discussed in the spring, and that Hyperbatus must have acted early in his term of office. Since there seems to have been no *synodos* in the autumn after the elections, the meeting must have been a *synkletos*. This seems implied also in the phrase ἀναδόντος 'Υπερβάτου τοῦ στρατηγοῦ διαβούλιον ὑπὲρ κτλ. (Cf. also 23.17.6.) It undoubtedly refers to the statement of the case made on the first of the three days of the meeting. In calling a *synkletos* Hyperbatus was probably stretching the law. The incident is significant as an indication of the influence normally exercised by a general. The decisions made at the earlier meetings had been in accordance with the policy of Lycortas; now Hyperbatus hoped to have one of the decisions reversed. Possibly, when he called the meeting, Hyperbatus still thought that Lycortas would be leaving for Egypt and would not be present at the meeting. The news of the death of Ptolemy, however, must have reached the Achaeans before the meeting, for Aratus, who earlier had been chosen to go to Egypt, was now one of the ambassadors chosen to go to Rome. At the meeting Lycortas and his supporters seem to have had the better of it, but Callicrates, one of the chief supporters of Hyperbatus, was one of the three ambassadors sent to Rome.

Ca. 180.—A *synodos* at Sicyon from about this time seems to be mentioned in *Inschriften von Olympia,* no. 46, line 57. The subject dealt with was boundary disputes involving Megalopolis, Thouria, and Messene. The editors have taken the *synodos* to be the meeting at Sicyon in 182 mentioned in Polybius 23.17.5. This meeting, however, as already noted, was a *synkletos*. Since *synodoi* were by no means infrequent, there seems no need of identifying this with any particular meeting mentioned in the literary sources. Nor need it cause any concern that it was held at Sicyon. The relative frequency of meetings at this city must have been due in part to its location. It was easily accessible from Corinth, the Argolid, and at least the eastern part of Achaea proper, and was at the head of routes north from Laconia and Arcadia.

174.—Livy (41.23–24) has preserved a rather lengthy account of a meeting which must have been a *synodos*. At the time all Macedonians were excluded from Achaean territory. The Macedonians naturally retaliated in kind. Perseus had sent a letter in an effort to get this changed. It was presented to the assembly by Xenarchus, the general of the time. The majority of those present were favorably impressed, but Callicrates argued that friendship with Macedonia might jeopardize the relations with Rome. Archon, the brother of Xenarchus, tried to refute Callicrates, but, according to Livy, the upshot was that the *principes* were offended because Perseus had not considered the matter as deserving an embassy but had only written a short letter. This must mean that the *damiourgoi* used this as a pretext for not allowing any action to be taken. To be sure, as Aymard (375 n. 1; cf. 339 n. 2) has pointed out, *principes* need not mean *damiourgoi,* but Livy's account implies that the majority were inclined to accept the overtures of Perseus. Most of those present considered the letter moderate and friendly (41.23.4), and those who had approved of the letter were in agreement with Archon (41.24.19). It looks as if Callicrates and his supporters had to make use of a subterfuge.

It appears that Perseus took the hint and sent ambassadors. These were refused a hearing at a *concilium* at Megalopolis (Livy 41.24.20). In this case it looks as if Callicrates insisted on the letter of the law excluding Macedonians. Undoubtedly the meeting was a *synodos.*

173.—This year a *synkletos* was called on the occasion of the visit of a Roman ambassador. The latter is reported to have praised the Achaeans for having retained their old decree about the exclusion of the Macedonian kings (Livy 42.6.1). At this time obviously, no matter what the law originally was, a *synkletos* was called for any accredited Roman ambassador who demanded it. Livy's word for the meeting is *conventus.* As Aymard (41 n. 3) points out, he uses the word both for *synodoi* and *synkletoi.* In the present case he may have chosen it because he has just used *concilium* to designate the Aetolian assembly.

172.—Livy (42.44.7–8) mentions a *concilium* (*synkletos*) called at Argos to confer with Roman ambassadors. At the request of the latter it was voted to send 1,000 troops to Chalcis to hold the city until the Roman army should arrive.

170.—In the late summer or autumn of this year Roman ambassadors again visited Achaea. According to the interpretation of Polybius (28.3.7–10) given above, they were reported to have thought of having the Achaean *ekklesia* called, but instead had the *boule* summoned to Aegium and addressed it.

169.—Envoys of Attalus of Pergamum appeared before the Achaeans at what must have been the first *synodos* of this year and also the first *synodos* of the strategic year 170/69 and pleaded for the restoration of the honors of his brother Eumenes (Pol. 28.7). From the point of view of the chief magistrates of the time this request came at an opportune moment. After the visit of the Roman ambassadors in 170 a group of Achaean leaders had held a conference and agreed to be timeservers and avoid trouble. They decided to run Archon for general and Polybius for hipparch and were successful in having them elected to office for 170/69 (Pol. 28.6). They therefore were glad to coöperate with Attalus. The latter sent envoys who appeared at the first *agora*. As Aymard (77 and nn. 1 and 2) points out, Polybius uses *agora* here and in 29.24.5 almost as synonym for *synodos*. Whether the *synodos* was the first after the arrival of the communication from Attalus, or the first of the year, makes no difference in this case. At the *synodos* it was decided to restore the legitimate honors of Eumenes.

At another *synodos* of the same year a decree was passed to send the entire military levy of the Achaeans to Thessaly for the campaign against Perseus. After this had been voted, it was decided that Archon was to remain at home, busied with the preparations, while Polybius was to head an embassy to communicate the offer to the Roman consul. It was voted further to send ambassadors to Attalus about the restoration of the honors of Eumenes, and to Ptolemy VI to congratulate him on his coming of age (Pol. 28.12). There is no name in the account for the assembly. The importance of the chief decision made suggests a *synkletos,* but the number and variety of the subjects handled indicates that it was a *synodos.* The explanation must be that the Confederacy was already at war with Macedonia and that details concerning the conduct of a war fell within the competence of a *synodos.* Action on the honors of Eumenes at a second meeting may mean that a detailed check of the honors had been made between the two meetings.

Later in the year, at what must have been a *synkletos,* the Achaeans considered the request from Appius Claudius Centho for 5,000 men to serve in Epirus. Quintus Marcius Philippus, the consul, who had refused the offer of the entire Achaean army, is reported by Polybius to have given the latter instructions to prevent the request of Appius Claudius from being granted. Polybius states that he kept these instructions secret and fell back on the recent *senatus consultum* to the effect that requests from commanders should not be honored unless authorized by the senate. In this manner he obtained the decision that the question should be referred to the consul (Marcius Philippus) (Pol. 28.13).

168.—For this year Polybius (29.23–25) reports a *synodos* at Corinth and a *synkletos* at Sicyon at which the question of sending military aid to the two Ptolemies was discussed. The ambassadors had arrived already in the winter, and so it is likely that the *synodos* was the first of the year. The request was for 1,000 foot and 100 horse under the command of Lycortas and Polybius. This was the meeting at which Callicrates prevented action by insisting that it was contrary to law to take counsel at the meeting on a question of military aid. The implication that Callicrates intimidated the magistrates suggests that the law may not have been too clear, and that in cases of the kind, if no one raised a point of order, the *synodos* might well take action. Moreover, whether the distortion is due to Callicrates or to Polybius, it looks as if the statement is not quite accurate. It may have been illegal for the *synodos* to take final action on certain questions, but not to discuss them. Discussion at a *synodos* followed, as in this case, by submission of the question to a *synkletos* cannot have been rare.

The question was later submitted to a *synkletos* at Sicyon to which all citizens over thirty were admitted. This is the only time we find the word applied by Polybius (29.24.6) to a meeting of an Achaean assembly. The significance of the account for our knowledge of Achaean institutions has already been discussed.

167.—The one meeting reported for this year was the one at which Roman ambassadors sought the surrender of Achaeans considered hostile to Rome. The statement of Polybius (30.13.11) that Aemilius Paulus sent ambassadors and letters suggests a *synkletos*. For the meeting we have only the unsatisfactory account of Pausanias (7.10.7–10).

154 (?).—Ambassadors from both Crete and Rhodes appeared before a *synodos* at Corinth to request aid for the war in progress against each other. Opinion is said to have favored supporting Rhodes, but Callicrates argued that the Achaeans should neither go to war nor send military aid without instructions from Rome, and his opinion prevailed (Pol. 33.16).

Ca. 150.—An inscription (*IG* VII, 411; *SIG³*, 675) contains reports of *synodos* and a *synkletos* held the same year. Oropus had appealed to the Achaean Confederacy for aid against Athens. The appeal was presented at a *synodos* at Corinth, but "the Achaeans" passed a decree ordering that a *synkletos* be summoned to Argos to deal with the question. The actual summons probably was issued by the general and the *damiourgoi* (Aymard, 320 f.). At this meeting ambassadors not only from Oropus but also from Athens and probably other states were present. The Achaeans decided to support the Oropians.

149.—The Achaeans, after the receipt of a letter from the Roman consul, Manilius, requesting that Polybius be sent to Lilybaeum, voted to send him. The action was probably taken at a *synodos* (Pol. 36.11.1).

148.—Pausanias (7.13.2–3) reports that Metellus, the Roman commander in Macedonia, instructed ambassadors who were on their way to Asia that they should first have a conference with Achaean leaders and instruct them not to make war on Sparta but to await ambassadors sent from Rome to judge between the Achaeans and the Spartans. When they had given their instructions to "Damocritus [the general for 149/8] and the Achaeans," they departed. Though a *synkletos* is not entirely excluded, it is probably more likely that the ambassadors merely had a conference with the general and the *damiourgoi*. Metellus later sent envoys to Diaeus, the next general, who promised to await the Roman ambassadors (Paus. 7.13.5).

147.—A meeting, apparently a *synkletos,* was called at Corinth in connection with the arrival of a Roman embassy headed by L. Aurelius Orestes. This must have been the embassy for which the Achaeans had been asked to wait. Orestes is said by Pausanias to have summoned to his quarters in Corinth the magistrates of each of the cities and Diaeus—probably, as Niccolini (*La Confederazione achea,* 191 n. 1) suggests, rather the *damiourgoi* and the general. He informed them that the Roman senate wished not only Sparta but a number of other cities to be detached from the Confederacy. The Achaean magistrates did not hear him to the end, but ran from the house and called the Achaeans to an *ekklesia.* As soon as the latter heard what was going on, they turned on and seized the Spartans who were present as well as others who were suspected of being Spartans. Orestes was unable to restrain the Achaeans and after warning them departed (Paus. 7.14.1–3; cf. Livy *Per.* 51; Dio Cassius 21.72.1; Justin 34.1.6–9). This may look as though no *synkletos* had been summoned, and as though there merely was action by a mob. Yet there are many reasons for taking the opposite point of view. It would be strange if there had been no arrangements for a meeting in connection with the long-awaited arrival of a Roman embassy which was to deal with so important a question. If Achaean magistrates had emerged unexpectedly from a conference, it is difficult to see how they could have gathered a mob so hurriedly. It is unlikely that even Pausanias would speak of an *ekklesia* unless there had been some sort of meeting. The presence of so many Spartans would be strange unless there had been arrangements for a meeting. Finally, the fact that the Spartans were not merely mobbed, but arrested, suggests a slightly more systematic action. Hence it is likely that a *synkletos* had been summoned, and that Orestes had invited the magistrates to a preliminary conference early in the morning of the first day of the meeting. Meanwhile, the assembly had gathered and was waiting for the general and the *damiourgoi* to come and open the meeting and introduce the Roman ambassadors. When the magistrates did come and did report, someone must have urged the immediate arrest of all Spartans in Corinth. The assembly obviously did not sit three days before it took action, but immediately transformed itself into a mob or a group of vigilantes. Even so, it looks as if the action taken on that day was later regarded as valid.

The events of this day called for further action by an assembly. A few days later the Spartans who had been seized were retained in prison; the non-Spartans, released; and an embassy was sent to Rome. Probably only the dispatch of the embassy required action by an assembly. Obviously the *synkletos* called to confer with the Roman embassy had broken up and another meeting was needed. Probably action was taken at the next *synodos*. The embassy sent, while on its way to Rome, met the next Roman embassy headed by Sextus Julius Caesar (Pol. 38.10.1–2; Paus. 7.14.3).

The latter after his arrival addressed the Achaeans at Aegium (Pol. 38.10) at a meeting which probably was the autumn *synodos* at which the elections were held. The account of Pausanias (7.14.3–4) implies that the ambassadors arrived before the elections. An address, not followed by any immediate action, would also fit the presentation of ambassadors to a *synodos*.

The same autumn, at the beginning of the term of office of Critolaus as general (147/6), Critolaus apparently had promised to call a *synkletos* at Tegea to which also the Spartans were invited. Romans and Spartans put in their appearance, but Critolaus, by arrangement with his fellows, came alone and came late. He stated that he could do nothing without the approval of "the many," and that he would refer the matter to the next *synodos,* which was to meet in six months. The Roman ambassadors naturally returned to Italy (Pol. 38.11.1–6; Paus. 7.14.4–5). They seem to have been quite right in concluding that Critolaus was acting in bad faith. To call a *synkletos* late in the autumn would have been unusual, but there is no reason to believe that it would have been illegal. In fact, there seem to have been two such meetings in 189. Moreover, Critolaus was holding over for a *synodos* a problem which might be held to call for action by an *ekklesia*.

146.—The one meeting which remains to be discussed is important and difficult. Polybius in his account (38.12–13; cf. Paus. 7.14.5) applies no technical name to the meeting, and its nature and composition has to be determined by its conduct and procedure. It has frequently been considered a *synkletos*. There was a larger gathering of workingmen and common people than normal, and the meeting was dominated by mob spirit. This looks like a meeting of a primary assembly. Moreover, it voted war against Sparta; and this too looks like an act of the *ekklesia*. Aymard (126–133), however, has pointed out that much suggests a *synodos*. It came at the time of the *synodos* of which Critolaus had spoken; it is unlikely that, after having refused to call a *synkletos* in the autumn, he should nevertheless have proceeded to call one before the next *synodos;* and on Aymard's theory that the *synodos* was a primary assembly it is easy to explain the large attendance and the mob spirit. It also seems necessary to grant that the language of Polybius implies that the large gathering was one of participants. It does not seem possible to get out of the dilemma by attributing the numbers and excesses to visitors.[8] In other words, it seems necessary to grant, in spite of the arguments for a *synodos,* that the meeting was a meeting of the primary assembly. It probably actually was, so to speak, a *synodos* and a *synkletos* combined. This is not too strange or too difficult to understand if we remember the history of the *synodos*. Down to 217 both the Achaean *boule* and *ekklesia* normally were present at regular *synodoi*. Then came the law that the *ekklesia* should not be summoned except to deal with questions of war and alliance. Thereafter the normal *synodoi* were meetings of the *boule* alone. At these meetings, and particularly, it seems, at the first meeting of the year, there was often a great variety of business brought up, and it was natural to bring before the *synodos* all business which had accumulated since the last meeting. Sometimes a problem was such that action by the *ekklesia* was called for and it was decided at the *synodos* that a *synkletos* should be summoned. Now in 146 it was known in advance that a subject calling for action by the *ekklesia* was to be brought up. What would then be more natural than that the *ekklesia* too should be summoned to meet at the same time as the *boule?* Thus, if the meeting was a *synodos,* it was like the one of 220 B.C. at which we know that the *ekklesia* was present (Pol. 4.7.1) and other early meetings. The specific action reported, the vote to go to war against Sparta (Pol. 38.13.6), must have been an action of the *ekklesia,* and the supplementary decree bestowing extraordinary powers upon the general probably was an action of the same body. It may well have been regarded as a detailed regulation concerning the manner in which the war already voted should be carried on and thus did not seem a violation of the rule that a *synkletos* should deal with one subject only.

Notes

TABLE OF ABBREVIATIONS

(Shortened forms of titles which are readily understood are not included.)

AJA	*American Journal of Archaeology*
AJP	*American Journal of Philology*
ATL	B. D. Meritt, H. T. Wade-Gery, and M. F. McGregor, *The Athenian Tribute Lists*, 1939–1953
BCH	*Bulletin de correspondance hellénique*
BSA	*Annual of the British School at Athens*
CAH	*Cambridge Ancient History*, 1923–1939
CIL	*Corpus inscriptionum Latinarum*
CP	*Classical Philology*
Dessau	H. Dessau, *Inscriptiones Latinae selectae*, 1892–1916
IG	*Inscriptiones Graecae*
IGR	*Inscriptiones Graecae ad res Romanas pertinentes*
JHS	*Journal of Hellenic Studies*
JRS	*Journal of Roman Studies*
OGIS	W. Dittenberger, *Orientis Graeci inscriptiones selectae*, 1903–1905
RE	*Paulys Real-Encyclopädie der classischen Altertumswissenschaft*, new ed. by G. Wissowa and others, 1894—
REG	*Revue des études grecques*
Schwyzer	E. Schwyzer, *Dialectorum Graecarum exempla epigraphica potiora*, 1923
SEG	*Supplementum epigraphicum Graecum*, 1923—
SGDI	H. Collitz and others, *Sammlung der griechischen Dialekt-Inschriften*, 1884–1915
*SIG*³	Dittenberger, *Sylloge inscriptionum Graecarum*, 3d ed., 1915–1924
TAPA	*Transactions of the American Philological Association*
Tod	M. N. Tod, *A Selection of Greek Historical Inscriptions*, 1933 (2d ed. 1946) and 1948

NOTES TO CHAPTER I
(Pp. 1–21)

[1] *IG* IV², 1, 68. 75 f. This document concerns the Hellenic League of early Hellenistic times (cf. pp. 49–52) and so does not strictly relate to a representative government, but rather shows that on one occasion, at least, Greeks went very far in permitting representatives in an interstate assembly to act for their constituents.

[2] By "active citizens" is meant those who have a right to vote and hold office. There may be others who enjoy the civil rights of citizenship but do not have the vote. This is illustrated by the constitutional inscription from Cyrene (*SEG* IX, 1) which shows that there was a property qualification for membership in the body of active citizens (*politeuma*), but that in addition to this group there were other citizens; cf. "Notes on the Constitutional Inscription from Cyrene," *CP* 24 (1929) 351–368, at 361. This important meaning of *politeuma* is scarcely noted in Ziebarth's short article, *RE* 21, 1401 f.

[3] On this point cf. Aymard, *CP* 45 (1950) 104.

[4] Cf. "The Origin and Significance of the Counting of Votes," *CP* 44 (1949) 164–181, at 175 and n. 28.

[5] For the Boeotian cities see *Hellenica Oxyrhynchia* 11.2; for Cyrene, *SEG* IX, 1.

[6] On this entire problem see the article cited in note 4 above.

[7] For the size of the Roman citizen body in the time of Augustus see T. Frank, *An Economic Survey of Ancient Rome,* V (1940) 1, and cf. his fundamental article, "Roman Census Statistics from 225 to 28 B.C.," *CP* 19 (1924) 329–341. On problems involving statistics no help is to be had from the works of Rostovtzeff.

[8] The fundamental handbook for the student of Greek political institutions is Georg Busolt, *Griechische Staatskunde* (1920–1926), in two volumes (paged continuously) and an index volume. The second volume was edited after the author's death by Heinrich Swoboda. The latter's *Lehrbuch der griechischen Staatsaltertümer* (1913), which is Vol. I, Pt. 3, of K. F. Hermann's *Lehrbuch der griechischen Antiquitäten,* 6th ed., is important for its definitions of the chief Greek political institutions and its detailed account of federal states. Shorter and more elementary are A. H. J. Greenidge, *A Handbook of Greek Constitutional History* (1896), and G. Glotz, *La Cité grecque* (1928), of which a translation, *The Greek City and Its Institutions,* was published in 1929. A new edition by Cloché has been announced.

191

[9] For representation in the *boule* see, for instance, J. B. Bury, *A History of Greece to the Death of Alexander the Great* (1900 and 3d ed. by Meiggs, 1951) 215; K. J. Beloch, *Griechische Geschichte,* I², 1 (1912) 397–398; W. S. Ferguson, *Greek Imperialism* (1913) 52; U. Wilcken, *Griechische Geschichte im Rahmen der Altertumsgeschichte* (1924) 197; M. Rostovtzeff, *A History of the Ancient World,* I (1926) 225–226; G. Glotz, *La Cité grecque* (1928) 213–215; G. De Sanctis, *Storia dei greci* (1939) I, 552; A. Aymard, *Les Premières Civilisations* (1950) 591; H. Bengtson, *Griechische Geschichte* (1950) 133; P. Cloché, *La Démocratie athénienne* (1951) 25–26; C. Hignett, *A History of the Athenian Constitution to the End of the Fifth Century* (1952) 150.

[10] In chapter i of my dissertation (available in the Harvard library), "A Study of Representative Government in Greek and Roman History, Pt. I: Greek History" (pp. xvi + 381); cf. Harvard University *Summaries of Theses, 1928* (Cambridge, Mass., 1931) 81–83.

[11] The evidence available in 1933 was summarized conveniently by A. W. Gomme, *The Population of Athens in the Fifth and Fourth Centuries B.C.* (1933) 56–65, with discussion 49–53. The evidence to become available later consists largely of prytany inscriptions. When S. Dow in 1937 published his *Prytaneis* (*Hesperia,* Suppl. I), a study of prytany inscriptions from 327/6 B.C. through the reign of Augustus, he included 121 entries, of which approximately half were Agora inscriptions published for the first time, while also some of the others had been found during the Agora excavations and had been published only a few years earlier. The work contained several prytany lists, but lists of *bouleutai* as distinct from prytany lists were omitted, and the entire problem of representation of demes was necessarily deferred. The publication of all the lists of *bouleutai* and a study of representation are now being prepared by H. J. Carroll and S. Dow.

[12] A member of the prytany was selected daily by lot to serve as the presiding officer. After 378 B.C., on days on which the council or the assembly met, there was selected to take charge of the meeting a committee of nine chosen by lot from among those members of the council who were from the non-prytanizing tribes; the actual chairman, in turn, was selected by lot from among the nine. The prytany, however, retained its former importance in connection with the preparation of the business to be brought before the larger bodies and probably did much of the work of the council as the council did that of the assembly.

[13] Ulrich Köhler, "Attische Prytanenurkunden," *Ath. Mitt.* 4 (1879) 97–106, noted that most demes were represented in proportion to their size, but seems to have attributed this not to the requirements of the law but to the energy with which the members of the various demes looked after their

interests. Only two years later A. Hauvette-Besnault, "Dédicace athéni-enne," *BCH* 5 (1881) 361–371, at 368, asserted that the lot was drawn not by tribes as a whole but by demes and that a definite number of seats was assigned to each deme in advance.

[14] *Aristotle on the Constitution of the Athenians,* ed. F. G. Kenyon (London, British Museum, 1891), at 62.1. This is a passage which was perfectly clear in the first edition and has not required serious emendation. According to the passage, also certain guards (*phrouroi*) continued to be chosen by demes. They remain a mystery. As for the authorship, it is now generally recognized that the work is the one which in antiquity was known as the Athenian *politeia* of Aristotle, but there are scholars who doubt that it is the work of Aristotle himself. Recently C. Hignett (*Hist. Ath. Const.* 29–30) has asserted emphatically that it cannot be, and has made extensive use of this conclusion in his reconstruction of Athenian constitutional history. I agree with Hignett that the *Constitution* is inferior to the *Politics,* and in case of conflict I normally prefer the evidence of the latter work. Never-theless, it looks as if Aristotle allowed the *Constitution* to go by his name, and whether he wrote it himself or turned the task over to a student, he must bear the responsibility. Hence I shall continue to cite it under the name of Aristotle.

[15] Representation in the council naturally gives a guide to the membership of the deme rather than to the population residing in a deme. Moreover, it gives information only about the citizens. Thus Peiraeus had a smaller representation than Acharnae, but doubtless, counting slaves and metics, was more populous.

[16] *IG* II², 1749. As printed there the list shows only 49 instead of 50 repre-sentatives, but incomplete representation is so rare that I follow the original editor, Hauvette-Besnault, *BCH* 5 (1881) 365 n. 6, in believing that the Ionidai had two and not merely one representative and that thus the total number is 50. Gomme too has treated the list as complete; cf., however, E. Gollob, *Wiener Studien,* 3 (1881) 214.

[17] The two inscriptions are *IG* II², 1747, another prytany inscription, and 1700, a list of the members of the *boule* arranged by tribes and demes. The number of representatives in the three lists is tabulated below, the demes being listed in the order in which they occur in 1749, the complete list.

	1747 Ca. 350	1749 341/0	1700 335/4
Erchieis	–	6	–
Gargettioi	4	4	–
Philaidai	3	3	–
Kydantidai	1	2	2
Ionidai	2	2	–

Ikarieis	. . . .	–	5	–
Hestiaieis	. . . .	–	1	1
Bateis	. . . .	2	1	1
Koloneis	. . . .	2	2	–
Kollyteis	. . . .	3	3	–
Plotheis	. . . .	1	1	1
Otryneis	. . . .	–	1	1
Erikeeis	. . . .	–	1	1
Halaieis	. . . .	5	5	–
Teithrasioi	. . . .	–	4	–
Phegaieis	. . . .	4	3	–
Araphenioi	. . . .	2	2	–
Myrinoutteis	. . . .	–	1	–
Ankyleis	. . . .	2	2	–
Diomeieis	. . . .	–	1	1

50

[18] Those who think that 1749 contained only one representative for Ionidai will find one additional example of disagreement.

[19] The latest editions of the Athenian decree are *Athenian Tribute Lists,* II, D 10 (cf. III, 254) and Hill-Meiggs-Andrewes, *Sources,* B 26. In these the year of the document is fixed convincingly by the restoration of the name of the archon as Lysikrates. This is based on the conviction that the name in line 2 beginning with a lambda is that of the archon. If so, the only possible name for this period is Lysikrates. This approach is much more likely to prove fruitful than attempts to date the document by the contents, as Accame does, *Riv. di. filol.* 80 (1952) 119–123.

[20] The only direct evidence for the thirty-year age qualification for members of the council of five hundred seems to be Xen. *Mem.* 1.2.35, but this detail finds support in indirect evidence such as the same age qualification in the constitution imposed upon Erythrae in 453/2 (cf. n. 19 just above). For permission to serve twice in a lifetime see Arist. *Const. Aths.* 62.3.

[21] G. De Sanctis, *Atthis,* 348 f.; Busolt, *Staatskunde,* 1022 n. 4.

[22] Statements about the population of Athens will be based upon Gomme, *The Population of Athens,* Table II on p. 29.

[23] The evidence for the alternates is interesting in itself. Aeschines (3.62) accused Demosthenes of becoming a member of the *boule* without having been drawn by lot either as a regular member or as an alternate, but through bribery. This statement merely proves that alternates were drawn by lot, but does not indicate whether they were chosen at the same time as the regular members or whether an alternate was only chosen later if an elected member died or was rejected. The lexicographer Harpocration

(s.v. ἐπιλαχών), in commenting on the passage, states that an alternate was selected for every councilor. In support of this he refers to the lost play *Hyperbolus* (frags. 166/7 Kock, *CAF* I, 643 f.) by the comedian Plato, which must have been performed during the Peloponnesian War. What appears to be the key passage has been preserved in a scholion on Aristophanes' *Thesmophoriazousai* 808. A slave reports that his master has almost been elected to the *boule,* since, it develops, he has been elected as an alternate for Hyperbolus. The implication is not that the latter has been rejected, but that the rejection is anticipated. Since the alternate has already been chosen, this implies further that he was chosen at the same time as the regular members, but it does not tell how many alternates were chosen. Perithoidai, the deme of Hyperbolus (Plut. *Alc.* 13; *Nic.* 11), had three representatives in the *boule* (*IG* II², 1700, 1745, and 1746). The scene would be equally to the point whether three alternates were chosen, one for each member, or whether there was only a single alternate for the deme. Thus it is legitimate to doubt that Perithoidai selected three alternates. To claim that the scene proves that there were three, means taking for granted more precision than is to be expected in a comedy. It is even more legitimate to doubt that the Acharnians selected 22. Thus, if we go back of Harpocration to the evidence he used, it seems very unlikely that the number of alternates chosen numbered 500. If it is safe to take for granted that the practice of demes was uniform, we can conclude from the scene from *Hyperbolus* that in the late fifth century demes used to select one or more alternates at the time of their sortition of their members in the council. The statement of Aeschines shows that the practice was continued in the fourth century.

[24] J. Sundwall, *Epigraphische Beiträge zur sozial-politischen Geschichte Athens* (*Klio,* Beiheft 4 [1906]) 1–18. Since Sundwall wrote, much additional material has become available. A new study of the entire problem has been undertaken by Carroll and will be included in the work by Carroll and Dow mentioned in note 11 above.

[25] Evidence for the subdivision of the *boule* and for committees similar to the Athenian prytanies serving as presiding committees is given by Swoboda, *Staatsaltertümer,* 129–130; Busolt, *Staatskunde,* 476–477 and 1581.

[26] First edited with important commentary by Wilamowitz, "Nordionische Steine," *Berlin Abhndl.* 1909, pp. 64–71, no. 25 (*SGDI* IV, pp. 873–875; Tod, no. 1). Wilamowitz dates it about 600 B.C., earlier rather than later than Solon; Tod and others follow Wilamowitz. This is not precise dating. Hence it is hard to see the point of Hignett's statement (p. 95): "the precision of the date suggested ... seems illusory."

[27] For the annual *boule* with 120 members see note 19 above; for the prytanies see Schwyzer, *Dialectorum Graecarum exempla,* no. 701 = Hill-Meiggs-

Andrews, *Sources*, B 116. Wilhelm (*Jahreshefte*, 12 [1909] 138) first dated the inscription in the early fourth century, but, when he had seen a facsimile, decided that it must belong to the first half of the fifth century (*ibid.* 14 [1911] 237).

[28] The conclusion that Erythrae had three tribes is based on a reference in Paus. 7.5.12 to the third tribe, Chalkis, and on the repeated occurrence in inscriptions of multiples of three in lists of generals, dicasts, etc. For the generals there are two third-century decrees each honoring nine generals who had served a four-month period (*SIG³*, 410 and 442) and two dedications by groups of nine generals probably best accessible in H. Gaebler, *Erythrä* (1892) 98 and 99. Of these the second is incomplete but undoubtedly if complete would show nine generals. On the other hand, judging by the description (*Ath. Mitt.* 21 [1896] 262), another dedication, listing six generals, appears to be complete, though it too is listed as incomplete by Wilhelm (*Jahreshefte*, 12 [1909] 130). There are at least three possibilities. The city may once have had only six generals, or the dedication was made by the generals from two tribes, or it was made by two of the three generals from each tribe. Busolt, *Staatskunde*, 259 n. 6, also cites Le Bas–Waddington, III, 1539, for six *epistatai* of dicasts and *Berlin Abhndl.* 1909, p. 56, for three judges sent by Erythrae to another city. Schwyzer, 701, the fifth-century inscription cited above in note 27, refers to nine dicasts per tribe, to *prytaneis*, and to the second prytany.

To turn to the modern literature, F. Lamprecht, *De rebus Erythraeorum publicis* (1871) 50–51, who wrote before these inscriptions were known, concluded from the evidence of Pausanias that Erythrae had at least three tribes, but was inclined to believe that the actual number was four as in other Ionic cities. H. Gaebler (*op. cit. supra*, 115) rejects the possibility of four tribes as irreconcilable with nine generals and concludes that there were three tribes and three *prytaneis*. E. Szanto (*Ausgewählte Abhandlungen*, 273) in his study "Die griechische Phylen" follows Gaebler. This comes immediately after his statement that Teos is the only Ionic city in which the presence of the four old Attic tribes can be demonstrated. K. Latte, in his article "Phyle," does not seem to have given special treatment to the question of the number of tribes at Erythrae, but indicates the great variation there was in Ionic cities (*RE* 20, 1000–1001). In view of this and of the repeated appearance of multiples of three, particularly in the lists of generals, it is practically certain that Erythrae had three tribes. M. P. Nilsson discusses the four Ionian tribes in *Cults, Myths, Oracles, and Politics in Ancient Greece* (Skrifter utgivna av Svenska Institutet i Athen, series in octavo, I [1951]) App. I: "The Ionian Phylae." He too fails to consider the tribes of Erythrae. Since evidence for the three tribes comes from the third century, it is also reasonably certain that Erythrae never imitated the later Athenian system of ten or more tribes. Moreover, since there is evidence for tribe and prytany in the first half of the fifth century, it is also reasonably certain that the system antedated the Athenian decree of 453/2. Since Schwyzer, 701, does not mention the number of tribes, it is only in a high degree likely but not absolutely certain that the tribes at that time too numbered three, particularly since the document in the reference to nine dicasts from each tribe shows the same obsession with multiples of three as the later documents. It is also likely that the second prytany of this document is the same as the middle or second four-month period—both terms are used—of *SIG*³, 442, and thus that the terms of service both of *prytaneis* and generals was four months, while the *bouleutai* served for a year (Wilhelm, *Jahreshefte*, 12, 135).

²⁹ *Hell. Ox.* 11.2 and cf. discussion in chap. ii of the present work, at pp. 31–32.

³⁰ For bibliography see Busolt, *Staatskunde,* 78, 630 d–e; *CAH* V, 517–518; Bengtson, *Griechische Geschichte,* 226–227. Add Mabel Lang, "The Revolution of the 400," *AJP* 69 (1948) 272–289; Franco Sartori, *La Crisi del 411 A.C.* (Padua, 1951; cf. *CP* 67 [1952] 189 f.); M. Cary, "Notes on the Revolution of the Four Hundred at Athens," *JHS* 72 (1952) 56–61; Gregory Vlastos, "The Constitution of the Five Thousand," *AJP* 73 (1952) 189–198; Hignett, *Hist. Ath. Const.* 276–280 and 356–378. In spite of objections from several scholars and most recently from Hignett, I still believe that this was the constitution actually adopted by the Five Thousand. One point of which Hignett makes much is that "the fusion of the treasury of Athena with that of the other gods" provided for in the constitution was not carried out before 406/5. This is not against the identification. If a constitution prepared in advance contains several administrative changes—and this reform is administrative rather than constitutional,—it may take some time to implement all of them, and the Five Thousand did not remain in control for long. Moreover, some such proviso, unless the proper authority takes the initiative, may remain a dead letter. Of the clauses in the constitution, the one providing that the generals must belong to the *boule,* and that thus no one—not even the precious Alcibiades—could be general more than once in four years, has been considered particularly impossible. But such a law might well be adopted by oligarchs inclined to believe in equality within their own group. There actually is evidence for a law at Thurii forbidding reëlection as general within five years (Arist. *Pol.* 1307b6). The positive evidence given by Hignett (279 and 378) for a council of 500 under the Five Thousand is of the most tenuous sort. The implication that it had to be done to please Alcibiades is not convincing, and even less convincing is the argument that in Andoc. 1.96 "the careful description of the boulē under the restored democracy of 410

is intended to distinguish it not only from the 400 but also from a previous
Council of *Five* Hundred which had not been chosen by lot." The emphasis on the use of lot would be equally natural, whether the preceding
council had 500 members or not.

[31] Cf. "The Judgment of Antiquity on Democracy," *CP* 49 (1954) 1–14.

[32] Cf. the article cited in the preceding note and literature listed there; also
Gregory Vlastos, "Isonomia," *AJP* 74 (1953) 337–366.

[33] The earliest that any of those who have recently discussed the development
of democracy would place its origin is under Cleisthenes. See particularly
V. Ehrenberg's important article, "Origins of Democracy," *Historia,* 1
(1950) 515–548.

[34] *IG* I²,114. For later studies of the text see particularly Wade-Gery, *BSA*
33 (1932–1933) 113–122 and cf. *SEG* X, 119.

[35] P. Cloché, "Le Conseil athénien de cinq cents et la peine de mort," *REG*
33 (1920) 1–50; R. J. Bonner and G. Smith, *The Administration of
Justice from Homer to Aristotle,* I (1930) 200–205; cf. Hignett, *Hist. Ath.
Const.* 153–154.

[36] Line references, according to Wade-Gery in *BSA* 33, are: for the five hundred, 20, 30, and 45; for the *boule,* 27, 40, and 49; for the *prytaneis,* 49; for
the *ekklesia,* 53 and 54.

[37] G. Glotz, *La Cité grecque* (1928) 198; Glotz and Cohen, *Histoire grecque,*
II (1931) 279; Hignett, *Hist. Ath. Const.* 153. The translation is that of
Bonner and Smith.

[38] Hignett seems to misunderstand the situation when he states (p. 155) that
Herod. 9.5.1–2 implies that in 479 the *boule* could have rejected Mardonius'
offer of peace without referring it to the *ekklesia* and expresses doubt that
it possessed the right to do so, except possibly by special authorization.
Herodotus reports that the ambassador of Mardonius appeared before the
boule of the government in exile on Salamis, that one member proposed
that the offer be accepted and a motion to that effect be submitted to the
people, and that he was lynched by members of the *boule* and "those outside." Here "those outside" certainly does not mean the men attending the
assembly, but those who were loitering around the meeting place of the
boule. Obviously no motion was brought before the people, and no such
motion was necessary, for the rejection of the peace offer by the *boule*
produced no change in the relations of Athens to the outside world. Such
actions cannot have been rare. Cloché makes better use of the passage when
he cites it (pp. 33–34) as proof that the people at this date possessed the
final decision on questions of foreign affairs. This is shown by the need of
laying the matter before the people if peace was to be made.

[39] Arist. *Const. Aths.* 22.2; for the date cf. the commentary of Sandys; Beloch,
Griechische Geschichte, I², 2 (1913) 167; T. J. Cadoux, *JHS* 68 (1948) 116.

⁴⁰ The attempt of A. E. Raubitschek in his article "The Origin of Ostracism," *AJA* 55 (1951) 221–229 (cf. A. C. Robinson, Jr., in *AJA* 56 [1952] 23–26), to prove that the measures listed in Arist. *Const. Aths.* 22.2–6 were due to Cleisthenes cannot be discussed in detail but must be considered unsuccessful. Clearly 22.1, Raubitschek and Kaibel to the contrary notwithstanding, contains a summary of the reforms described in the preceding chapter but adds as a sort of afterthought a reference to the law of ostracism, which had not been mentioned in the previous account. Undoubtedly this happens because the chapter contains an account of the first use of the law. When this report occurs (22.3) the law is represented as having been in existence a considerable time before it was used. There is no evidence for the authorship of the later measures mentioned in the chapter.

⁴¹ For the election of magistrates by the Areopagus we have the direct evidence of Arist. *Const. Aths.* 8.2 and the indirect evidence of Arist. *Pol.* 1274a16, where the election of magistrates is listed as one of the chief powers granted the people by Solon; cf. *CP* 44 (1949) 169 n. 13. If before Solon's time not the assembly but some other body elected the magistrates, what body could that be except that council which later was known as the Areopagus? To discuss whether there was continuity or not between the Areopagus of the period after Solon and the earlier council of nobles is meaningless. Even if by some specific act the old council was abolished and a new council took its place, this new council served as a substitute for the old and thus there was factual continuity.

Recently Hignett (*Hist. Ath. Const.* 78–79) has rejected the election of magistrates by the Areopagus. In doing so he has overlooked or disregarded *Pol.* 1274a16 and has ruled out the evidence of *Const. Aths.* 8.2 on the grounds that the statement that the best man was appointed to each post is too good to be true and that the passage echoes Isoc. 7.22. In the first place, it is bad methodology to reject evidence simply because it represents the system described as working better than it possibly could have done. In the second place, there is little point in the reference to Isocrates, who is dealing with the later use of *prokrisis* and not with the earlier method of elections. Moreover, some similarity in statements by two oligarchic writers would not be surprising. For positive evidence, Hignett cites *Pol.* 1273b41–1274a2, where it is stated that Solon left the election (*hairesis*) of magistrates unchanged. However, it is only necessary to look back to 1273b40, where *hairesis* is classified as aristocratic, to see that Aristotle is speaking about *hairesis* in opposition to election by lot and is not at the moment concerned with the electing body. The information on that point, as already noted, comes a few lines later.

⁴² Our knowledge of the council of four hundred organized by Solon is very slight. Thus, we do not know how the members were chosen or for how

long a term. However, to reject it as a forgery like the constitution of Draco (Hignett, *Hist. Ath. Const.* 93) is going too far.

[43] "Aristotle on the Electors of Mantinea and Representative Government," *CP* 45 (1950) 180–183. The chief passage discussed there is *Politics* 1298a40–b2. To this I can now add two other passages. In a discussion of forms of government in which participation is based on property, one alternative suggested is that, if two groups of citizens, one numbering 1,000 and one numbering 500, own equal amounts of property, each group should choose an equal number of representatives and place them in charge of elections and the courts (1318a15). Whether this is pure theory or based on observation of actual practices, it indicates that Aristotle did not consider representative government strange or unnatural. In another passage, which is not too clear, the author seems to imply that in democracies which lack pay, the *boule* is extremely strong; when there is pay, the *boule* is stripped of its power (1317b28). The latter statement might fit the experience of Athens, except that there the power of the *boule* was limited long before pay was introduced for attendance at the meetings of the *ekklesia* and apparently even before pay was introduced for jury service. Nevertheless the observation of the connection between pay and extreme democracy certainly is correct.

[44] The phrase δήμου κεκλημένου in line 7 seems to refer to the summoning of a primary assembly but probably rather refers to the meetings of the *boule* (so Wilamowitz, 67, and commentary in *SGDI*), which is seen from other parts of the document to have had authority to act for the *demos*.

[45] Swoboda, *Staatsaltertümer,* 128 n. 7; Tod, commentary on line 16.

[46] This original meaning is not always given much prominence in dictionaries. Bailly, however, gives "ce qu'on veut etc." as the literal meaning. H. Ebeling, *Lexicon Homericum* (1880–1885), gives "voluntas, sententia, consultum" as the first meaning and lists numerous examples. Of course, it may not always be easy, for instance in *Iliad* 1.5, to distinguish among "will," "wish," and "plan."

NOTES TO CHAPTER II
(Pp. 22–46)

[1] *CP* 40 (1945) 78 n. 72.

[2] For brief statements and bibliographies see in the *Oxford Classical Dictionary* the articles "Sympoliteia" and "Symmachia."

[3] See Lexicon, and Buck-Peterson, *Reverse Index,* p. 134; *IG* XII, 2, 59 cited in the latter work dates from the time of the Roman Empire.

⁴ It occurs in a decree from Araxa in Lycia (*JHS* 68 [1948] 46–48; cf. pp. 99–100 of the present work), which probably is to be dated early in the second century.

⁵ To cite recent manuals, R. Cohen, *La Grèce et l'hellénisation du monde antique,* 3d ed. (Paris, 1948), uses "ligue" for both types; H. Bengtson, *Griechische Geschichte* (Munich, 1950), uses "Bund" for both.

⁶ See particularly H. Francotte, *La Polis grecque* (1907), esp. 150 and 162; A. E. R. Boak, "Greek Interstate Associations and the League of Nations," *American Journal of International Law,* 15 (1921) 375–383. A. Aymard in *Les Assemblées de la Confédération achaienne* (1938) uses "confédération" for federal states and "ligue" for alliances.

⁷ E. A. Freeman's *History of Federal Government in Greece and Italy,* 2d ed. by J. B. Bury (London, 1893), written at the time of the American Civil War, is still important as the one general history of Greek federalism, but is no longer the best guide for the study of institutions. From the point of view of the student of representative government the work has two drawbacks. In the first place, much of the epigraphic evidence was not available when Freeman wrote. In the second place, he held the theory of the Teutonic origin of modern free institutions including representative government (cf. H. J. Ford, *Representative Government* [New York, 1924] 51–62) and so rejected or misinterpreted what little evidence was available at the time. Of later handbooks on constitutional antiquities, H. Swoboda, *Lehrbuch der griechischen Staatsaltertümer* (1913, Vol. I, Pt. 3, of K. F. Hermann, *Lehrbuch der griechischen Antiquitäten,* 6th ed.), deserves special mention for its excellent account of Greek federal states. The pertinent part of G. Busolt's monumental *Griechische Staatskunde* (1920–1926), the second volume of which was edited after Busolt's death by Swoboda, adds little except some more recent material and occasionally a different interpretation. Both fail to include accounts of the Lycian Confederation and the Macedonian republics organized in 167 B.C., though they are as Greek as much of what is included.

⁸ For early Achaean history see Herod. 1.145; Strabo 8.383–384; Pol. 2.41 and 4.1.5; cf. "The Early Achaean League," *Studies Presented to David Moore Robinson,* II (1953) 797–815. Strabo reports that the Ionians conquered the country once known as Aigialeia and that they were in turn expelled by the Achaeans. Herodotus also reports the early occupation of the country by the Ionians and their expulsion by the Achaeans. In the catalogue of ships the district called Aigialon, and its towns Pellene, Aigion, and Helike, are listed as parts of the domain of Agamemnon (*Iliad* 2.574–575). M. P. Nilsson, in "The Prehistoric Migrations of the Greeks" (Skrifter utgivna av Svenska Institutet i Athen, series in quarto, II [1953] 1–8), suggests that the traditions may contain more history than formerly was thought,

and that the Ionians may once have occupied the entire Peloponnesus and have been expelled to the coast by the Achaeans. To continue beyond Nilsson's reconstruction, in order to produce the conditions we find later— Achaeans speaking a Northwest Greek dialect but still calling themselves Achaeans—it is necessary to suppose that the Ionians were expelled also from the coast by the Achaeans, and that later a sufficient number of immigrants infiltrated or overran the district to change the language, though the name of the Achaeans was retained. Both Polybius and Strabo imply that the country passed directly from monarchy to a republican federal government. This is not impossible and is not contradicted by the tendency of Pellene to go her own way.

[9] See, for instance, the map (from Buck, *Greek Dialects*) in Bury-Meiggs, *History of Greece,* opposite p. 72; or the one in Bengtson, *Griechische Geschichte,* opposite p. 48. There seems to be disagreement whether the dialect is to be classed as Doric or Northwest Greek; cf. A. Thumb, *Handbuch der griechischen Dialeckten,* 2d ed. by Kieckers, I (1932) 228–230.

[10] For the Ionian League see particularly U. von Wilamowitz-Moellendorff, "Panionion," *Kleine Schriften,* V, Pt. 1, 128–151; M. Caspari (Cary), "The Ionian Confederacy," *JHS* 35 (1915) 173–188; Ida Calabi, *Ricerche sui rapporti tra le poleis* (Florence, La Nuova Italia, 1953) 26–36; C. Roebuck, "The Early Ionian League," *Classical Philology* for January, 1955.

[11] On this point see A. Momigliano, "Il Re degli Ioni nella provincia romana di Asia," *Atti del III Congresso nazionale di studi Romani,* I (1934) 429–434.

[12] C. Roebuck, "The Economic Development of Ionia," *CP* 48 (1953) 9–16, estimates that the free population of Chios was *ca.* 80,000; Miletus, *ca.* 64,000; Samos, *ca.* 48,000. These figures are based on the contingents furnished to the fleet at Lade. By the same method of computation, Teos with 17 ships as compared with the 100 of Chios (Herod. 6.8) would have a free population of about 13,600. These statistics are, of course, conjectural and only approximate but probably give a correct impression of the relative sizes of the cities.

[13] By B. Haussoullier (Paris, 1884).

[14] Herod. 6.7. We find *probouloi* also in the congress at the Isthmus in 481 (Herod. 7.172.1) and in the Hellenic League as reorganized at Plataea in 479 (Plut. *Arist.* 21.1; cf. pp. 48–57 of the present work).

[15] *CP* 40 (1945) 70–74.

[16] *Oxyrhynchus Papyri,* V (1908), ed. B. P. Grenfell and A. S. Hunt, no. 842. Subsequent editions of the *Hellenica Oxyrhynchia* are Grenfell and Hunt (Oxford, 1909), F. Jacoby (*Die Fragmente der griechischen Historiker,* no. 66 [1926]), E. Kalinka (Leipzig, 1927), M. Gigante (Rome, 1949).

[17] For an introduction to the problem see particularly H. Bloch, "Studies in

Historical Literature of the Fourth Century b.c.," *Harv. Stud. Class. Phil.* Suppl. 1 (1940) 303–376; cf. also Gigante's edition, pp. xxxvi–lv.

[18] A number of studies of the Boeotian constitution naturally appeared soon after the publication of the *Hell. Ox.* For references to earlier works see Busolt, *Staatskunde,* 1415 n. 2. A more recent account is given by P. Cloché, *Thèbes de Béotie, des origines à la conquête romaine* (Namur and Paris, n.d. [1951 or later]), 71–74.

[19] See particularly Busolt, *Staatskunde,* 1417 and n. 1, and literature cited there.

[20] Swoboda, *Klio* 10 (1910) 319, reaches the same conclusion but on different grounds.

[21] R. J. Bonner, "The Boeotian Federal Constitution," *CP* 5 (1910), 405–417, at 407; Swoboda, *Klio* 10 (1910) 317 f., *Staatsaltertümer,* 258; E. M. Walker, *The Hellenica Oxyrhynchia* (Oxford, 1913) 144–146; Busolt, *Staatskunde,* 353 and nn. 4 and 5; Glotz, *La Cité grecque,* 341.

[22] In an inscription dealing with the sympolity of the two cities, Melitea and Perea, one of the provisos in case the two separate is that the people of Perea, the smaller of the two, are to retain one *bouleutes* and ἐμφερόντω τὰ ἐ[ν] τοὺς Αἰτωλοὺς γινόμενα κατὰ τὸν βουλευτάν (*SIG*³, 546b. 20–21). This must mean that the united cities contributed to the Aetolian treasury in proportion to the number of their councilors, and that the Pereans are to continue to pay the contributions that went with their one representative in the federal council.

[23] J. Kromayer and G. Veith, *Heerwesen und Kriegführung der Griechen und Römer* (1928) 66, count the peltasts with the citizen soldiers and believe that the Boeotian state at the time organized other light-armed troops also. These are mentioned not only at Delium; for the campaign against Argos in 418 the Boeotians are reported to have sent 5,000 hoplites, the same number of light-armed troops, 500 horsemen, and the same number of ἄμιπποι (Thuc. 5.57.2). The mention of these special troops, the development of light-armed troops, and the drawing up of the Theban hoplites at Delium 25 deep (Thuc. 4.93.4) justify the conclusion that Thebes had already begun that development of her military system which was to make her supreme in the fourth century.

[24] In the foregoing statement the towns included in *Hell. Ox.* 11.3 are listed except for those grouped with Plataea under Thebes. From other sources there are known to have been other small towns or villages in the territory of some of the larger cities. The fullest discussion is that in E. Meyer, *Theopomps Hellenika* (1909) 95–99.

[25] Thus, to give an illustration, Glotz, *BCH* 32 (1908) 277–278, considers Eutresis and Thisbe, which are grouped with Thespiae, as each constituting one half unit, so that each would supply thirty councilors. He has a similar treatment of the towns once grouped with Plataea.

²⁶ The people of these towns were σύμμοροι (Thuc. 4.93.4) or συντελεῖς (Thuc. 4.76.3; *Hell. Ox.* 11.3) with the people of the larger cities. The first word undoubtedly means that that they were grouped in the same federal μέρη or representational units; the second, that they belonged together for the purposes of federal taxes and administration. I cannot see that either word necessarily means that the smaller towns were subject to the larger. συμπολιτευμένων is used about the former union of a group of cities with Plataea (*Hell. Ox.* 11.3); the verb could probably be equally well used about the other groupings.

²⁷ Swoboda, *Klio*, 10 (1910) 316 and n. 5; *Staatsaltertümer*, 257 and n. 5; Busolt, *Staatskunde*, 1415.

²⁸ *Op. cit.* at end of volume.

²⁹ The statement about meetings reads: τὰ συνέδρια ⌈καὶ⌉ τὰ κοινὰ τῶν Βοιωτῶν ἐν τῇ Καδμείᾳ συνεκάθιζεν. Grenfell and Hunt deleted the καί and explained the passage as referring to "general meetings of the federal boule in the Cadmea" (*Oxyrh. Pap.* V [1908] 228). Later editors have followed them in this, and it surely must be correct. It would hardly be possible to retain the conjunction and see a reference to meetings of both a council and an assembly. The language would be strange, and there is no other evidence for a federal assembly in addition to the council. Moreover, the reference in *Hell. Ox.* 12.2 to a political clique as influential both at Thebes and in the *boule* of the Boeotians clearly shows that the *boule* was the important power in the federal government.

³⁰ ἅπαν τὸ κῦρος ἔχουσιν is difficult to translate, but κῦρος obviously refers to authority to make a binding decision and this authority belonged in its entirety to the "four *boulai* of the Boeotians."

³¹ The view that the federal council had little authority began with the original editors (*Oxyrh. Pap.* V [1908] 224) and was maintained by E. Meyer, *Theopomps Hellenika* (1909) 93; E. M. Walker, *The Hellenica Oxyrhynchia* (1913) 139 ff.; and M. Gelzer, *Wochenschrift für klassische Philologie*, 31 (1914) 127, in review of Walker. For arguments on the other side see W. A. Goligher, *CR* 22 (1908) 80–82; G. Glotz, *BCH* 32 (1908) 274 f.; H. Swoboda, *Klio*, 10 (1910) 315 f.; R. J. Bonner, *CP* 5 (1910) 408–410 and 10 (1915) 381–385. Some later statements: Busolt, *Staatskunde*, 1417 f.; Glotz, *La Cité grecque*, 341; R. Cohen, *La Grèce et l'hellénisation du monde antique*, 3d ed. (1948) 313; and especially Cloché, *Thèbes de Béotie*, 73.

³² For the earlier literature see Busolt, *Staatskunde*, 1421 n. 1. Busolt himself made it a "Mittelding zwischen einem Staatenbunde und Bundesstaate," which means that he recognized it was a more close organization than a symmachy but, in his opinion, did not quite rank as a sympolity. Swoboda, on the other hand, in *Zwei Kapitel aus dem griechischen Bundesrecht* (*SB*

Vienna, 199 [1923]) 31 ff., had shown that for all practical purposes it was a sympolity. So also Glotz (*La Cité grecque*, 340), Cohen (*La Grèce*, 3d ed., 313), and Cloché (*Thèbes de Béotie*, 71), who refer to it as a "confédération."

[33] On both points this interpretation follows Grenfell and Hunt; on both, Swoboda disagrees. He speaks of a direct tax (*Klio*, 10 [1910] 326, and *Staatsaltertümer*, 260) and of pay for the *bouleutai* from federal funds (*Staatsaltertümer*, 258 f.). Except for him, there seems to be agreement on the taxes. See particularly Busolt, *Staatskunde*, 1420 and n. 4, where Swoboda is refuted, and where the latter, in editing the manuscript, has indicated no disagreement with Busolt's view. Also Beloch, *Griechische Geschichte*, II², 1 (1914) 181, speaks of "Matrikularbeiträge"; cf. also Glotz, *La Cité grecque*, 342, who mentions "des contributions matriculaires, dont le montant est le même pour tous les districts"; Cohen, *La Grèce*, 3d ed., 313. The statement about the councilors reads as follows: [ἔκαστον μέρος] παρείχετο δὲ καὶ βουλευτὰς ἑξήκοντα κατὰ τὸν βοιωτάρχην, καὶ τούτοις αὐτοὶ τὰ καθ' ἡμέραν ἀνήλισκον (*Hell. Ox.* 11.4). Every possible interpretation has been offered. For pay by the cities or constituents: besides Grenfell and Hunt, also Bonner, *CP* 5 (1910) 414; for pay by the federal government: Swoboda and Busolt, *Staatskunde*, 1417 f.; for no pay, Glotz, *BCH* 32 (1908) 272 and 275–277, Cloché, *Thèbes de Béotie*, 73. The last view seems impossible; which of the other two is correct makes little practical difference, for the districts contributed to the federal treasury in proportion to their representation. However, it seems best to take αὐτοί as referring to the citizens of the μέρος. There is a similar shift in construction in the statement which follows immediately after the sentence quoted.

[34] Probably there were similarly officers in charge of the cavalry of each division of the Confederacy, but, if so, they cannot have played the important part in federal affairs that the Boeotarchs did. The reference to "the hipparch of the Boeotians" in Thuc. 4.72.4 proves only that there was a commander-in-chief of the cavalry in that particular battle. He may well have been selected for the occasion or the campaign. If there normally was a commander of the cavalry with a definite term of office, he must have been chosen by the Boeotarchs or the federal *boule*. Since the more important Boeotarchs were chosen locally, we cannot imagine that a federal election was held to elect a hipparch, nor, with the chief executive put into a commission, was there any room in the Boeotian Confederacy—as in the later Aetolian and Achaean confederacies—for a hipparch who was virtually the vice-president.

[35] On this point see Bonner, *CP* 5 (1910) 410.

[36] See particularly Bonner, *CP* 5, 411; Bengtson, *Griechische Geschichte*, 197.

[37] Sparta did not conscientiously dissolve all federal states, but allowed the

Achaean Confederacy, which was friendly to herself, to survive; cf. "The Early Achaean League," *Studies Presented to D. M. Robinson,* II (1953) 797–815, at 814.

[38] See particularly Meyer, *Theopomps Hellenika,* 237–249; for another interpretation cf. Silvio Ferri, "Il significato di Tagia," *Riv. di fil.* 58 (1930) 300–305.

[39] The ἄνευ τοῦ πάντων κοινοῦ of Thuc. 4.78.3 is almost untranslatable and is difficult to interpret. Some sort of action by or on behalf of all Thessalians is implied. It seems most natural to take it to refer to action by a primary federal assembly.

[40] *A Handbook of Greek Constitutional History* (1896) 223.

[41] For the older literature see A. B. West, *The History of the Chalcidic League* (Madison, Wis., 1918); Busolt, *Staatskunde,* 1501–1507; for the newer, F. Hampl, "Olynth und der Chalkidische Staat," *Hermes,* 70 (1935) 177–196; D. M. Robinson, *RE* 18, 325–342, s.v. "Olynthos."

[42] *TAPA* 69 (1938) 52–55, no. 6; dated first half of fourth century; quotation from p. 54.

[43] *SIG³,* 135 = Tod, 111.

[44] Tod, 158, after Robinson in *TAPA* 65 (1934) 103–122, no. 1 with emendations by Segré. Tod (pp. 173 f.) remarks: "The phrase τὰς ἀρχὰς τὰς ξυνάς (l. 3) refers to the federal magistrates of the Chalcidian League, and disproves F. Hampl's contention (*Hermes* lxx, 177 ff.) that Olynthians and Chalcidians are the same and that there was never a federation of Chalcidian cities." In justice to Hampl, it should be noted that this inscription was not known to him when he wrote.

[45] The validity of this argument is denied by Hampl (*op. cit.* 196) on the grounds that in documents bestowing citizenship on individuals *epigamia* and *enktesis* are listed. This is hardly a parallel, since in such grants the separate mention of these rights may have a meaning. It might mean, for instance, that the person honored may enjoy these privileges even if he does not register as a citizen and assume active citizenship.

[46] Cf. note 42 above. See also his statement *RE* 18, 327.

[47] Swoboda, *Staatsaltertümer,* 217 and n. 1; cf. Busolt, *Staatskunde,* 1505, where the evidence is not even cited.

[48] West, *The History of the Chalcidic League,* chap. xiv.

[49] Cleigenes of Acanthus as quoted by Xenophon (*Hell.* 5.2.14) speaks of the Olynthians—that is, the Chalcidians—as already having not less than 800 hoplites and many more peltasts; moreover, if the Acanthians join them, their cavalry will number more than 1,000. Though the small number of hoplites is somewhat counterbalanced by the peltasts, the prominence of the cavalry is clear. Though the Acanthians did not join them, they were able to send 600 horsemen on a raid against Apollonia (Xen. *Hell.* 5.3.1),

and there are other indications of the prominence of cavalry in fighting around Olynthus. Such a state is not likely to have had a democratic government.

⁵⁰ *SGDI*, 1336; cf. Beloch, *Griechische Geschichte,* III², 2, 182. The grant was made by οἱ σύμμαχοι τῶν 'Απειρωτᾶν and applied ἐν 'Απείρωι. Here it is clear that the grant was not made by the allies of the Epirotes, but by the Epirotes who were united as "allies." Actually, then, *symmachoi* is a misnomer if normal Greek usage be kept in view, for the nature of the grant itself shows that we are rather in the presence of a federal state, and one headed by a king at that. Unfortunately the study of Epirote institutions, interesting in themselves, does not yield much definite information about assemblies and representation. Thus the most interesting feature remains the fact that Epirus had a constitutional federal monarchy. See, in addition to the literature cited by Busolt, *Staatskunde,* 1478, also Geoffrey Neale Cross, *Epirus: A Study in Greek Constitutional Development* (Cambridge, 1932). The latter is a valuable study but the author is misled by the σύμμαχοι of the inscription cited into thinking that the organization of the time was a loose one (39 f., 113).

NOTES TO CHAPTER III
(Pp. 47–65)

¹ For the earlier literature on symmachies see particularly Busolt, *Staatskunde,* 1310 ff.; somewhat more recent is Schwahn's article, "Symmachia," *RE* 4A, 1 (1931) 1102–1134; V. Martin, *La Vie internationale dans la Grèce des cités* (Paris, 1940) Pt. II, chap. i (pp. 121–281), discusses the alliances in the light of interstate relations as a whole; Ida Calabi, *Ricerche sui rapporti tra le poleis* (Florence, 1953), has little to offer on symmachies; Hans Schaefer, *Staatsform und Politik: Untersuchungen zur griechischen Geschichte des 6. und 5. Jahrhunderts* (Leipzig, 1932), while stimulating, is too negative and subjective (cf. *CP* 28 [1933] 320–322); L. I. Highby, *The Erythrae Decree: Contributions to the Early History of the Delian League and the Peloponnesian Confederacy* (*Klio,* Beiheft 36, Leipzig, 1936), devotes a large part of his study to a refutation of Schaefer; Larsen, "Federation for Peace in Ancient Greece," *CP* 39 (1944) 145–162, discusses the role of symmachies in the movement for Greek unity.

Select literature on individual leagues:

THE PELOPONNESIAN LEAGUE: U. Kahrstedt, *Griechisches Staatsrecht,* Vol. I (the only one published): *Sparta und seine Symmachie* (Göttingen, 1922); Larsen, "Sparta and the Ionian Revolt," *CP* 27 (1932) 136–150;

idem, "The Constitution of the Peloponnesian League," *CP* 28 (1933) 257–276 and 29 (1934) 1–19.

THE DELIAN LEAGUE: Larsen, "The Constitution and Original Purpose of the Delian League," *Harv. Stud. Class. Phil.* 41 (1940) 175–213; B. D. Meritt, H. T. Wade-Gery, and M. F. McGregor, *The Athenian Tribute Lists* (hereafter cited as *ATL*), III (1950) Pt. III.

THE SECOND ATHENIAN LEAGUE: Silvio Accame, *La Lega ateniese del sec. IV A.C.* (Rome, 1941), is indispensable and can serve as guide to the extensive earlier literature. F. H. Marshall, *The Second Athenian Confederacy* (Cambridge, 1905), is still useful.

THE HELLENIC LEAGUE OF CA. 337–300 B.C.: M. N. Tod, *A Selection of Greek Historical Inscriptions,* II (1948), commentary on no. 177, gives an excellent introduction with bibliography. A sketch of the growth of our knowledge as the result of the discovery of inscriptions is given by Larsen in *Ninth International Congress for Historical Sciences,* Vol. I: *Rapports* (Paris, 1950) 401–405, and in connection with it also some of the more recent literature is cited. An article on the aspect of the League which most concerns the present study is Larsen, "Representative Government in the Panhellenic Leagues," *CP* 20 (1925) 313–329 and 21 (1926) 52–71.

[2] In *CP* 27 (1932) 136–150 I argue for a date about 505 B.C. as the time of the transformation on the grounds that the League as such cannot have existed when Cleomenes in 507 or 506 called on the allies of Sparta to follow him without consulting them or even informing them of his plans; its formation is represented as a result of the opposition to Cleomenes. G. De Sanctis, *Storia dei greci* (1939) I, 574, at the end of an excellent account of the growth and formation of the Peloponnesian League, argues for an earlier date; cf. also Bengtson, *Griechische Geschichte,* 124 n. 1, and Calabi, *Ricerche,* 39 n. 1, who seems to have misunderstood my interpretation of the connection of Cleomenes with the event. The early date is itself thoroughly acceptable, and the exact date is of little importance for the present investigation, but I still feel that the chief argument against it carries considerable weight. The arguments of De Sanctis are discussed briefly in *CP* 39 (1944) 149 n. 10.

[3] Thucydides (1.23.1) wrote of the Persian War as ending with Plataea; cf. A. W. Gomme, *Commentary,* on the passage, and my remarks *CP* 44 (1949) 260 and 39 (1944) 151 n. 14.

[4] This has recently been questioned by Calabi (*Ricerche,* 62–69), who, however, concentrates too much on refuting me and on proving that the decree of Aristeides as reported by Plutarch (*Arist.* 21.1–2) is not genuine, and therefore does not give sufficient weight to the other evidence. The discussion in *ATL* III, 101–104, is excellent particularly in showing that the obligations of the covenant were still being discussed in 427. The de-

cree of Aristeides as given by Plutarch can hardly be correct in all details; cf. my doubts *CP* 28 (1933) 264. Yet it is very likely true that Aristeides took a lead in drawing up the arrangements which were accepted. P. A. Brunt, "The Hellenic League against Persia," *Historia,* II (1953) 135–163, argues that it was the league organized in 481 which endured to 462/1. His study of material frequently overlooked is to be welcomed, even if not all his conclusions can be accepted.

⁵ The date is established by the fact that the Aristoteles decree inviting states to join the League (*SIG³*, 147; Tod, 123) was passed in the seventh prytany of 378/7 B.C., that is, February or March, 377. This is the decree in which Athens promises good behavior in the future. Since the decree takes the existence of the League for granted, it is almost certain that it was founded in 378. As far as the indications of the inscription are concerned, January or February, 377, would seem possible, but there was a convention of delegates in connection with the founding (Diod. 15.28.3), and it can hardly have been held in the middle of the winter.

⁶ *CP* 28 (1933) 265–270. The case for permanency, which depends in part on evidence for the early use by the Greeks of treaties made for all time, has since been strengthened by the proof that Athens near the middle of the fifth century made treaties for all time with Rhegium and Leontini (Meritt, "The Athenian Alliances with Rhegion and Leontinoi," *Class. Quart.* 40 [1946] 85–91; cf. *ATL* III, 276 f. and 304 f.).

⁷ Arist. *Const. Aths.* 23.5; Plut. *Arist.* 25.1; cf. *CP* 28 (1933) 267 f. and *Harv. Stud. Class. Phil.* 41 (1940) 187 n. 5. In these accounts I do not speak of "red-hot iron," since the emphasis is on the fact that the object will not float, and since the precise meaning of μύδρους does not seem too certain. At times the word means "anvil," but the examples given in Liddell-Scott-Jones make it likely that in the present passages and in Herod. 1.165 it means "red-hot iron." Martin, *La Vie internationale,* 152 n. 1, emphasizes this phase and challenges the interpretation that the rite signifies perpetuity. A pledge of that nature he considers out of place in a League organized with a limited and specific objective, and so he is inclined to take the rite to be a symbol of the solemn and binding character of the oath. The distinguished scholar here seems to have made the mistake of relying more on logic than on the evidence. Herodotus—and he, if anyone, should know— is emphatic that the rite means a pledge not to do something before the *mydros* appears again on the surface of the water. Calabi, *Ricerche,* 43 f., echoes Martin and adds a discussion of Herod. 1.165. She realizes that Herodotus took the rite to be a symbol of perpetuity, but she rejects his interpretation on the grounds that he has not taken into consideration the heating of the iron before it was thrown into the sea, and that the act followed upon the imprecations in the oath taken. As Beloch might have

said (I quote from memory), "die Modernen verstehen es natürlich viel besser." The rejection of the reconstruction of an ancient author is often warranted, particularly when he deals with something remote in time or place, but in the present instance Herodotus was very close to the atmosphere to which the rite belongs.

[8] Accame, *La Lega ateniese*, 48–53. His reconstruction is accepted by Tod (no. 123). V. Martin, "Le Traitement de l'histoire diplomatique dans la tradition littéraire du IVe siècle avant J.-C.," *Museum Helveticum*, I (1944) 13–30, at 29 n. 22, who argues that the King's Peace and the *koine eirene* are identical, considers it extremely plausible.

[9] Oath of the Athenians as given in Tod, 177; the text of the same given by Calabi, *Ricerche*, 153, is extremely convenient because it is printed line by line so that it is easy to tell at a glance what parts of the document are preserved and what are restored. The restoration in 11–12: οὐδὲ τ]ὴν βασιλείαν [τ]ὴν Φ[ιλίππου καὶ τῶν ἐκγόν]ων καταλύσω must be essentially correct. The phi, which is preserved, is enough to make it certain that we have a pledge not to overthrow the kingdom of Philip and someone else. Given the space and a noun in the genitive plural, the someone else cannot well be anyone but his descendants or successor.

[10] The organization of a *synedrion* of the allies at Corinth is reported directly only by Diodorus (14.82 and 84.5), but its existence is confirmed by Xenophon (*Hell.* 4.8.8) when he reports that Pharnabazus and Conon sailed to the Isthmus of Corinth to address the allies and bring them subsidies. See now S. Accame, *Ricerche intorno alla Guerra corinzia* (1951) chap. iv.

[11] *SIG*³, 665. 19–20; cf. my brief discussions, *CP* 34 (1939) 378 and 39 (1944) 160 n. 27, and the fuller treatment of C. Roebuck, "The Settlement of Philip II with the Greek States in 338 B.C.," *CP* 43 (1948) 73–92, at 91–92. The conclusion has been questioned by Calabi, *Ricerche*, 139–144, who makes the mistake of not taking into consideration the tendency of a prominent individual and especially a king to be in the limelight. Undoubtedly the boundary settlements between Sparta and her neighbors were due to Philip personally, and authors were more likely to mention him than the assembly of the allies. Hence a failure to mention the allies should not be interpreted as a negation. When Calabi writes: "In tale tradizione diffusa ... sono dunque solamente il passo di Polibio e l'epigrafe *Syll.*³ 665 che possono far pensare al sinedrio della lega di Corinto," she seems to fail to realize how much weight this positive evidence should carry.

[12] Tod, 177, conveniently given by Calabi, p. 153.

[13] For this point of view see *ATL* III, 141. The reader will easily detect that, as far as this aspect of the Delian League is concerned, no evidence is cited, but that the argument is based altogether on probability.

[14] Here the case is not quite so clear. In *IG* II², 232. 6–7, there is a reference to the *synedros,* Aratus; in *IG* II², 233b. 29–30, there is possibly a reference to the *synedroi* of Tenedos, but the connection of the expression has been lost. In *SIG*³, 256 n. 17, this is taken as a reference to the several delegates of Tenedos: Aratus is first singled out for praise, and then the entire group. Probably the plural was used in a reference to the *synedroi* of several cities, as in Tod, 131.

[15] Accame, *La Lega ateniese,* 109 f.

[16] So W. Schwahn, *Heeresmatrikel und Landfriede Philipps von Makedonien* (*Klio,* Beiheft 21, 1930) 47; Kahrstedt, *RE* 4A, 1334.

[17] *SIG*³, 150; Tod, 126. For the argument that in the case of Acarnania the reference to delegates from each *polis* does not mean separate representation from each city in Acarnania, but rather that the Acarnanian Confederacy is regarded as a *polis,* see *Studies Presented to D. M. Robinson,* II, 812. Corroborative evidence is found in the entry of the Acarnanians as a single unit in the list of allies appended to the Aristoteles decree (Tod, 123. 106).

[18] In Kahrstedt's article on the subject in *RE* 4A, 1333–1350, the first *synedrion* discussed is that of the Amphictionic League, the next that of the Second Athenian League.

[19] In *ATL* III, 138, "councils" is used in the translation of the statement of Thucydides about the Delian League. Since the authors obviously do not mean a group of councils, like the four councils of the Boeotians, this seems to bring out admirably the fact that the word refers to a series of meetings rather than to the body attending the meetings.

[20] See particularly S. B. Smith, "The Athenian *Proedroi,*" *CP* 25 (1930) 250–276.

[21] Larsen, "A Study of Rep. Govt." (diss.) 135.

[22] J. H. Oliver, *AJA* 40 (1936) 461 ff., no. 2; amended text, Accame, *La Lega ateniese,* 230.

[23] Accame's interpretation (pp. 118–119) is quite different. He believes that the *synedrion* was subject to call by the Athenian authorities and that a chairman was selected by lot after the *synedrion* had gathered. This is an interpretation of the relation of the power holding the hegemony to the *synedrion* which was natural before the discovery of new evidence first for the Hellenic League and then for the Second Athenian League itself, that is, at a time when many of our ideas concerning the functioning of symmachies were derived from Thucydides' accounts of the meeting of the assembly of the Peloponnesian League in 432.

[24] F. H. Marshall, *The Second Athenian Confederacy* (1905) 35–37, with references to earlier literature; also Accame, *La Lega ateniese,* 138–140, is inclined to see a reference to a joint court.

[25] This is the explanation given by Glotz and Cohen, *Histoire grecque,* III, 123-124, and followed by M. Feyel, *Rev. phil.* 71 (1945) 156, who states that the passage "doit signifier que la sentence sera rendue d'abord par un tribunal athénien, puis confirmée par le Synedrion des Alliés." Feyel (*loc. cit.* 152-157) himself, however, tries to get a mixed court by restoring [βο]λἐι for [πό]λει in *SIG*³, 173 (Tod, 142) line 49. The restoration depends on the use of **E** for **H**, but though this is common enough in itself, it does not seem to occur in the present inscription; cf. the copy in *IG* II, 5, 54b. Thus the emendation is most improbable, not to say impossible. Even less probable is the suggestion that the same symmachy should have a deliberative executive assembly called *synedrion* and a federal law court distinct from it called *boule.*

NOTES TO CHAPTER IV
(Pp. 66-85)

[1] The Aetolian council actually is called *synedrion* more frequently than *boule,* but the latter word too was used.
[2] See "The Early Achaean League," *Studies Presented to D. M. Robinson,* II, 797-815.
[3] See the article just cited, at 812 f.
[4] "The Judgment of Antiquity on Democracy," *CP* 49 (1954) 1-14, at 6-10.
[5] The source accounts for Aetolian history are summarized and an excellent brief account given by G. Klaffenbach, *IG* IX², 1 (1932) pp. ix-xlviii. For the political institutions Holleaux's article, "Sur les assemblées ordinaires de la Ligue aitolienne," *BCH* 29 (1905) 362-372, is fundamental. See also Larsen, "The Assembly of the Aetolian League," *TAPA* 83 (1952) 1-33, with references to other recent literature.
[6] W. W. Tarn, *Hellenistic Civilization,* 3 ed. by Tarn and G. T. Griffith (1952) 71.
[7] The proof is based on *SIG*³, 546B, an inscription of the third century, but, in view of what is known of the history of the institution in general, it is almost certain that the system goes back to the first organization of the Confederacy.
[8] *IG* II², 358, formerly dated 327/6 B.C., but placed in 333/2 by W. B. Dinsmoor, *The Archons of Athens in the Hellenistic Age* (1931) 357 f. The latter date seems to be generally accepted, e.g., by W. K. Pritchett and O. Neugebauer, *The Calendars of Athens* (1947) 48.
[9] The *synedroi* mentioned in the record of gifts for the conduct of the Sacred War (*SIG*³, 201; Tod, 160) are hardly members of a Boeotian federal council.

[10] *SIG*³, 183 = Tod, 132; for the date see Cary, *JHS* 42 (1922) 188–190. Tod's commentary gives a good summary of the controversy concerning the date.

[11] *History of Federal Government*, 2d ed., 156 n. 1.

[12] See particularly Busolt, *Staatskunde*, 1406. See also Glotz-Cohen, *Histoire grecque*, III, 155, and Cohen, *La Grèce*, 3d ed., 317. The most important evidence favoring the taking of *myrioi* as a real numeral is the statement of Diodorus (15.59.1) that Lycomedes persuaded the Arcadians to organize a single state and to have a federal assembly consisting of ten thousand men.

[13] A. Aymard, *Les Assemblées de la Confédération achaienne* (Bordeaux and Paris, 1938; pp. xv + 450). The reader is referred to this work for the earlier literature. It will be cited by the name of the author alone, while other works by him will be cited by title.

[14] *Aratos of Sicyon* (Cambridge, 1933) 27.

[15] In *CR* 53 (1939) 139–140 Walbank discusses both *Les Assemblées* and Aymard's *Les Premiers Rapports de Rome et de la Confédération achaienne*, also published in 1938. He makes a few more reservations with regard to the second of these than the first.

[16] W. W. Tarn, *Hellenistic Civilization*, 3d ed. (1952) 74 and n. 2.

[17] Cary, *JHS* 59 (1939) 154 f.; Larsen, *CP* 36 (1941) 406–409.

[18] "A Study of Rep. Govt." (diss.) chap. vi, part 2.

[19] Cf. βουλὴν . . . γερόντων in *Iliad* 2.53.

[20] *TAPA* 83 (1952) 18 f. The conference of officials is to be found in Pol. 10.42.4.

[21] This is approximately the view of Caspari (Cary), *Eng. Hist. Rev.* 29 (1914) 215 n. 25.

[22] Aymard, 310 n. 2; Walbank, *Aratos*, 91; W. H. Porter (*Plutarch's Life of Aratus* [1937]) commentary on 39.2.

[23] Pol. 4.7.1: καθηκούσης αὐτοῖς ἐκ τῶν νόμων συνόδου κατὰ τὸν καιρὸν τοῦτον.

[24] Pol. 4.14.1: εἰς τὴν καθήκουσαν σύνοδον. The same phrase is used in 4.26.7 about the fourth *synodos*. In the one place where this phrase is used by Polybius concerning a meeting of the Aetolian Confederacy, the meeting appears to be an extraordinary one (cf. *TAPA* 83 [1952] 5 f. and nn. 10 and 11), but the phrase when applied to the Achaean Confederacy appears to mean a regular meeting, though it is not quite as clear in the two passages cited as in 4.7.1. In fact, I do not know of any case in which Polybius applies *synodos* to an extraordinary meeting of the Achaeans.

[25] Any attempt to fix the time of the Achaean elections for the period in which generals took office in the spring must be based on the election of the four years 220, 219, 218, and 217. See Beloch, *Griechische Geschichte*, 2d ed., IV, 2, 230, and esp. Aymard, 250–260. Beloch's account is excessively brief and starts from the assumption that the *archairesiai* were a spe-

cial kind of assembly distinct from the others. Aymard believes that the elections were held at regular *synodoi* and that the time varied. This appears to be correct, so far as it is possible to judge from the evidence available.

[26] Any hesitation on the point is due to the fact that Greeks could send aid to defend an ally against attack without thereby involving their own state in war. Examples from earlier Greek history are the aid sent by Corinth to Potidaea in 432 and the participation of the Athenians in the Mantinea campaign of 418. In the present case there is no indication that Messene was an ally, and aid sent to the city was likely to lead to serious complications, as it actually did. Action on questions as serious as this must have been reserved for the primary assembly.

[27] For this meeting see Appendix at p. 167 of the present work.

[28] The contention that a *synodos* at times included an *ekklesia* as well as a *boule* was the chief point of the article by Caspari (Cary), "The Parliament of the Achaean League," *Eng. Hist. Rev.* 29 (1914) 209–220.

NOTES TO CHAPTER V
(Pp. 86–105)

[1] Pol. 29.24.5 has ἐν ἀγορᾷ. It is clear that he does not use the name as a technical term for a primary assembly.

[2] συγκλήτου συναχθείσης εἰς τὴν τῶν Σικυωνίων πόλιν, ἐν ᾗ συνέβαινε μὴ μόνον συμπορεύεσθαι τὴν βουλὴν ἀλλὰ πάντας τοὺς ἀπὸ τριάκοντ' ἐτῶν (Pol. 29.24.6).

[3] Schweighaeuser, *Lexicon Polybianum,* s.vv. ἀγορά, σύγκλητος ; G. De Sanctis, *Riv. di fil.* 36 (1908) 255; G. Niccolini, *La Confederazione achea* (1914) 216; Busolt, *Staatskunde,* 1555 n. 3 on 1556 col. 1; Beloch, *Griechische Geschichte,* 2d ed., IV, 2, 232; Larsen, "A Study of Rep. Govt." (diss.) 330.

[4] Aymard (73 f.) translates: "…une synklètos…ou se réalisa la réunion, non seulement de la boulè, mais de tous ceux qui avaient dépassé trente ans."

[5] Unfortunately the two extant Achaean decrees (*SIG*³, 490, and *Inschriften von Magnesia,* 39) do not give any information concerning the composition of the body by which it was passed.

[6] *Inschriften von Olympia,* 46.

[7] Livy reports the apology of the ambassadors in the following words: "Achaei maxime concilii negati crimen excusabant recitando legem, quae nisi belli pacisve causa, et cum legati ab senatu cum litteris aut scriptis mandatis

venirent, vetaret indici concilium" (39.33.7). When Livy has "belli pacisve" instead of a reference merely to war, this apparently is practically a hendiadys meaning a question whether to have peace or war. Thus it does not add anything to Polybius' statement. This does not really matter, for the account is so obviously based on Polybius that it can have no independent value as evidence. This applies also to his omission of any reference to questions of alliance.

[8] In 190 the Achaeans, gathered in an *ekklesia,* renewed the alliance with Eumenes and voted to send 1,000 infantry and 100 cavalry to his aid (21.3b); in 183 Flamininus asked the *damiourgoi* to assemble the Achaeans in an *ekklesia* (23.5.16); in 170 Roman ambassadors were reported to have planned to have the *ekklesia* of the Achaeans summoned and to accuse Archon and Polybius before it, but are said to have given up the plan and instead to have had the *boule* summoned to Aegium and to have addressed it there (28.3.7–10).

[9] On the treaty see Aymard, *Les Premiers Rapports,* 261–267, who argues for 194/3 as the date, and E. Badian, "The Treaty between Rome and the Achaean League," *JRS* 42 (1952) 76–80, who argues for 192/1.

[10] Aymard, "A propos d'une assemblée achaienne," *Mélanges Glotz,* 49–72, at 63–68; *Les Assemblées,* 188–204; but cf. my own brief statement, *TAPA* 83 (1952) 16 n. 28.

[11] Pol. 29.24.5, where *agora* is used instead of *synodos* but used as a synonym of the latter word, which had been used in 29.23.8. Cf. Aymard, 190.

[12] In his account of the refusal of the Achaean officials in 185 to call a meeting of the *ekklesia* and the subsequent defense of this action by Achaean ambassadors before the senate, Polybius (22.10.11 and 12; 22.12.5, 6, 7, and 9) does not use σύγκλητος a single time about the Achaean assembly, but six times about the Roman senate.

[13] The Index of *SIG³* (Vol. IV, pp. 564 f.) lists one example for Athens and one for the Achaeans, but has approximately a column of citations for the Roman senate.

[14] For 200 see Livy 31.25.2–10, and cf. Aymard, 347 and 419; for 198, Livy 32.19–23, and Aymard, 338–342 and 419.

[15] So Walbank, *Philip V,* 300 n. 3, and earlier B. Niese, *Geschichte der griechischen und makedonischen Staaten,* II, 461; H. Nissen, *Kritische Untersuchungen,* 137; and De Sanctis, *Storia dei Romani,* III, 1, 221. Aymard (238–247) is less positive, but points out that the change was made before 208.

[16] See Appendix to the present work: "The Meetings of the Assemblies of the Achaean Confederacy."

[17] J. H. Lipsius, *Verhandlungen der sächsischen Gesellschaft,* 50 (1898) 172; Francotte, *La Polis grecque* (1907) 240 f.; Caspari, *Eng. Hist. Rev.* 29

(1914) 214; G. Niccolini, *La Confederazione achea* (1914) 220; Busolt, *Staatskunde*, 1555 n. 3; Larsen, "A Study of Rep. Govt." (diss.) 339 n. and 341 n. 2; Schwahn, *RE* 4A, 1254; W. H. Porter, *Plutarch's Life of Aratus* (1937) ci.

[18] The crucial words are: οἱ δὲ περὶ τὸν Γάιον, συναχθείσης τῆς τῶν ᾿Αχαιῶν ἐκκλησίας, ἐλέγοντο μὲν βεβουλεῦσθαι κατηγορήσειν ... συναχθείσης αὐτοῖς τῆς βουλῆς εἰς Αἴγιον.... (Pol. 28.3.7–10). The statement about the *boule* clearly indicates that it was summoned specifically for the ambassadors. As for the statement about the *ekklesia*, ἐλέγοντο indicates that Polybius is repeating gossip circulating at the time of the visit of the ambassadors to the Peloponnesus. At that time it was being said that the latter had formed a plan, after the *ekklesia* had been gathered, to accuse the Achaean leaders. From the point of view of the gossips, these acts were all in the future, and the plan was not carried out. Thus what Polybius reports is a plan attributed to the ambassadors but not carried out and a substitute plan which was put into execution.

[19] Freeman, *Federal Government*, 2d ed., 525, remarks, "They [the Romans] ... did not appear before the Assembly, but contented themselves with addressing a few words of compliment and exhortation to the Senate," but indicates in a footnote that he is not certain that the interpretation is correct; J. L. Strachan-Davidson, *Selections from Polybius*, 46, follows Freeman and states that the ambassadors "did not meet the Assembly at all, and only made a friendly speech in the Senate"; Francotte, *Polis*, 241, remarks, "A la rigeur, on pourrait comprendre que les députés renoncèrent à s'adresser à l'assemblée générale et se contentèrent d'une entrevue avec le Conseil," but rejects this explanation and prefers to think that the text contains an error; Aymard, 77 n. 6, notes the various interpretations and considers the problem as practically insoluble.

[20] See particularly Aymard, 331 ff. More recently Tarn-Griffith, *Hellenistic Civilization*, 74 f., has adopted the view that the members of the *boule* in all likelihood were paid. However, it is not easy to reconcile the well-known conservative and aristocratic outlook of the Achaean Confederacy, which obviously was dominated by men of wealth, with a system of pay for attendance at meetings. Moreover, as Aymard has pointed out, there is no question in the debate of relief for the normal Athenian budget. In another place (*Econ. Surv. Rome*, IV, 366 f.) I have suggested as one reason for rejecting the offer that the sum was so big that an effort to invest it would have upset the business world.

[21] For estimates of the possible number of members of the Achaean *synodos* see De Sanctis, *Riv. di fil.* 36 (1908) 257 n. 1; Schwahn, *RE* 4A, 1256. For the donations to the Lycian Confederacy, *CP* 40 (1945) 91 ff.; cf. *Econ. Surv. Rome*, IV, 363–368, for gifts to set up endowments in Greece in

Hellenistic times, and note how relatively small they were as compared with the sum offered by Eumenes.

[22] A list of *nomographoi* in *IG* IV², 1, 73, was adduced by Swoboda (*Hermes*, 57 [1922] 519–522) as proof that the board was made up on the principle of representation in proportion to population. This was accepted by Busolt, *Staatskunde*, 1561 n. 6 on 1562; Larsen, "A Study of Rep. Govt." (diss.) 327 and 334; Schwahn, *RE* 4A, 1249. However, Aymard (383–385 and esp. 384 n. 3) has demonstrated that for no period in the history of the Confederacy would the distribution of cities in this list be satisfactory according to that principle. Hence it is necessary to conclude that for the *nomographoi*, as well as for the smaller board of *damiourgoi*, this principle was not applied.

[23] For the procedure see particularly Livy 32.19–23, a report of the meeting at Sicyon in 198 B.C. In addition, for the rule that motions must be formulated on the second day, see Pol. 29.24.10; for evidence that only a single question could be considered at any one meeting, Livy 31.25.9.

[24] The possibility that the same rule was in use for extraordinary meetings at an earlier date may be suggested, but is unlikely. On the other hand, it looks as if the *boule* functioned as a probouleutic body at an extraordinary meeting in 229 (Pol. 2.46.6).

[25] Pol. 4.15.8–11, reporting a meeting of the Aetolians; cf. *TAPA* 83 (1952) 5–6.

[26] The inscription was first published by E. G. Bean, "Notes and Inscriptions from Lycia," *JHS* 68 (1948) 40–58, at 46 ff. See also J. and L. Robert, *Bulletin épigraphique* (1950) no. 183; Luigi Moretti, "Una nuova iscrizione da Araxa," *Riv. di fil.* 78 (1950) 326–350. The arguments of A. H. M. Jones (quoted by Bean), the Roberts, and Moretti make out a strong case for an early date. The Roman ambassadors mentioned in the document are best taken as members of the commission of 188. Events related in the document may well belong to the period of Ptolemaic control before the occupation by Antiochus in 197. As to the cult of Rome, the reference to 'Ρώμη Θεᾶ 'Επιφανεῖ suggests that it was established after the Roman intervention. *CIL* I², 725, which undoubtedly should be dated about 167 B.C., shows that the cult was in existence at that time. Since the events recorded cannot belong in the period of Rhodian control between 188 and 167 B.C., all the events recorded except those connected with the upkeep of the cult of Roma must be placed earlier. The establishment of the cult may well fall after the battle of Magnesia but before the disillusion which followed the subjection of Lycia under Rhodes.

[27] Our knowledge of the institutions depends on a few references in Livy and the following inscriptions: *IG* V, 1, 29; IX, 1, 513–517; *Inschriften von Magnesia*, 31. The latter document, dating from the last part of the third

century, uses *chilioi* for the primary assembly and supplies part of the evidence for the practice of taking votes in the assembly by cities. See particularly Busolt, *Staatskunde*, 1466 n. 2.

[28] Busolt, *Staatskunde*, 1492–1493.

[29] On the Lycian Confederacy cf. "Representation and Democracy in Hellenistic Federalism," *CP* 40 (1945) 65–97.

[30] Aymard, "L'Organisation de la Macédoine en 167 et le régime représentatif dans le monde grec," *CP* 45 (1950) 96–107, at 105, argues against the establishment of representative government in Thessaly at this time. It is true that *multitudo* in Livy 42.38.7 may be more appropriate to a primary than to a representative assembly, but this does not itself constitute a proof. As for the reference to *comitia, conventus,* and *concilium* in Livy 34.51.5, it is natural to believe that primary assemblies are included, but the statement covers so much that it cannot be held to prove that the federal government after 194 B.C. possessed a primary assembly. More concrete is the following statement about Flamininus: "a censu maxime et senatum et iudices legit potentioremque eam partem civitatium fecit" (Livy 34.51.6). Aymard points out that *maxime* indicates that the senate did not constitute the entire government. But does not *civitatium* indicate that Livy is talking about the local government of the cities and that the passage thus does not give any direct information about the nature of the federal government? On this point cf. Swoboda, *Staatsaltertümer,* 171 and 241; Busolt, *Staatskunde*, 1496.

[31] See *"Consilium"* in Livy xlv.18.6–7 and the Macedonian *Synedria," CP* 44 (1949) 73–90, and the article by Aymard cited in the note just above. Aymard on the whole agrees with my analysis of the evidence for the *synedria,* but is inclined to believe that there were primary assemblies also. Consequently he dates the introduction of representative government somewhat later than I do—so late, indeed, that it amounts to little more than the elimination of the primary assemblies from governments which no longer governed.

[32] Thirlwall, *History of Greece,* VIII, 441.

[33] Pol. 2.37.7–11. On the single περίβολος, cf. *Studies Presented to D. M. Robinson,* II, 810 n. 55.

NOTES TO CHAPTER VI
(Pp. 106–125)

[1] See particularly M. N. Tod, "The Progress of Greek Epigraphy," appearing from time to time in the *Journal of Hellenic Studies;* J. and L. Robert, *Bulletin épigraphique,* appearing annually in *Revue des études grecques*

and remarkable for its inclusiveness; and *L'Année épigraphique,* now edited by A. Merlin. The last-named work appears annually as a separate publication as well as in *Revue archéologique.* It reports epigraphical publications bearing on Roman institutions, whether the inscriptions are in Latin or Greek. The annual and decennial indexes are extremely useful. Of these the *Bulletin épigraphique* has already been cited several times.

² The standard general work remains Paul Guiraud, *Les Assemblées provinciales dans l'Empire romain* (Paris, 1887). See also E. G. Hardy, "The Provincial Concilia from Augustus to Diocletian," in *Studies in Roman History,* first series (1910) 235–282, and F. F. Abbott and A. C. Johnson, *Municipal Administration in the Roman Empire* (1926) chap. xii: "Provincial Assemblies," by Johnson.

³ E. Beurlier, *Le Culte impérial* (1891); Lily Ross Taylor, *The Divinity of the Roman Emperor* (1931).

⁴ This view is still to be found in Cohen, *La Grèce,* 3d ed. (1948) 640.

⁵ For discussions of the account of Pausanias and the settlement of 145 B.C. see *Econ. Surv. Rome,* IV, 306–309, and the more recent work of Silvio Accame, *Il Dominio romano in Grecia dalla Guerra Acaica ad Augusto* (Rome, 1946) esp. chap. ii.

⁶ See "Roman Supervision of Greece between Wars," *Econ. Surv. Rome,* IV, 286–290, and, for a more generalized statement, M. Rostovtzeff, *The Social and Economic History of the Hellenistic World* (1941) 1016 f.

⁷ *L'Année épigraphique,* 1900, no. 130; corrected text *CP* 44 (1949) 89; discussion: *CP* 40 (1945) 67 f. and nn. 13 and 14; 44 (1949) 88–89; *Concordia Theological Monthly* 17 (1946) 123–125. See also the important study of D. Kanatsoulis, Τὸ κοινὸν τῶν Μακεδόνων καὶ τὰ συνέδρια τῶν μερίδων, in Προσφορὰ εἰς Στίλπωνα Π. Κυριακίδην (Thessaloniki, 1953) 294–304 (Δημοσιεύματα Ἑταιρείας Μακεδονικῶν Σπουδῶν).

⁸ Charles Edson, "A Note on the Macedonian *Merides,*" *CP* 41 (1946) 107.

⁹ On the provinces of Greece and Macedonia under the Principate see *Econ. Surv. Rome,* IV, 437–441; on the units of local government, *ibid.,* 441–449; on the transfer of Thessaly to Macedonia cf. L. Robert, *Hellenica* 5 (1948) 29 f.

¹⁰ To the material cited in *Econ. Surv. Rome,* IV, 450–452, add *IG²,* 4114 (*SIG³,* 767), and *IG* VII, 2878. The first of these two documents, dated 34 or 33 B.C., shows that the organization is not "first heard of towards the end of the reign of Tiberius" but is considerably older, though the *koinon* of this document included only the Boeotians, Euboeans, Locrians, Phocians, and Dorians. It should also be noted that A. Momigliano, *JRS* 34 (1944) 115–116, has shown that *SIG³,* 796, should be dated under Nero, not Tiberius, and should be connected with Nero's proclamation of the freedom of the Greeks. See further U. Kahrstedt, "Das Koinon der Achaier,"

Symbolae Osloenses 28 (1950) 70–75; L. Moretti, "Un nuovo proconsole d'Acaia?" *Arch. Class.* 5 (1953) 255–259.

[11] For Augustus as general of the Thessalian Confederacy see *IG* IX, 2, 415b; for the date see A. S. Arbanitopullos, *Arch. eph.* 1917, p. 149; for Claudius in the Magnesian Confederacy, *IG* IX, 2, 1115, and cf. 1117 and 1120, both referring to the generalship of an emperor of unknown identity. It may be Claudius again.

[12] For an effort to evaluate Greek and Macedonian contributions to the wars of the period see "The Effects of the Wars between 146 and 30 B.C.," *Econ. Surv. Rome,* IV, 422–435.

[13] Additions to the Confederacy: Paus. 10.8.3. Cf. Busolt, *Staatskunde,* 1494 and n. 3; freedom of Thessaly: *Econ. Surv. Rome,* IV, 447–448.

[14] Not only the name but the coins show that Nicopolis was Greek; cf. *Econ. Surv. Rome,* IV, 446.

[15] Cf. *CP* 47 (1952) 14 and n. 42.

[16] He is referred to as high priest in two inscriptions: *Inscr. Corinth Lat.* 68, and *IG* II², 3538 (cf. *Econ. Surv. Rome,* IV, 451 n. 14). In the latter he appears as ἀρχιερεὺς Θεῶν Σεβαστῶν καὶ γένους Σεβαστῶν ἐκ τοῦ κοινοῦ τῆς Ἀχαίας διὰ βίου πρῶτος τῶν ἀπ' αἰῶνος and in the former as *archiereus . . . in perpetuum primus Achaeon.* The title, high priest for life, is clearly the honorary title retained after the year of office is over. In the Greek inscription it is perfectly obvious that "first" is chronological. It is possible that Spartiaticus was not the first high priest but only the first to acquire the title of high priest for life (Cormack, *JRS* 33 [1943] 40). However, by the middle of the first century after Christ it is likely that the official designation of offices was so developed that this title was adopted as soon as the cult was organized. Chronologically it makes little difference, for we have seen that the organization was purely secular at the beginning of the reign of Gaius. The date A.D. 55 as the *terminus ante quem* is derived from the reference in the Latin inscription to Spartiaticus as *procurator Caesaris et Augustae Agrippinae.* A. B. West, the editor, remarks that the inscription "was presumably erected before the disgrace of Agrippina in 55 A.D."

[17] So much new material has been discovered that the account in *Econ. Surv. Rome,* IV, 452–453, is badly out of date. For references to this material, improved versions of some documents, and discussions see particularly J. M. R. Cormack, "The Nerva Inscription in Beroea," *JRS* 30 (1940) 50–52; "A Letter of Hadrian in Beroea," *ibid.* 148–152; "High Priests and Macedoniarchs from Beroea," *ibid.* 33 (1943) 39–44. Add the important collection of inscriptions from Beroea in *Jahrbuch des deutsch. arch. Inst., Anzeiger* 57 (1942) 175–184. The inscriptions are published without commentary. An excellent summary and brief commentary are given by J. and L. Robert, *Bulletin épigraphique,* 1942, no. 96; cf. also *L'Année épigraphique,* 1946, nos. 179–182, where the texts of three are given.

[18] No. 9 of the inscriptions published in *Arch. Anz.* 57 (1942) 175–184; *L'Année épigraphique,* 1946, no. 180. On Licinius Rufinus cf. L. Robert, "Un juriste romain dans une inscription de Beroia," *Hellenica* 5 (1948) 29–34.

[19] *CP* 47 (1952) 8 f.

[20] *Econ. Surv. Rome,* IV, 294–300.

[21] No. 4 of the inscriptions in *Arch. Anz.* 57.

[22] *Ibid.* no. 21; cf. no. 17.

[23] *Ibid.* no. 20.

[24] It has occasioned some surprise that Macedoniarchs have appeared at Thessalonica, a free city. This seems to be based on the supposition that membership in a "provincial assembly" indicates subjection. If, as conjectured above, the League was originally a political organization which later voluntarily established an imperial cult, there is no reason why a free city should not belong. Thessalonica had been the capital of the second of the four *merides* (Livy 45.29.9), and there seems to be no reason why later privileges granted the city need have caused a severing of the ties. Moreover, the example of Corinth and the Panachaean League shows that even Roman colonies could belong to organizations of the kind.

[25] For a discussion of some aspects of the organization with references to earlier literature see "Cyrene and the Panhellenion," *CP* 47 (1952) 7–16.

[26] For a relatively late reference to an *archon* with no mention of the high priesthood, see *L'Année épigraphique,* 1947, no. 88.

[27] See, for instance, the career of Cn. Cornelius Pulcher, as shown in *Inscript. Corinth Greek,* 80; cf. *Pros. imp. Rom.,* 2d ed., C no. 1424.

[28] P. Monceaux, *De communi Asiae provinciae* (Paris, 1885) 7.

[29] G. Fougères, *De Lyciorum communi* (Paris, 1898); the work of Monceaux on Asia cited just above; cf. also the works by Guiraud and Beurlier cited in notes 2 and 3 to this chapter. Important on Asia is also V. Chapot, *La Province romaine proconsulaire d'Asie* (Paris, 1904).

[30] David Magie, *Roman Rule in Asia Minor* (Princeton, 1950). The preface is dated March 1, 1948. The work will be cited as: Magie, *Asia.*

[31] For a statement of the case for the identity of the two offices see *CP* 40 (1945) 85 n. 103; for Magie's point of view, esp. *Asia,* n. 54 on pp. 1388–1389. I have nothing to add to my earlier argument except that I started out with the belief that the two offices were distinct. It is easy to find documents in which a Lyciarch who is not identical with the high priest of the year is mentioned. Later I was convinced, chiefly by the arguments presented by Fougères in *Mélanges Perrot,* that in such cases the Lyciarch is a former high priest.

[32] For Asia Minor the holders of such titles as well as the high priest and high priestesses are conveniently tabulated by Magie, *Asia,* 1601–1612.

[33] Magie, *Asia,* 449–450 and 1298–1301, argues that the title of Asiarch is to be connected with individual cities rather than with the province as a whole. This seems unlikely. Every title of this kind must have some connection with the province, or rather Commonality, as a whole. Since the men who held office in confederacies and commonalities were also locally prominent, it is not surprising that Asiarchs are known best from inscriptions in their home cities and that they frequently were honored for local benefactions. Even the fact that some local benefaction was performed ἀντ' 'Ασιαρχίας does not prove that the title of Asiarch was merely a local dignity. The benefaction may have been a part of the campaign before election or an expression of gratitude after election.

[34] *IGR* I, 707, 732, and 1451; *L'Année épigraphique,* 1932, no. 25; 1939, no. 184; 1940, no. 30; 1944, nos. 81 and 142; 1948, no. 20; *Digest* 49.1.1; a brief discussion by P. Collart, *BCH* 62 (1938) 421–428.

[35] ἔθνους ἱεραρχία, οἷον 'Ασιαρχία, Βιθυναρχία, Καππαδοκαρχία, παρέχει ἀλειτουργησίαν ἀπὸ ἐπιτροπῶν, τοῦτ' ἔστιν ἕως ἂν ἄρχῃ (*Digest* 27.1.6.14). Frequently scholars have cited only the first part of this statement and omitted the latter and more important. So Monceaux, *De communi Asiae proviniciae,* 58; Chapot *La Province romaine proconsulaire d'Asie,* 468; Magie, *Asia,* 1299.

[36] Examples for Lycia can be found in the index of *IGR* III, p. 645; note that nos. 500 and 739 each contain several examples. For Asia, see *IGR* IV, 1226. For the latter there is evidence for some who held the office twice or thrice; these are listed by Magie, p. 1301. Similar evidence for Bithynia, *ibid*.

[37] For a different interpretation and bibliography see Magie, *Asia,* 449–450 and 1298–1301.

[38] *Inscr. Sardis (Sardis:* Publications of the American Society for the Excavation of Sardis, Vol. VII, Pt. 1 [1932], ed. W. H. Buckler and David M. Robinson), no. 8, doc. 7.

[39] For an example from Olbia see *SIG³,* 730.

[40] See Magie, *Asia,* 448; cf. *CP* 47 (1952) 14.

[41] Guiraud, *Les Assemblées provinciales,* 140 and n. 1; Hardy, *Studies,* first series, 268.

[42] Guiraud, *Les Assemblées provinciales,* Liv. II, chap. vii; E. G. Hardy, ed., *C. Plinii Caecilii Secundi Epistulae ad Traianum* (1889) pp. 29–49.

[43] Accusations brought by Asia: against C. Silanus (Tac. *Ann.* 3.66–69), Lucilius Capito (Tac. *Ann.* 4.15), P. Celer (Tac. *Ann.* 13.33), P. Suillius (Tac. *Ann.* 13.43); Bithynia: Iunius Cilo (Dio Cassius 60.33), Cadius Rufus (Tac. *Ann.* 12.22), Tarquitius Priscus (Tac. *Ann.* 14.46), Iulius Bassus (Pliny *Ep.* 4.9), Varenus Rufus (Pliny *Ep.* 5.20; 6.5; 6.13; 6.29.11; 7.6; 7.10).

⁴⁴ Crete: Cestius Proculus (Tac. *Ann.* 13.30); Cyrene: Caesius Cordus (Tac. *Ann.* 3.38, 70), Pedius Blaesus (Tac. *Ann.* 14.18). In such cases as these and the accusations brought by the Bithynians there is a tendency on the part of modern scholars to treat them as accusations by the entire province— province in this case meaning the *governor's* province.

⁴⁵ For Lycia see *CP* 40 (1945) 86 f. for evidence of competition for office; for Thessaly, see "A Thessalian Family under the Principate," *CP* 48 (1953) 86–95.

⁴⁶ See particularly *CP* 48 (1953) 92 and n. 7; cf. A. Stein, "Zur sozialen Stellung der provinzialen Oberpriester," *Epitymbion Heinrich Swoboda dargebracht* (1927) 300–311.

NOTES TO CHAPTER VII
(Pp. 126–144)

¹ Cf. Aymard, *"Arca provinciae,* et non *concilii," Revue des études anciennes,* 43 (1941) 229–239. Aymard starts from the criticism of the restoration *in[p]endio co[n]ci[lii]* in an inscription discovered a few years ago and argues correctly that the treasury did not belong to the assembly, but to the organization it represented, as indicated by the expression, long known, *arca Galliarum.* Though this treasury was controlled by the assembly, it did not belong to the assembly and was not *arca concilii.*

² The scholars who have made most of the *Commune Siciliae* are Th. Mommsen, *Römische Geschichte,* I³, 543 f.; *Gesammelte Schriften,* V, 553; J. Marquardt, *Ephemeris epigraphica,* 1 (1872) 202; *Römische Staatsverwaltung,* 2d ed., I (1881) 510; Kornemann, *RE* 4, 805. The evidence comes from Cicero *ii in Verrem* 2. For the games see sections 51–52, 114, 154; statues erected, 114, 168; payments to the *commune,* 145; common actions of all Sicily or of all cities, 103, 146. For a polemic directed against Marquardt and Mommsen see A. Holm, *Geschichte Siciliens im Altertum,* III (1898) 91–92 and 384–385. The latter goes much too far, for instance, when he questions that the games were celebrated by the *commune.* It is true that they were held at Syracuse and sometimes are referred to in such a way that they might have been municipal, but in section 114 *apud Siculos dies festi aguntur* in connection with the Verria is convincing, particularly since it immediately precedes a statement about statues dedicated by the province.

³ For changes in the governments of cities see Cic. *ii in Verrem* 2.121–125. The earliest reform listed was that effected by Scipio at Agrigentum. This would be in the latter part of the Second Punic War.

[4] For the constitution of the Italic allies see Diod. 37.2; Strabo 5.241. The passages in Livy are 8.5.5; 23.22.4–6; 23.6.6–8; cf. *CP* 49 (1954) 11.

[5] Besides Guiraud's *Les Assemblées provinciales* see particularly M. Krascheninnikoff, "Ueber die Einführung des provinzialen Kaisercultus im römischen Westen," *Philologus* 53 (1894) 147–189; Ernest Carette, *Les Assemblées provinciales de la Gaule romaine* (Paris, 1895); Kornemann, *RE* 4, 809–812, s.v. "Concilium"; A. L. Abaecherli, "The Institution of the Imperial Cult in the Western Provinces of the Roman Empire," *Studi e materiali di storia delle religioni,* 11 (1935) 153–186. Carette's book is thoughtful but suffers from numerous minor errors (cf. "Additions et corrections," pp. 477–503).

[6] So Dio Cassius 54.32.1 and Livy *Epitome* 139. On the other hand, Suet. *Claud.* 2 points to 10 B.C. As Hirschfeld argues in *CIL* XIII, Pt. 1, p. 227, it is clear that 12 B.C. should be accepted because Livy indicates a connection with the census of that year. He was so near to the scene that he cannot have made a mistake on so fundamental a point. To be sure, for our purposes, it makes no difference whether the date was 12 or 10 B.C.

[7] *L'Année épigraphique,* 1947, no. 69, where text and bibliography are given; cf. *CP* 39 (1944) 197 f.

[8] *CIL* XII, 6038; Dessau, 6964; *Fontes iuris Romani antejustiniani,* I² (1941) 199–202, no. 22. For a discussion of the nature of the document with references to earlier literature see *"Signandi ius* in the Charter of the Provincial Assembly of Narbonensis," *Studies in Honor of B. L. Ullman* (1955) 1–11. It has recently been dated under Vespasian by J. Gagé, "Vespasien et la mémoire de Galba," *Revue des études anciennes,* 54 (1952) 290–315, at 314–315.

[9] *Histoire de la Gaule,* IV, 426 n. 5; cf. Daremberg-Saglio, II, 1180 f., s.v. "Flamen." Jullian makes much of an inscription from Spain (*CIL* II, 4248; Dessau, 6937), in which, according to him, a *sacerdos* is given special permission to have his statue set up *inter flaminales viros.* It looks as if Jullian has mistranslated the document. Hübner (commentary on *CIL* II, 4248; cf. suppl., p. 973) has another and more plausible explanation. The statue was already there but was to be further adorned. Yet a difficulty remains; there is a *sacerdos* in a province in which the usual title for the high priest is *flamen.*

[10] *CIL* X, 7599 with a *flamen divorum Augustorum* appears to be earlier than 7917 with a *sacerdos provinciae Sardiniae.* Kornemann (*RE* 4, 812.7) cites Sardinia as an example of a change from *flamen* to *sacerdos.* The first of the two inscriptions is discussed in *CP* 26 (1931) 322–323.

[11] For examples see the index of *CIL* II, p. 1132. The form is not always quite the same.

[12] F. Geiger, *De sacerdotibus Augustorum municipalibus* (Halle, 1913) 45–56.

[13] Dessau, 6811 and 6812. The era is commonly taken to be that of the imperial cult of the province, but see Abaecherli, *op. cit.* (in note 5 *supra*), 173–181.

[14] *CIL* XIII, 1698, without emendations, reads:

AURICO Q LICIN
ÇIS HONORIBUS FUN
RIB PROVINCIS GA
IO LICIN SABI

Let us look at this without the restorations of the editors. The first line shows that the name of the man honored was in the dative. The second line shows part of a phrase indicating that he had held municipal offices in his home community. The editor restores *apud suos publi*]*cis honoribus fun*[*cto.* In line 3 the restoration *t*]*rib. Provinci(i)s Ga*[*lliis* can be considered certain. This cannot well refer to anything but an election to office by the provinces, and the most likely office is the high priesthood. The editor restores *sacerdoti ad aram Rom. et Aug.* The inscription cannot record a dedication by the three provinces. In that case their name would certainly appear in the nominative and be placed in the last line.

Similarly, *CIL* XIII, 1700 reads:

ORI · LICINI
GINTI · ANNO
S SACERD
RERE · P
VINCIAE
ORI LEMO

In this there is a reference to *sacerdos* or *sacerdotium.* In line 5 *tres pro*]*vinciae* [*Galliae* can be considered a certain restoration. The last line shows that the monument was dedicated by the Lemovices, and so it is clear that the provinces are mentioned for some other activity, probably in connection with the granting of permission to serve as high priest at an early age. No. 1699, which refers to the same individual, contains a reference to a *sacerdotium . . . apud aram* and also to a number of which *duo et* is preserved. The age thus must be twenty-two and the following restoration of 1700 probably gives the meaning of the document:

Q. Licinio Ult]*ori Licini* [*Taurici filio*
cui duo et vi]*ginti anno*[*s nato ex con*
cilii consen]*s. sacerd*[*otium ad aram*
Rom. et Aug. ge]*rere p*[*ermiserunt*
        tres pro]*vinciae* [*Galliae*
Liciniis Taurico Sabino Ul]*tori Lemo*[*vices publice*

The restoration is that of Hirschfeld in *CIL* except for the substitution of p[*ermiserunt* for p[*ermissum est.*

For Narbonensis there is *CIL* XII, 392, which will be quoted in Hirschfeld's version except with *flamen* and *flamonium* substituted for *sacerdos* and *sacerdotium*. If Hirschfeld had had an opportunity to revise the volume after the publication of the charter of Narbonensis (*CIL* XII, 6038), which appears at the very end of the volume in a sort of supplement, he undoubtedly would have made this change himself. The fragments of the first and last two lines will be omitted.

> *omnibus honoribus*] functo · in
> *patria sua tribun*]o · militum
> ...   *praefect*]o alae Longi
> *niae flamini*] templi · Divi
> *Aug. quod est Nar*]bone in · quod
> *flamonium univ*]ersa provin
> *cia consentiente adl*]ectus est

[15] For a short-lived experiment with something approaching the modern system in the Roman elections in the time of Augustus see *CP* 49 (1954) 12.

[16] O. Hirschfeld, "Zur Geschichte des römischen Kaiserkultus," *Kleine Schriften,* 471–504, at 494 f.; Kornemann, *RE* 4, 813.

[17] Below is given a list of the number of high priests attested for each of the fifteen tribes at the altar area and in local inscriptions. All the evidence, except one inscription, is from *CIL* XIII, the numbers given in parentheses being the numbers of the inscriptions. The list has been prepared with the aid of the statement by Hirschfeld, *CIL* XIII, 1, p. 228, a rapid survey of the part of the volume published later, and a final check by means of the recently published index.

	ALTAR AREA	LOCAL INSCRIPTIONS	TOTAL
Aedui	1 (1714)	1 (5353)	2
Segusiavi	3 (1701, 1711, 1712)	1 (XII, 1851)	3
Arverni	2 (1706, 1715)	1 (1463)	3
Santoni	1 (1716)	2 (1036, 1042–1045)	3
Petrucorii	2 (1704)	3 (939, 11042)	3
Lemovices	2 (1698, 1699–1700)		2
Carnutes	2 (1672, 1694)		2
Senones	1 (1676)	1 (2940)	1
Cadurci		1 (1541)	1
Viducasses		1 (3162)	1
Tricasses	1 (1691)		1
Veliocasses	1 (1717)		1
Nervii	1 (1702)		1
Sequani	1 (1674–1675)	1 (2870)	2
Coriosolites		1 (3144)	1
	18	13	27

In some cases, as can be seen from the totals for the tribes and the grand
total, the same men are listed both at the altar area and locally. The one
priest known from a literary source (Livy, *Epitome* 139) was an Aeduan.
This brings the total from this tribe up to three and the grand total to
twenty-eight. In addition, the following eight inscriptions from the altar
area contain references to high priests without indicating their origin: *CIL*
XIII, 1684, 1687, 1692, 1696, 1710, 1718, 1719, 11174.

Such a list can claim no more than approximate accuracy. It is easy to
disagree on whether there is enough evidence to include an imperfectly
preserved inscription in a certain class or not. Therefore I have not discussed doubtful inscriptions, but simply given the results. Anyone who goes
over the evidence is likely to disagree on certain details but to reach the
same general conclusion.

[18] Provincial high priests from Narbonensis are cited below. When not otherwise indicated, the evidence consists of inscriptions in *CIL* XII.

Nemausus (3183, 3184, 3212–3213, 3275)	4
Near Toulon (392)	1
Narbo (4393)	1
Vienna (*CIL* VI, 29688)	1
Tolosa (Q. Trebellius Rufus, cf. pp. 130–132)	1
Ruscino (E. Espérandieu, *Inscr. lat. de Gaule*, 634)	1
City unknown (4323)	1
	10

Most of these are discussed briefly *CP* 39 (1944) 197 f.

[19] On this point cf. note 8 to this chapter.

[20] Carette, *Les Assemblées provinciales de la Gaule,* 90–91; Kornemann, *RE*
4, 813 f.

[21] *CIL* XIII, 3162, the famous and troublesome Thorigny inscription. The last
edition is by H. G. Pflaum, *Le Marbre de Thorigny* (Paris, 1948); cf. *CP*
45 (1950) 254–256. Pflaum's edition, important in other ways, has little to
offer students of provincial assemblies.

[22] For efforts to draw up lists of members see Ernest Desjardins, *Géographie
de la Gaule romaine,* III (1885) 167–173; A. Allmer and P. Dissard,
Musée de Lyon: Inscriptions, II (1889) 6–19; Kornemann, "Die Zahl der
gallischen Civitates in der römischen Kaiserzeit," *Klio,* 1 (1901) 331–348;
Jullian, *Histoire de la Gaule,* IV, 90 n. 8. The latter, in contrast to the
others, finds room only for Gallic tribes. Also Hirschfeld, *Kleine Schriften,*
222 and 132, in articles first published in 1896 and 1904, believes that the
Iberians were excluded.

[23] See Guiraud, *Les Assemblées provinciales,* 45, and the works by Arbois de
Joubainville cited by him. The theory was elaborated further by Hirsch-

feld, *Kleine Schriften,* 129–132; cf. a partial palinode, "Der Dedicationstag des Augustus-Altars bei Lugudunum," *Westdeutsche Zeitschrift für Geschichte und Kunst,* 23 (1904) 89–91. This article was not included in the author's *Kleine Schriften.*

[24] The etymology is accepted by A. Holder, *Alt-celtischer Sprachschatz;* cf. also H. Hubert, *Les Celtes depuis l'époque de la Tène* (1932) 286.

[25] Desjardins, *Géographie de la Gaule romaine,* II, 541 ff.; Carette, *Assemblées,* 1–18.

[26] The following meetings can be noted

Spring 55	*B.G.* 4.6.5
Spring 54	*B.G.* 5.2.4
Autumn 54	*B.G.* 5.24.1
Late autumn 54	*B.G.* 5.54.1
Spring 53	*B.G.* 6.3.4
Autumn 53	*B.G.* 6.44.1

Of these meetings the extra meeting in the autumn of 54 seems to have been occasioned by disturbances. Note the words *concilio Galliae primo vere, uti instituerat, indicto* used in connection with the spring meeting of 53.

[27] For the *allectus arcae* see *CIL* XIII, 1688, 1709; for the *iudex arcae, CIL* XIII, 1686, 1707, 1708; for the *inquisitor Galliarum, CIL* XIII, 1690, 1695, 1697, 1703, 3528.

NOTES TO CHAPTER VIII
(Pp. 145–161)

[1] The standard edition remains Th. Mommsen and P. M. Meyer, *Theodosiani libri XVI cum constitutionibus Sirmondianis et leges novellae ad Theodosianum pertinentes* (Berlin, 1905). Valuable aids to students are the new English translation by Clyde Pharr and others, *The Theodosian Code and Novels and the Sirmondian Constitutions* (Princeton, 1952), and A. Berger, *Encyclopedic Dictionary of Roman Law* (Transactions of the American Philosophical Society, Vol. 43, Pt. 2 [1953]). The latter work will be cited by the author's name alone.

For literature on the assemblies see, besides the general works on provincial assemblies already cited, Larsen, "The Position of Provincial Assemblies in the Government and Society of the Late Roman Empire," *CP* 29 (1934) 209–220.

[2] See the list with dates of first and last mentions given by Guiraud, *Les*

Assemblées provinciales, 56–58. Undoubtedly a careful search for evidence would lead to an expansion of the list and the fixing of later dates for some. Thus, to give only one example, the Magnesian Confederacy is not included in his list.

[3] See the chronological list in the Mommsen-Meyer edition, I, 1, pp. ccix ff.; cf. also Berger under "Codex Theodosianus."

[4] Two rulings on the same point would be possible, but two addressed by different emperors to the Thessalian Confederacy would be most unlikely. Moreover, the similarity of language and particularly the phrase *Graece rescripsit* indicate not only that it is the same document but that the two jurists took it from the same earlier compilation.

[5] For lists see Guiraud, *Les Assemblées provinciales,* 223–226; Kornemann, *RE* 4, 821 f.; Joseph Zeller, "Concilia provincialia in Gallien in der späteren Kaiserzeit," *Westdeutsche Zeitschrift für Geschichte und Kunst,* 25 (1906) 258–273, presents evidence for additional Gallic provinces including Lugdunensis III and IV. Zeller considers the existence of assemblies in such provinces as these proof that the institution must have been universal throughout the Empire.

[6] For the text see Ernest Carette, *Les Assemblées provinciales de la Gaule romaine,* 460–463; for discussion Zeller, *Westdeutsche Zeitschrift,* 24 (1905) 1–19.

[7] Th. Mommsen, "Epigraphische Analekten," *Gesammelte Schriften,* VIII, 1–188, at 32–34; Kornemann, *RE* 4, 822 f.; V. Chapot, *Le Monde romaine* (1927) 132 f.

[8] *Cod. Th.* 12.12.1. The document contains two words used in unusual ways; *potestas* is used about the right, authority, or opportunity of the assemblies to consult as they wish. The modifier *libera* probably means "free from interference." Any possible meddler who might interfere is called *dictator.* This word cannot be used here in any technical sense.

[9] Guiraud, *Les Assemblées provinciales,* 228 f., on the basis of this edict argues that the emperors did not order the formation of diocesan assemblies, but permitted their formation where they were desired.

[10] *Cod. Th.* 12.12.12. The first part of the document refers to the extraordinary assemblies, but the statement about the attendance seems to apply to all provincial assemblies.

[11] An edict of 403 authorizing all provincials to use force against deserters instructs a pretorian prefect to bring this authorization *ad notitiam primatium urbium vicorum castellorumque* (*Cod. Th.* 7.18.13).

[12] *CP* 29 (1934) 215 and n. 22.

[13] On *sacerdotes* and *sacerdotales* see Guiraud, *Les Assemblées provinciales,* 246–252; Carette, *Les Assemblées provinciales de la Gaule,* 271–300; Beurlier, *Le Culte impérial,* 290–297.

[14] A. Alföldi, *The Conversion of Constantine and Pagan Rome* (1948) 116 f.

[15] *CP* 40 (1945) 81–85; cf. 91–93.

[16] These are discussed briefly in *CP* 49 (1954) 12. For other literature and interpretations of the *Tabula Hebana* see Ernst Meyer, "Neuere Erkentnisse und Forschungen auf dem Gebiete des römischen Staatsrechts," *Die Welt als Geschichte* (1953) Heft 3, 137–148. See now also J. H. Oliver and R. E. A. Palmer, "Text of the Tabula Hebana," *American Journal of Philology* 75 (1954) 225–249.

NOTES TO APPENDIX
(Pp. 165–188)

[1] For the chronology of 209 and 208 see F. W. Walbank, *Philip V of Macedon* (1940) 304 f.

[2] The statement about the time of the meeting is based on the reference of Polybius (11.10.9) to a period of not quite eight months before the battle of Mantinea, during which Philopoemen remade the Achaean army. It is implied that the address came at the beginning of this period. A different order of events is found in the more detailed statement of Plutarch (*Philopoemen* 9), which also is derived from Polybius. The latter version is followed by Aymard (96 n. 3). I prefer the former for the reason that a mistake may have been made by Plutarch in reproducing the story. The date of the meeting, of course, does not matter for the present purpose.

[3] For all questions of Achaean chronology for this period see Aymard, "Les Stratèges de la Confédération achéenne de 202 à 172 av. J.-C.," *Revue des études anciennes*, 30 (1928) 1–62.

[4] See particularly Aymard, 302–305, and his earlier article, "A propos d'une assemblée achaienne," *Mélanges Glotz,* 49–72; Walbank, *Philip V,* 333. Aymard is inclined to consider the meeting a *synkletos*. A reason for considering the meeting a *synodos* is that legislation on procedure was not among the questions reserved for the *ekklesia*. Moreover, Nobilior seems to have brought up also the question of Sparta, and, though a Roman might take liberties, this introduction of a new subject fits a *synodos* better than a *synkletos*.

[5] Aymard (156 n. 4) has demonstrated that the account of Diodorus (29.17) has no independent value.

[6] See particularly P. Usteri, *Ächtung und Verbannung im griechischen Recht* (1903) 95–116; Busolt, *Staatskunde,* 236.

[7] Ferguson, *Hellenistic Athens,* 323 f.; P. Roussel, *Délos colonie athénienne* (1916) 16 f.; Aymard, 113 n. 2.

[8] The presence of visitors would not in itself be impossible. In all likelihood the normal *synodoi* were not secret meetings. There is no direct evidence so far as I know. For the Aetolian Confederacy the secrecy of the meetings of the *apokletoi* (Livy 35.35.5), who constituted a *sanctius consilium* (35.34.2), suggests that the meetings of the less august *consilium*, namely the *boule-synedrion*, were not secret. In the Achaean Confederacy secret meetings probably were confined to the *damiourgoi* and higher magistrates.

Index

INDEX

[In the notes only a few points not discussed in the text are indexed separately. In these references the numbers of the notes are included.]

Commonality, meaning in this book, 106, 116 f.

Commune, used as equivalent of *koinon* and applied to commonalities, 117, 126

Commune Siciliae. See Sicilian Commonality

Concilium: applied in text of Livy to meetings of Achaeans, 170, 172, 173, 175, 177, 182; to meetings of Aetolians, 182; to meetings of allies, 170; used for assemblies of western provinces of the Roman Empire, 126; for Gallic assemblies, 142

Confederacy, meaning in this book, 25. *See also* Federal state

Constantine the Great: and provincial assemblies, 145; edict of 331 *ad universos provinciales,* 149; deified after his death, 153

Copae, city in Boeotian Confederacy, 34

Corcyra: in Second Athenian League, 56

Corinth: scene of Achaean meetings, 87, 88, 91, 184, 185, 187 f.; member of Panachaean League, 112 f.

Corinthian War: temporary symmachy of allies, 51

Cornelius, Cn. Cornelius Pulcher, high priest of Panachaean League, 113

Coronea, city in Boeotian Confederacy, 34

Crete and Cyrene: Roman province or provinces, 114; prosecution of governors, 124

Critolaus, Achaean general, 187 f.

Croesus, king of Lydia: relation to Ionians, 29

Curia, city council: in Late Empire, 152 (cf. 127)

Curiales, members of *curiae:* in provincial and diocesan assemblies of Late Empire, 152–154, 157

Cycliadas, Achaean general, 171

Cyrene: its "Ten Thousand," 3; *boule,* 13; representation in Panhellenion, 116; prosecution of governors, 124

Cyrus, king of Persia: relation to Ionians, 29, 30

Damiorgoi of Arcadian Confederacy, 73

Damiourgoi of Achaean Confederacy, 174, 182

Damocritus, Achaean general, 185

Deification of emperors. *See* Imperial cult

Delian exiles citizens of Achaean Confederacy, 176

Delian League, 47 and chapter iii *passim;* founded as permanent organization, 49 f., 60; assembly, 53 f., 57, 58; one vote for each state, 54; Athens had vote, 58; *synodos* used of meetings, 57; tribute, 60; Hellenotamiae, 60

Delium, battle of, 33, 38 f.

Demes at Athens, 6–11, 28

Democracy: primary assembly fundamental, 3; democracy and democratic